# AN ECOSYSTEM FOR ENGAGED SCHOOLS

Looking at the potential for research-use by educators to improve schools for all young people, *An Ecosystem for Research-Engaged Schools* presents a range of ground-breaking research and fascinating case studies. It carefully explores the elements and dimensions of research-engaged schools using an ecosystems perspective to study the layers and interconnections that occur amongst the people and institutions that exist within the ecosystem. Allowing the reader to consider how to ensure independent elements of the ecosystem are maintained to ensure an effective balance, this book brings together contributions from international experts working in a variety of fields such as school leadership, professional development and accountability.

Key issues facing the research-use ecosystem both theoretically and empirically are covered, with examples of innovative practice, new theories and value systems. The book also provides an insight into the exciting possibility of such a system of learning and innovation in our schools where structures, cultures, practices and policies align to promote research-informed school improvement.

With chapters bringing together issues from different aspects of the system, this book:

- expands the analysis of evidence and research-informed practice, considering the wider environment within which it is undertaken
- shows the interplay and tensions between aspects of the ecosystem and illustrates how different aspects of the ecosystem affect evidence use
- reconciles all aspects of the ecosystem within an overarching framework which attempts to explain the complex totality of the ecosystem.

Designed to both challenge and inspire, *An Ecosystem for Research-Engaged Schools* truly bridges the gap between theory and practice. It will be an invaluable asset to those currently working in the area, allowing them to think more deeply about their work and the theoretical mechanisms that underpin it. Policy makers, practitioners and teachers will also find this book a fascinating read.

**David Godfrey** is a Lecturer at UCL Institute of Education, UK where he is also Co-Director of the Centre for Educational Evaluation and Accountability and Programme Leader for the MA Leadership.

**Chris Brown** is Professor of Education at the University of Portsmouth, UK.

# AN ECOSYSTEM FOR RESEARCH-ENGAGED SCHOOLS

## Reforming Education Through Research

*Edited by David Godfrey and Chris Brown*

Routledge
Taylor & Francis Group

LONDON AND NEW YORK

First published 2019
by Routledge
2 Park Square, Milton Park, Abingdon, Oxon, OX14 4RN

and by Routledge
52 Vanderbilt Avenue, New York, NY 10017

*Routledge is an imprint of the Taylor & Francis Group, an informa business*

*British Library Cataloguing-in-Publication Data*
A catalogue record for this book is available from the British Library

*Library of Congress Cataloging-in-Publication Data*
Names: Godfrey, David, 1968- editor. | Brown, Chris, 1975- editor.
Title: An ecosystem for research-engaged schools : reforming education
    through research / David Godfrey, Chris Brown.
Description: Abingdon, Oxon ; New York, NY : Routledge, 2019. |
    Includes bibliographical references.
Identifiers: LCCN 2018054701| ISBN 9781138574458 (hbk) |
    ISBN 9781138574465 (pbk) | ISBN 9780203701027 (ebk)
Subjects: LCSH: Educational change—Research. | Teaching—Research. |
    Teachers—Training of—Research. | School improvement programs—
    Research.
Classification: LCC LB2806 .E27 2019 | DDC 371.2—dc23
LC record available at https://lccn.loc.gov/2018054701

ISBN: 978-1-138-57445-8 (hbk)
ISBN: 978-1-138-57446-5 (pbk)
ISBN: 978-0-203-70102-7 (ebk)

Typeset in Bembo
by Swales & Willis Ltd, Exeter, Devon, UK

Printed and bound in Great Britain by
TJ International Ltd, Padstow, Cornwall

David and Chris dedicate this book to the memory of Professor Geoff Whitty, former Director of the Institute of Education. Not only was Geoff a wonderful human being, he was also a world-leading sociologist of education.

# CONTENTS

# ABOUT THE EDITORS

Dr **David Godfrey** is a lecturer in Education, Leadership and Management at UCL Institute of Education in London. He is Co-Director of the Centre for Educational Evaluation and Accountability and Programme Leader for the MA Leadership. An advocate of research-informed practice in education, his projects and publications include research-engaged schools, school peer review, inspection systems and lesson study. David has had an international career as an educator, including in a leadership position at a large sixth form college as an Assistant Director and research coordinator, during which he helped them to win the country's first 'research-engaged' school/college award from the National Foundation for Educational Research. David then dedicated his time through doctoral research to investigate this field further, switching to an academic career at UCL. During this period he has developed his thinking about research-informed practice and ecosystems through numerous articles and in the development of innovative research–practice initiatives, including 'research-informed peer review' (RiPR). In July 2017, David was acknowledged in the *Oxford Review of Education* as one of the best new educational researchers in the UK.

Professor **Chris Brown** is Professor of Education at the School of Education and Sociology, University of Portsmouth. With a long-standing interest in how evidence can aid education policy and practice, Chris has written/edited eight books (including *Leading the Use of Research and Evidence in Schools*), scores of papers and has presented on the subject at a number of international conferences in Europe, Asia and North and South America. Chris has extensive experience of leading a range of funded projects, which seek to help practitioners to identify and scale up best practice, including a significant grant by the Education Endowment Foundation to work with 100+ primary schools in England to increase their use of research. Other projects include an evaluation of England's progress towards an evidence-informed school system (funded by England's Department for Education). Chris has received numerous awards for his work in this area including, in 2019, a Siftung Mercator Foundation Senior Fellowship. Such Fellowships are awarded to just six people each year, identified by a panel of experts as 'exceptionally talented and outstanding researchers and practitioners'. The purpose of the Mercator Fellowship programme is to offer selected fellows the space and freedom to also devote themselves to exploratory and unconventional research and practical projects (typically for six months). Previous fellows include advisors to former US President Obama and current French President Macron.

# ACKNOWLEDGEMENTS

Chris and David would like to thank the contributors for working so hard to make this book the insightful and compelling text it has become. We are truly lucky to have been able to work with all of you to produce this state-of-the art set of perspectives on how an ecosystems approach can help schools become research-informed.

# CONTRIBUTORS

**Kelly Bairos**, M.Ed., has studied Knowledge Mobilisation (KMb) since 2011 in both professional and academic capacities. As the Network Manager for the first phase of the Knowledge Network for Applied Education Research (KNAER), Kelly created connections between projects and organisations across Ontario, in addition to working as part of a team that created multiple KMb resources and workshops for a variety of audiences and stakeholders. In her current role as the Secretariat's Knowledge Mobilization Manager in phase 2 of KNAER, Kelly continues to build capacity in KMb across the province and works to connect a wide variety of education stakeholders with one another to strengthen the relationship between research and practice and build system-wide capacity for knowledge mobilisation.

**Tim Cain** is Professor in Education at Edge Hill University. Prior to taking this post, he taught for 19 years in four secondary schools. He subsequently worked at Kingston University, Bath Spa University and the University of Southampton, before moving to Edge Hill University in 2011. Here, he directs the research centre for Schools, Colleges and Teacher Education (SCaTE) and teaches research methods on undergraduate and postgraduate programmes. His research interests are in teacher education and how teachers, particularly in schools, use research findings and collaborative research methods to develop their practice. His latest work in this area is a book, published by Routledge: *Becoming a Research-Informed School: Why? What? How?*

**Carol Campbell** is Associate Professor of Leadership and Educational Change, and Co-Director of the Knowledge Network for Applied Education Research (KNAER), at the Ontario Institute for Studies in Education, University of Toronto. She is a member of the International Council of Education Advisors for the Scottish Government and a Board member of the International Congress for School Effectiveness and Improvement (ICSEI). Originally from Scotland, Carol has held education, academic and government roles in Canada, the UK and the

USA. Her recent co-authored books are: *Teacher Learning and Leadership: Of, By and For Teachers* (Routledge), *Empowering Educators in Canada* (Jossey-Bass) and *Empowered Educators: How High-Performing Systems Shape Teaching Quality Around the World* (Jossey-Bass). She is an active contributor on Twitter @CarolCampbell4.

**Clive Dimmock** was appointed Chair in Professional Learning and Leadership at the University of Glasgow in October 2013. Prior to this he was Professor of Education at the National Institute of Education, Nanyang Technological University, Singapore, and Professor Emeritus at University of Leicester. He is also Senior Research Fellow at the Asia Pacific Centre for Leadership, Hong Kong Institute of Education. He has held earlier appointments at Cardiff University, The University of Western Australia and The Chinese University of Hong Kong. His undergraduate degree was completed at the London School of Economics and doctorate in Comparative Education and Policy at the Institute of Education, London University.

**Valerie Drew** is a Senior Lecturer in the Faculty of Social Sciences at the University of Stirling where she is Programme Director for the MSc in Educational Leadership (leading to Specialist Qualification for Headship) and the MSc in Professional Education and Leadership. Her research interests and publications encompass professional learning and leadership, with a particular interest in the methodology of critical collaborative professional enquiry. She leads on School-based Curriculum Making through Critical Collaborative Professional Enquiry projects in partnership with local authorities in Scotland and Wales.

**Melanie Ehren** is a Professor in Educational Accountability and Improvement at the UCL Institute of Education and Head of the Centre for Educational Evaluation and Accountability (www.educationalevaluation.net). Her academic work focuses on the effectiveness of accountability and evaluation systems and aims to contribute to a greater understanding of the interplay between accountability and the broader education system in tackling inequality and improving student outcomes.

**Graham Handscomb** is Honorary Professor with University College London (UCL) and was Professor of Education and Dean of The College of Teachers. His has an extensive career of senior leadership of local authorities and schools and 20 years teaching experience. Graham has made a considerable contribution to the development of school-based practitioner enquiry and pioneered the concept of the *Research-Engaged School*. He wrote the criteria to establish the national Research Mark Award for the National Foundation for Educational Research. As an educational consultant he works with schools, Teaching Schools Alliances and Trusts throughout the UK and has also a range of international experience. He was a senior member of Hughes Hall, University of Cambridge, and is a fellow of numerous universities. Graham has made a major contribution to professional development policy and practice, is editor of *Professional Development Today* and on the editorial boards of a number of journals.

**Doris McWhorter** is the former Director of the Education Research and Evaluation Strategy Branch of the Ontario Ministry of Education where she was

responsible for leading the ministry's research and evaluation strategy, the Brian
Fleming Research Library and Records Management for the Learning Ministries.
Doris has a longstanding commitment to research partnerships and the mobilization of quality evidence to improve school and system effectiveness. As an educator, school district Research Officer and MISA (Managing Information for Student
Achievement) Leader, Doris was instrumental in building capacity for data management and evidence use among classroom teachers, school and system leaders. She has championed research capacity building, knowledge mobilization and
collaborative partnerships between education researchers and practitioners across
Ontario as past Co-Chair of the Ontario Education Research Panel (OERP),
Past President of the Association of Educational Researchers of Ontario (AERO)
and Co-Chair of the 2017 International Congress for School Effectiveness and
Improvement (ICSEI). Doris has extensive experience as an organizer, facilitator
and presenter at provincial, national and international education research conferences. These include the annual Ontario Education Research Symposium (OERS)
as well as the 2019 and 2020 ICSEI conferences in the role of Executive Director.

**Gareth Mills** leads the Enquiring Schools programme at the National Foundation
for Educational Research. He designed the programme to build bridges between
research evidence and classroom practice. It uses teacher-enquiry as a vehicle
for professional development and school improvement. Gareth is also an experienced curriculum developer. He has worked with schools and organisations,
such as UNESCO, the International Baccalaureate Organization and the British
Council, developing curriculum and professional development programmes for
teachers and school leaders. When Head of Futures and Innovation at England's
National Curriculum Authority, he led developments in the school curriculum so
that it might better prepare young people for life and work in the 21st century.
He is the author of the National College of School Leadership's publication, 'Why
Curriculum Innovation Matters', a document that explores the key features of suc-
cessful leadership of curriculum and pedagogy.

**Katina Pollock** is an Associate Professor, Educational Leadership and Policy in the
field of Critical Policy, Equity, and Leadership Studies at the Faculty of Education,
Western University, and Co-Director of the KNAER Secretariat. As a scholar in
leadership and policy, Katina has been awarded several research grants and contracts. Three of these projects are funded by the Social Sciences and Humanities
Research Council of Canada. In addition to her traditional scholarship efforts,
Dr Pollock has also been involved in large-scale knowledge mobilisation initiatives that connect research to practice. Katina is also the inaugural Director for
Western's Centre for Education Leadership. This Centre focuses on supporting
aspiring, new and experienced education leaders by reducing the gap between
applied educational research and leadership practice. Katina's recently co-authored
books include, *How School Leaders Contribute to Student Success* (Springer).

**Mark Priestley** is Professor of Education and Director of the Stirling Network for
Curriculum Studies, an international network set up in 2016 to connect curriculum
scholars, policy makers and practitioners. His research interests lie in the school

curriculum – theory, policy and practice – and especially the processes of curriculum making across different layers of education systems. He is Lead Editor of *The Curriculum Journal*. His publications include the edited collection *Reinventing the Curriculum* (with Biesta) and monograph *Teacher Agency: An Ecological Approach* (with Biesta and Robinson). Priestley advises three national governments (Ireland, Scotland, Wales) on curriculum matters. He is a Co-Convener of the EERA network 3, Curriculum Innovation and a board member of the European Association for Curriculum Studies.

**Lesley Saunders** holds visiting professorships at UCL Institute of Education, London, and Newman University, Birmingham, and an honorary research fellowship at Oxford University Department of Education. She is a qualified teacher and an honorary member of the Chartered College of Teaching. She worked for 13 years at the National Foundation for Educational Research, where she set up and headed the NFER's School Improvement Research Centre. After holding a short-term secondment at the World Bank, she was appointed senior policy advisor for research at the General Teaching Council for England. She now works as an independent part-time consultant, with clients ranging from Save the Children in Kosovo to individual university departments of education. She has consistently sought to find ways of promoting and supporting teaching as a scholarly and research-informed profession.

**Roos Van Gasse** is a postdoctoral researcher at the Faculty of Social Sciences, Department Training and Education Sciences at the University of Antwerp, Belgium. Her general research interests involve policy making, data use, assessment in schools and teachers' professional development. She finished her PhD on teacher interactions in data use, and the effects of data use interactions on teachers' professional development. Furthermore, she has been involved in D-PAC (Digital Platform for Assessment of Competences), which focuses on the merits of Comparative Judgement for competence assessment. Within D-PAC, her general research interests involve large-scale assessment and learning gains, formative (peer) assessment and assessor professionalisation.

**Jan Vanhoof** received his PhD in Educational Sciences at the University of Antwerp in 2007 and is currently Associate Professor at the Faculty of Social Sciences, Department Training and Education Sciences at the University of Antwerp, Belgium. He is a member of the EduBROn research group (www. edubron.be). His current research activities focus on school policy and quality care in general and on school self-evaluation, data driven school policy and professional learning in particular. Jan Vanhoof is Co-Founder and Vice-Chair of the ICSEI (International Congress for School Effectiveness and Improvement) data use network. He has published a variety of articles in the area of school management, professional learning, quality care and data use by schools.

**Peter Van Petegem** received his PhD in Educational Sciences at the University of Ghent in 1997 and is currently full Professor at the Department of Training and Education Sciences, Faculty of Social Sciences at the University of Antwerp (Belgium). He is a member of the EduBROn research group (www.edubron.be)

and former Head of the Centre of Excellence in Higher Education (www.uantwer pen.be/echo). He is also Visiting Professor at the Norges teknisk-naturvitenskapelige universitet (NTNU, Trondheim, Norway) His research interests include school and education policies, environmental education and education for sustainable development. He co-authored more than 100 articles in international peer-reviewed journals, such as *Learning & Instruction, School Effectiveness and School Improvement, Sustainability, Environmental Education Research* and *Journal of Cleaner Production*. He is Editor-in-Chief of *Studies in Educational Evaluation*.

**Erica van Roosmalen** received her PhD in Sociology in 1993 from the University of Alberta. She is the Director of the Education Research & Evaluation Strategy Branch and the Knowledge Network for Applied Education Research with the Ontario Ministry of Education. She is an Adjunct Professor of Practice, Masters of International Education (School Leadership), Charles Sturt University. Since 1996, Erica has been a leader in building and engaging multisectoral, multidisciplinary partnerships of researchers, practitioners and community members in the fields of health, social services and education, provincially, nationally and internationally. A dynamic educational leader and change agent with experience in elementary, secondary and post-secondary contexts, Erica works at the intersection of research, practice and policy ensuring research evidence is meaningful, scalable and practical to a wide variety of stakeholders.

**Geoff Whitty** (1946–2018) taught in primary and secondary schools before moving to the higher education sector, initially as part of Bath Spa University's initial teacher education provision. This was followed by posts at the University of Wisconsin–Madison, King's College London, Bristol Polytechnic and Goldsmiths College. He joined the Institute of Education, University of London as Karl Mannheim Professor of Sociology of Education in 1992 and served as the Institute's Director from 2000 to 2010. From 2010 he was the Institute's Director Emeritus and later held posts at the Universities of Bath, Bath Spa and Newcastle, Australia. Over the course of his career he would be President of the British Educational Research Association and of the College of Teachers. In 2011 he was awarded a CBE for services to teacher education.

**Emma Wisby** is Head of Policy and Public Affairs at the UCL Institute of Education. Prior to that she was Committee Specialist to the House of Commons Education Select Committee and a researcher in the field of education policy, during which time she undertook a review of school councils and pupil voice for the government. Following a PhD at the University of Sheffield, which examined the post-Dearing shift to standards-based quality assurance in the UK higher education sector, she spent her early career conducting consultancy research for government departments and their agencies across schools, further education and teacher education policy.

# FOREWORD

When I worked as part of a team commissioned by the Department for Education to review the development of evidence-informed teaching in England (Coldwell et al., 2017), three aspects of the study struck me as particularly noteworthy in relation to the themes in this book.

Firstly, when we set out to recruit a sample of schools as case study sites for the research, we wanted to achieve a balance between schools that were more and less engaged with research and evidence. So we invited school leaders nationally to complete a short questionnaire about how they and their staff used research and evidence. Based on these responses we selected 15 case study schools, thinking that we had identified five that were highly engaged, five that were averagely engaged and five that were not significantly engaged with research. In practice though, when we visited the schools and interviewed a range of staff, we found that only one of the 15 schools could be said to be genuinely highly engaged.[1]

Secondly, when we analysed the data, we concluded that about a third of the case study schools had what we called a 'leadership research evidence culture', as opposed to a whole-school evidence culture. In these schools, senior leaders saw it as their job to engage with research and to use this to inform their decision-making. In some cases they might then engage staff in the research as part of a whole-school approach, while in others they might use the research to justify a particular decision to staff. Beyond this, these leaders felt that teachers were too busy to engage with research and saw it as their job to buffer teachers from such distractions.

Thirdly, we interviewed former and current staff in a small number of schools that had historically been active in engaging with research, but which had nevertheless seen a decline in terms of student attainment data and/or Ofsted outcomes. What this strand of work showed is how quickly a school's approach can change, for example in the face of new demands from the exosystem, or when a few key staff leave. It also indicated that research-engagement is not a panacea, at least in

England's highly accountable school system: schools must integrate and embed it within a wider improvement model that ensures improved progress and outcomes for all students.

For me these three snippets highlight some of the issues and challenges associated with understanding why, where and how research does and doesn't inform practice in schools: issues which are picked up and addressed in different ways and from different perspectives throughout this valuable book. These issues include the conceptual challenges we face in defining what is meant by evidence and evidence-informed practice, and in understanding how any such evidence is drawn on – directly or indirectly – by practitioners and schools to inform their thinking and work. They also include the challenge of analysing the ways in which the wider ecosystem (a helpful conceptual framework that is used to link the different contributions to this book) influences and interacts with teachers' use of evidence.

Starting with the first of these challenges – how to understand evidence and its use – the book provides a rich variety of perspectives. At one end of the spectrum, Van Gasse et al. include almost any form of data in their analysis of practices in Flanders, where the absence of the kinds of standardised assessment and accountability metrics that are common in England, Scotland and the Netherlands, means that schools must compile and evaluate evidence from multiple sources. At the other end, there is a widespread rejection by all the authors of any instrumental 'what works' notion that research and evidence can be applied without adaptation to context and culture, but there are shades of view in terms of how far research and evidence should be seen as primarily a tool in the pursuit of school improvement or a wider prompt for conceptual and critical thinking by teachers as reflective professionals.

These perspectives inevitably shape the discussions on evidence use, but what I find most encouraging is how many of the authors are able to exemplify the uses that they advocate and to show how research-informed practice can be developed, even in the face of an ecosystem that contains countervailing pressures. So, for example, Tim Cain (Chapter 8) provides powerful examples of how research and enquiry can help trainee teachers to reflect on and enhance their practice in focused but potentially sustainable ways. Equally, Mark Priestley and Valerie Drew (Chapter 10) describe their use of Critical Collaborative Professional Enquiry (CCPE) and an ecological perspective to help school teachers and leaders in East Lothian to develop research engagement and agency. Similarly, the chapters by David Godfrey, Chris Brown and Roos Van Gasse et al. provide other practical interventions.

Turning to the wider ecosystem, a number of chapters highlight the ways in which accountability and performativity can limit a broad notion of evidence use. Therefore, it is helpful to have Melanie Ehren's analysis of accountability frameworks and their tendency to promote isomorphism as well as the potential for more 'participatory' models of evaluation. Equally, chapters by Gareth Mills and Lesley Saunders, Graham Handscomb and Katina Pollock et al. explore other aspects of the wider ecosystem, while Clive Dimmock's excellent chapter on school-level leadership addresses this important and recurring theme.

In his chapter, Graham Handscomb states that 'The third millennium school is required to be self-evaluating, open to scrutiny, evidenced-based, data rich'. This may be true, but in their powerful concluding chapter, Emma Wisby and Geoff Whitty not only remind us that this terrain is often fraught and contested, but also that in our current 'post-truth' world where expertise is often dismissed, there are forces that might take us away from Handscomb's ideal. By providing rich discussion and evidence on this theme within a powerful ecological framework and drawn from work in England, Canada, Flanders and Scotland, this important and timely book enriches our understanding and helps us to appreciate how Handscomb's vision might yet be achieved.

Toby Greany
Professor of Education, University of Nottingham
October 2018

## Note

1 i.e. in the sense that all staff were expected and supported to engage in and with research – see Coldwell et al. (2017) for a fuller discussion.

## Reference

Coldwell, M., Greany, T., Higgins, S., Brown, C., Maxwell, B., Stiell, B., Stoll, L., Willis, B. and Burns, H. (2017) *Evidence-informed teaching: an evaluation of progress in England. Research Report July 2017* (DFE- RR-696) London: Department for Education.

# INTRODUCTION

This book looks at the potential for research-use by educators to improve schools for all young people. What makes it unique is the ecosystems perspective we have adopted to consider the actualisation of research-use. We assume that for a research-use ecosystem to be optimal, we need to examine its many levels of scale and the numerous interconnections that occur amongst the people and institutions that inhabit it. Once we understand these, we can then work to ensure interdependent elements of the ecosystem cohere effectively, nourishment is afforded where needed and tensions addressed. To rise to this challenge, we use the book to bring together contributions from experts working in a variety of fields connected to the key elements of the ecosystem (for instance school leadership, professional development and accountability). In setting out their thoughts, our experts have engaged with what they identify as the key issues facing the research-use ecosystem both theoretically and empirically. Often groundbreaking research is presented to describe the issues under discussion. Elsewhere case studies exemplify interesting and innovative practice. New theories and values systems are also posited. Together our 13 chapters thus provide a first glimpse of the exciting possibility of an ecosystem of learning and innovation in our schools; where structures, cultures, practices and policies align to promote research-informed school improvement.

This book has three overall aims:

1. to expand the analysis of evidence- and research-informed practice, considering the wider environment within which it is undertaken;
2. to show the interplay and tensions between aspects of the ecosystem and to illustrate how different aspects of the ecosystem affect evidence use;
3. to reconcile all aspects of the ecosystem within an overarching framework which attempts to explain the complex totality of the ecosystem.

To meet these aims the book begins, in Chapter 1, by defining our key elements: i.e. the concept of a research-engaged school and of the ecosystem. One of the authors of this first chapter is responsible for the coining of the term research-engaged school and the co-author has also written extensively, following in this tradition. The contribution of the idea of an ecosystem to thinking about such schools, is also outlined in detail. While all chapters make reference to the various interconnections in the whole ecosystem, they move generally from upper to lower levels of the ecosystem, starting at the exosystem and working down towards the meso and microsystems of schooling. Thus, we look at a knowledge network for schools in Canada (Chapter 2) and then the accountability systems surrounding the schools (Chapter 3). This is followed by examining leadership at every level of research-engaged schools (Chapter 4) and then by the role that is and could be played by teacher professional bodies in their growth and sustainability (Chapter 5). In Chapter 6, we outline two innovative approaches to school collaboration, based on shared principles for bringing research knowledge to bear in school improvement alongside other sources of enquiry and information.

Moving more clearly to examining the mesosystem, we then look at how schools can increase their ability to make data-informed improvements to practice with the aid of data brokerage (Chapter 7). Then follow four chapters that are more closely focused on the practice of teachers (the microsystem). We start this by looking at pre-service professional education (Chapter 8), then in-service professional learning and research (Chapter 9), a case of teachers learning through professional enquiry (Chapter 10) and then by looking at the decision-making processes of teachers through the lens of optimal rationality (Chapter 11). In the penultimate chapter (Chapter 12) the values dimension in research-practice ecosystem is examined, in particular the need to maintain openness to a range of research methodologies, an inclusive research focus and towards a principled agenda. Finally Chapter 13 synthesises the learning of the chapters in the body of the book, integrates them into the ecosystems literature and suggests a new conceptual framework for the ecosystem of research-engaged schools.

As we hope is apparent, the purpose of the book then is to both challenge and infuse: to challenge those currently working in the area to begin to think more deeply about their work and the theoretical mechanisms that underpin it; to infuse by providing theoretical tools to assist them in doing so. As such, our audience is primarily those studying and writing about this area, however a secondary audience will be policy makers, practitioners and the departments, organisations, schools and chains that employ them. Whilst the book's primary domain is education, the concept of evidence-informed practice has salience across a number of sectors, notably health and social care. There are also a number of organisations and current initiatives that are likely to express an interest in this book, related to the work of government Departments for Education and Higher Education Institutions, in particular those departments or functions that are responsible for enhancing knowledge use. This book should also be of interest to those studying postgraduate taught degrees and PhDs in relevant fields. Furthermore, the reach of this book is international; within this volume we have references to work conducted in England, Canada, Germany, the United States, Singapore and Belgium, among others. Our authors have worked in a wide range of national contexts and this, we feel, is further testament to the global relevance of the arguments expressed in this book.

Finally, although pleased with the work we have produced, we feel that the potential for the ecosystem framework has yet to be fully exploited. We therefore recognise this book as a good first attempt at deepening such thinking and invite further responses and contributions from the research community. Thank you for engaging with this work.

David Godfrey and Chris Brown

# 1

# EVIDENCE USE, RESEARCH-ENGAGED SCHOOLS AND THE CONCEPT OF AN ECOSYSTEM

*David Godfrey and Graham Handscomb*

## Aims of the chapter

- To sketch out different levels of the school ecosystem.
- To outline the ecosystem concept of the research-engaged school.
- To propose theoretical frameworks to understand the ecological conditions for a research-engaged school system.
- To foreground subsequent chapters in this book.

## Introduction

This chapter explains how research can be integrated into the lives of teachers and school leaders as part of the structures and cultures of the organisation. *Research-engaged schools* (RES) promote enquiry stances by teachers, and the use of published research and other school evidence; they are outward looking and connect to the research community. This engagement occurs through interconnections from the macro to the micro-level of the school ecosystem and ultimately affects the lives of young learners. The dimensions and elements of such a system are described here and subsequent chapters elaborate on chosen aspects of these levels. The chapter also opens up thinking about theoretical lenses that can be used to understand and research (social) ecosystems, applying these to research-engaged schools.

## Ecosystems and levels

In this section we outline the basic ecosystem concept for the school system that is later built upon in subsequent chapters. This is informed by work published else-where, where it is argued that it is helpful to understand research-engaged schools as operating within an ecosystem (Godfrey, 2016a, 2017; Godfrey and Brown, 2018). This work has been influenced by Urie Bronfenbrenner's (1992) ecosystems model used in developmental psychology. Bronfenbrenner suggested that in order to study children in a way that led to high 'ecological validity', i.e. generating authentic findings and theories that could be applied to real life contexts, and not just in 'ideal' or 'laboratory' conditions, then we needed to take account of the various subsystems within which children developed. For instance, if we were studying children's classroom behaviour or mental health, we may wish to analyse their peer group interactions (the microsystem) and their family's economic and social context (mesosystem). In addition, if the child misses school or otherwise gets into difficulties adapting to school life, policies to do with truancy or exclusion may have an impact on how he or she is subsequently punished or supported by the school (the exosystem). In turn, cultural and societal beliefs about school and family life (the macrosystem) influence the exo, meso and microsystems by shaping the way that schools are valued, funded, organised and evaluated. The developmental rate of the changes at each level – e.g. the child's physical, cognitive and emotional development (the chronosystem) could also be studied in relation to their transition through school years, or alongside curriculum reforms. Bronfenbrenner believed that by studying children in such a way we avoid over-simplifying the causal links that lead to various outcomes in their lives; we also consciously connect the values and beliefs of society to the eventual impact they have at the micro-level.

This model has much potential when applied to a school system. Here the 'institution' or 'organisational' level is in sharpest focus (meso-level) and we are challenged to think about the nature of influence of political values on the types of schools we have, the working environments they create for staff and children and the ways that schools work together to meet the aims of the education system. Ultimately, these higher-level elements of the ecosystem will have an effect on the microsystems that most impact on children's lives, shaping the way that teachers and other adults 'educate' them. Box 1.1 outlines how such a model can be applied to the school system and later sections in this chapter focus on how such an ecosystem can be enhanced or enriched through research engagement.

---

### Box 1.1  Ecosystem levels as applied to the school system

- The macrosystem: This consists of the overarching beliefs and values in society that affect the school system, such as belief that parents should be able to choose their children's schools and that schools need to be measured, ranked and held accountable for 'outcomes'.
- The exosystem: This is the concrete manifestation of the macrosystem. This might include government policies to increase school autonomy and the use of school inspections and the publication of school league tables. This level is

*(continued)*

*(continued)*

also sometimes used to describe the indirect environment, for instance networks or other organisations that connect to the school (as in Chapter 2 in this book).

- The mesosystem: This is the interaction between elements of the microsystem with the immediate environment, specifically the 'workings' of a school as an organisation or institution. This could include a school policy to set up professional learning communities or in the use of data to inform decisions by school leaders.
- The microsystem: This is the immediate educational environment of the child, especially the child as 'learner' in the classroom, their relationships with teachers, peers, parents and other staff. The above levels may influence the methods by which children are taught and assessed, placed into ability groups and so on.
- The chronosystem: The pace of change or development at each and any sub level of the ecosystem. For instance, a child's cognitive maturation can be studied alongside transitions from the primary phase to the secondary phase of education. Attempts to improve or change teaching practice can be contrasted or set within the context of often rapid policy changes introduced by new governments, eager to force through reforms to the school system.

## Some key issues

This ecosystem frame addresses three key issues that we consider essential to the study of research-engaged schools: First, the need to connect all school change ultimately to its intended educational impact on children, and by corollary to society; second, to ensure that elements of the system – especially at the individual school level – are not viewed reductively or in isolation, and third, to see system change as both interconnected and working in patterns of multidirectional cause and effect.

The first issue addresses the need to understand the way the macrosystem indirectly impacts on the microsystems of school children. As such, tracing the effect of educational policies purely on the performance of schools in inspection reports or league tables is insufficient – this both stops short of the child's microsystem and too narrowly measures outcomes. In order to link the values that drive school policies to their eventual impact on students, each reform must be judged in terms of its stated aim; for instance to develop children's mental and physical well-being, to eliminate inequalities in student educational outcomes, or to build citizens fit to enter democratic society and to have the means to influence it. Without addressing these issues explicitly, we are in danger of reverting to measuring what is easy to measure – for example examination results – and to simplistic suggestions about 'what works' in schools (Biesta, 2007).

In terms of the second issue, we recognise that research-engaged schools are meso and exo-level organisations / institutions with numerous vertical and horizontal connections in the ecosystem. We know from previous work on school effectiveness that the effect of the teacher on a child's academic attainment is more than the indirect effect of the school's overall effectiveness (Barber and Mourshed, 2007). More generally, we might conclude that the quality of the child's parenting and the home environment has considerable effect on educational outcomes for children and is more important than teaching and that teaching has more importance than the quality of school leadership (Robinson, 2011). Thus the extent to which the school contributes to a system that fosters high quality teaching, support and parental engagement to emerge, should be our main concern. In turn, we need to consider that there are factors outside of the school itself, e.g. the support of local educational authority/district or the role of teacher professional bodies, that also impact on the quality of teaching, the ability of parents to engage in their children's education and so on. If the unit of the individual school is too much the focus, this can lead to unfairly comparing one school's performance with another and in creating a blame culture in which individual schools are disproportionately held accountable for outcomes outside of their control.

The above point also links to the third area that the ecosystems approach addresses, the interconnectivity of levels and multiple directions of cause and effect. For many nations we see a macrosystem emphasising school autonomy, parental choice and external accountability (Sahlberg, 2011). Commonplace in many nations' education policies (exo-level) has been the promotion of school-led improvement, coupled with the encouragement of new types of networks of schools (Greany and Higham, 2018). Such policies emphasise horizontal connections in the ecosystem, specifically at the meso- and exo-levels, through school-to-school collaborations or teachers and school leaders working across schools. Evidence suggests that professional learning networks can positively impact on schools' innovation potential (e.g. Berkemeyer et al., 2008); the professional development of teachers (e.g. Berkemeyer et al., 2011); improved teaching practice (Darling-Hammond, 2010) and student outcomes (e.g. van Holt et al., 2015).

With such new forms of lateral work evolving, the role of the exo- and macro-level (i.e. local and central government) will need to enable this lateral collaboration to flourish.

Lastly, focusing on the chronosystem helps remind us of the need to examine the relative developmental pace of change from the actors' perspective at different levels in the ecosystem. For instance, governments can impose policy changes that have dramatic implications for the school curriculum in the space of a few weeks. However, it can take teachers months or years to implement the new curriculum due to the need to build new skills, introduce new materials and refine strategies to context. The chronosystem can also be projected backwards and forwards – tracing backwards to the historical antecedents of the present system and forwards towards a new, imagined future for schooling in the late 21st century (and for those interested, one way for examining policy and systemic evolution in the chronosystem can found in Ball's work on critical policy sociology: e.g. Ball, 2008).

Such thinking also necessitates theoretical approaches that acknowledge the complex and open nature of systems within which schools operate and the factors that impact on young people's educational outcomes. No one factor at any level can be taken to have a function in isolation of the wider ecosystem; and the effects of particular features – for instance the promotion of research use by school principals – must be taken alongside other elements, such as the nature of initial teacher training.

Below we offer a more thorough conceptualisation of the research-engaged school in relation to this ecosystem model. Later we outline models to think about two further issues: how to create a highly research-engaged school ecosystem and also how to study it.

## The research-engaged school

In Chapter 9, Handscomb reflects on the value of enquiry and research being an integral part of the continuing professional development for practitioners – and the personal, professional dividends that can accrue. However it has also been suggested that there are implied benefits for the whole school and indeed for the wider system. The concept of the research-engaged school is helpful here in articulating how practitioner enquiry, embedded within professional learning, is in a symbiotic and dynamic relationship with other cultural elements within the school ecosystem (Godfrey, 2016a; Godfrey and Brown, 2018).

When the term 'research-engaged school' was first coined it was identified as having four interrelated dimensions: it would have a *research-rich pedagogy* – i.e. manifest in the school's teaching and learning and classroom practice; it would have a *research orientation* – exemplified in the school's values and culture; it would *promote research communities* – within and beyond the school; and research would be at *the heart of school policy and practice* (Handscomb and MacBeath, 2003). There has been much exemplification and development of these features since. For Wilkins (2011) the term research-engaged entailed the practitioner combining the undertaking of one's own action research whilst concurrently accessing and making judicious use of published research, echoing the Research Learning Community practice mentioned in Chapter 6. Godfrey (2016b, p. 268) used the focus on research orientation to emphasise that 'such schools create a culture in which research provides a richer professional discourse'. This is particularly significant in helping to illuminate the reciprocal relationship between practitioner research and professional learning. Engaging in enquiry and research provides teachers with the language and context with which they can explore and evaluate their own practice, and share and critique these insights within their professional communities.

Combining the work of various authors, there are five key aspects of a RES:

1. They promote practitioner research among staff (especially teachers)
2. They encourage staff to read and make sense of published research

3.  They welcome participation in research projects led by outside organisations such as universities
4.  They use research to inform decision-making at every level of the school – individual, departmental, whole school and in collaborative work
5.  They have an outward looking orientation, which may be aided by maintaining research-based links with other schools, universities or professional/academic entities.

> *(Handscomb and MacBeath, 2003; Sharp et al., 2005; Wilkins, 2011)*

Dimmock (see also Chapter 4, this volume) develops the notion of the RES as a unifying concept, addressing three systemic concerns:

1.  How to bridge the research–policy–practice gap by mobilising knowledge more effectively through knowledge producers and consumers working collaboratively
2.  Valuing and integrating both tacit knowledge and academic coded (explicit) knowledge
3.  Raising the professionalism and reflectivity of teachers and leaders

> *(adapted from Dimmock, 2014, p. 1)*

**TABLE 1.1** Key Characteristics of Research-Engaged Schools Mapped onto the Mesosystem of Research-Informed Practice in Schools (from Godfrey, 2016b, p. 53)

| *Features of research-engaged schools (Handscomb and MacBeath, 2003; Sharp et al., 2005; Wilkins, 2011)* | *Human and organisational infrastructure for research-engaged schools (Dimmock, 2014)* | *Mesosystem dimensions of research-informed practice* |
| --- | --- | --- |
| 1.  Promotes practitioner research among its staff | | |
| 2.  Encourages its staff to access, read, use and engage critically with published research | Research-engaged teachers and leaders | Research-informed professional practice |
| 3.  Uses research to inform its decision-making at every level | Use of design-research-development | The school as a learning organisation |
| 4.  Welcomes being the subject of research by outside organisations | | |
| 5.  Has 'an outward looking orientation' | Schools and networks as PLCs | Connectivity to the wider system |

Dimmock (2014, p. 3) argues that RESs provide a way to leverage the mobilisation of knowledge across the school system, and they do so by: facilitating research-engaged teachers and leaders; creating schools and networks as research-engaged professional learning communities (PLCs) and using a methodology that enables research to be scaled up, while being tailored to context.

We can map the five features of RESs and Dimmock's 'linchpin' concept onto three overlapping dimensions at the meso-level of the ecosystem of research-informed practice (see Table 1.1).

## Interplay between enquiry, leadership and professional development

Building on the first dimension above, we prefer to use *research-informed practice* over Dimmock's 'research-engaged teachers and leaders'. By doing so we focus on two concerns:

1. The need to encompass the practices of a wider range of professionals – other than teachers – that work in and with schools and that have a direct effect on learners, such as teaching assistants (TAs) and other support staff. Chapter 7, for instance, looks at the important role of 'knowledge brokers' in enhancing data use in schools. In this book, we have generally excluded the role of 'non-professionals' such as parents and pupils from our analysis, although these groups can potentially play an important part in the process of enquiry and school transformation (Rubin and Jones, 2007). There is likely to be further scope to investigate the role of wider groups of stakeholders in a research-informed ecosystem beyond this volume.

2. The need to see leadership alongside professional practice – sometimes as a 'separate' practice and sometimes as integral to the idea of the professional endeavour. Thus, there is an important role of formal leadership in establishing, maintaining and building research engagement in schools (e.g. Brown, 2015 and Sharp et al., 2006). However, a broader view of leadership also takes into account a distributed model, including how teacher leadership can be enhanced through engagement with research (e.g. Frost, 2000). Thus, it is not always possible to separate out membership of 'leaders' from the work of practitioners.

There is a compelling case for enabling research engagement as a core element of all staff development programmes. Indeed some have seen this in terms of a fundamental professional expectation and right:

> All teachers should have an entitlement to research training in order to develop their role as critical users of research . . . All schools and colleges should have an entitlement, and perhaps a responsibility, to participate in a relevant research partnership for appropriate periods.
>
> *(Dyson, 2001, p. 4)*

More recently such an entitlement has been seen as a fundamental feature within the context of the self-improving school system. Thus the BERA-RSA Inquiry into the role of research in teacher education made the case for the development of self-improving education systems in which all teachers become research literate and many have frequent opportunities for engagement in research and enquiry (Furlong, 2014).

Sachs (2011) reflects the views of many that sadly much CPD does not enable teachers to be 'researchers of their own and their peer's practice' (p. 162) and thus contribute to increased understanding and transformation of practice. To redress this she calls for a range of learning opportunities 'supported by school cultures of inquiry and be evidenced-based, where evidence is collected and evaluated' (Sachs, 2011, p. 163). This appeal resonates with the British Education Research Association's call for 'close to practice' research, in which educational research is based on problems in practice, often involves researchers working in partnership with practitioners, may address issues defined by the latter as relevant or useful, and will support the application of critical thinking, and the use of evidence in practice.[1]

There is clearly much more ground to make up. On the positive side there is significantly greater awareness of the vital part the development of an inquiry outlook can have for professional learning and that a research evidenced-based culture can have for school improvement. However, such awareness has not yet resulted in the kind of momentum where inquiry becomes the bedrock of professional learning in all schools. These issues are explored more fully in this book in terms of: 'Teachers' professional bodies and the role of research' (Chapter 5); 'Research-informed initial teacher education' (Chapter 8); 'Professional learning and research' (Chapter 9) and 'Professional enquiry: an ecological approach to developing teacher agency' (Chapter 10).

Perhaps the common element in all the explorations of what a research-engaged school might comprise is agreement around the central tenet that 'research and enquiry is at the heart of the school, its outlook, systems, and activity' (Handscomb and MacBeath, 2003, p. 10). This in turn brings into sharp focus the crucial contribution of leadership to school-based enquiry and to professional development, and indeed to the relationship between them.

The leadership role is seen as pivotal not just in terms of an authoritative 'gate-keeping' function, whereby leaders permit, enable and support teachers' research engagement (Sharp and Handscomb, 2007), but also by the way in which they foster a culture of research engagement through their own outlook, values and behaviour (see also Chapter 4). Stoll, 2015a suggests senior leaders provide role modelling through, for instance, actively looking for a range of perspectives, consciously seeking relevant information from many diverse sources and constantly exploring new ways to tackle recurrent problems. Indeed the relationship between leadership and research engagement can be seen to be in a mutually beneficial reciprocal relationship with professional development dividends for leaders themselves: 'Research engagement provides an opportunity for school leaders to share leadership and for staff to develop their leadership skills' (Sharp et al., 2006, p. 9).

The interplay between these ecosystem elements of enquiry, leadership and professional development is also implicitly bounded within the overall ethos of the school as a learning enterprise. Thus teachers are characterised as leaders of learning and as continually learning themselves through enquiry: 'teachers see themselves increasingly as learning from their students, as well as being leaders of learning, of both their students and one other' (Durrant, 2014, p. 54).

## Enquiry, self-evaluation and accountability

For the second meso-level dimension, the school is a learning organisation in as much as it connects research knowledge, alongside other forms of knowledge, to internal school decision-making and practices. This is also complementary, when schools are seen as interconnected and outward looking institutions, to Dimmock's (2014) point that school innovations sometimes need to be 'scaled up', for instance by using a research-design-development methodology (Bryk and Gomez, 2008). Learning organisations also need to engage in rigorous cycles of self-evaluation. Knowing thyself has never been so important. In the febrile accountability culture in England, of unannounced inspection, maintaining robust self-evaluation processes has become crucial. So there is much perceived value in being able to harness the enquiry and reflection of its staff to feed in to this.

The move from a stark overreliance on external inspection towards an emphasis on schools continuously evaluating themselves is a very welcome development that has taken many decades to gestate in England. Other schools systems have also engaged in self-evaluation to a greater or lesser degree. However, self-evaluation carries with it the risk of schools establishing their own crude overbearing internal inspection regimes:

> With the imperative for self-evaluation there is a danger that managers will scurry to precipitate judgements about their schools without taking . . . a due regard to the evidence. This requires a set of skills that clearly sit within the realm of enquiry and research.
>
> *(Handscomb and Ramsey, 2008, p. 4)*

Effective self-evaluation entails taking the opportunity to grow a rich school ethos of enquiry as part of its professional learning culture. Indeed there is clearly a fertile reciprocal correspondence between these two vibrant forces of research engagement and self-evaluation, with increasing evidence that research cultures significantly enhance schools' capacity for self-evaluation and improving themselves: 'Teachers and students thrive in the kind of settings that we describe as research-rich, and research-rich schools and colleges are those that are likely to have the greatest capacity for self-evaluation and self-improvement' (Furlong, 2014, p. 5–6).

In Chapter 3, Melanie Ehren explores further the relationship between external accountability, self-evaluation and a culture of enquiry.

## Only connect!

Thus, the final dimension looks at *'connectivity' to the wider system*. Here, we can analyse meso-level interactions with levels above and below this level, as well as laterally. 'Connections' can be seen as an inclusive term to look at 'collaborations' as well as other kinds of interactions, forms of communication, spreading of ideas and knowledge, and so on. Chapter 2, for instance, examines a knowledge network in Canada.

Godfrey (2016a, p. 67) states that in order for teachers to become 'research literate, enquiring professionals' they need to be 'supported in developing the skills of research through in-house and externally supported expertise'. This raises the significant contribution of collaboration within and beyond the school. The forming of research communities was seen as an integral part of the research-engaged school. It has perhaps gained increased profile with the dawn of new forms of school organisation and the proliferation of alliances, trusts and other school improvement collaboratives: 'In England, increasingly, evidence-based teacher enquiry and joint practice development between schools are perceived by teaching school alliances as impetus for CPD and part of the mainstream school-to-school improvement' (Handscomb et al., 2014).

Often school-university partnerships play an important part in effective research and professional learning collaboration. This can take the form of teacher research coordinators operating across and between schools and universities (McLaughlin and Black-Hawkins, 2007), or the role of 'the 'blended professionals' who work across institutional boundaries' (Whitchurch, 2009). Such partnerships are not always smooth sailing because of the cultural differences between schools and universities (see the 'mind the gap' critique in Handscomb et al., 2014). However, much of the literature on successful research partnerships points to a common set of conditions which include 'the importance of shared leadership, shared goals, development of social and intellectual skills needed for collaborative work, and adequate time' (Arhar et al., 2013, p. 627). Chapter 6 outlines two research projects that have utilised university-school collaborations to inject published research into school practitioners' thinking in order to lead to improvements at the whole school (and to an extent network) level. Such initiatives require skill and time to foster, develop and embed but have provided both sides with highly satisfying experiences of collaborative work that spans research and school practice.

Perhaps one of the biggest challenges is how to foster and utilise the potential of collaboration between schools. The educational landscape has changed dramatically from that which would have been unrecognisable at the turn of the century:

> The pattern of education in England is shifting. Schools that once were islands are becoming connected. Indeed, it is increasingly rare to find outstanding schools that do not have a web of links with other schools. Competition remains, but now co-exists with collaboration and the creation of formal alliances through federations and chains.
>
> *(Matthews et al., 2011, p. 5)*

Such an environment has been uniquely termed 'coopetition' (Muijs and Rumyantseva, 2014). Many other countries will find this a familiar picture. Within this collaborative environment the imperative is to draw upon the expertise that resides within the self-improving school system, 'to learn from each other, within and between schools, to tap into the professional expertise that lies latent in the system, and to learn from what works!' (Handscomb, 2012, p. 3). However, this is no easy task because the sharing of knowledge to bring about genuine 'transfer' of practice from one setting to another has always been difficult and highly problematic (Hargreaves, 1998). It is here that professional development grounded in enquiry can make a significant contribution.

For this to happen there needs to be a shift in perspective in both policy and practice which sees enquiry not just as a desirable add on but also as a fundamental part of how we develop educational professionals. When considering schools as ecosystems we need to envisage the forces of collaboration, enquiry and professional learning in dynamic interplay within an intimate relationship:

> For teacher development . . . to occur commitment to certain kinds of collaboration is centrally important. However, collaboration without reflection and enquiry is little more than working collegially. For collaboration to influence personal growth and development it has to be premised upon enquiry and sharing.
>
> *(Harris, 2002, p. 58)*

A range of initiatives have begun to explore what this would look like in practice within collaborative research settings (Brown, 2017; Stoll, 2015b). It will entail asking searching questions about not only what effective research engagement across an alliance looks like but also what being part of an alliance brings to enhance the capacity of a school to be research engaged.

## An ecosystem for research-engaged schools: theoretical and conceptual issues

This section addresses some of the potential conceptual issues that relate to the ecosystem of research-engaged schools. These include: the nature of research and evidence and its potential or proposed role in the ecosystem; and the theoretical and conceptual tools that can help to understand the process of maintenance and enhancement of an ecosystem. It is not meant in any sense to be the final word or an exhaustive coverage of the theme and in the last chapter we will seek to further develop ecosystems thinking around this topic and point to further avenues of action and interest for practitioners, policy makers and researchers working in the field of school research engagement.

## Schools as institutions or organisations?

Recent orthodoxy has tended to talk in terms of schools as 'organisations'. Stemming etymologically from 'organism', this can connote dynamism, growth and adaptability.

Simultaneously, being 'organised' suggests the existence of well-defined structures, processes, systems and roles that enable efficient operation (effectiveness). However, referring to schools as organisations can also feed into an instrumentalist, managerial narrative that sees them as merely vehicles for delivering academic targets that we measure and control through the use of a narrow range of performance indicators. By referring to schools as institutions we can focus on their historical, social and political antecedents, functions and roles (Glatter, 2015). As institutions, schools are less about specific buildings and the staff and students within their four walls; instead they represent something more ideas-based, including the values that they promote and their role in the formation, reproduction and development of past, present and future versions of society.

In a number of case studies of research-engaged schools (Godfrey, 2016b), schools were viewed as 'activity systems' that are both dynamic as well as containing historically and socially situated practices (Blackler, 2007). Importantly, such activity occurs as a result of, and in the context of, a specific 'object' (Engeström, 1996) through which it is teleologically defined. In other words, school education is not just for a purpose, but only makes sense when it is viewed through the lens of its specific object or aims. So, while referring to the notion of research-engaged schools, we may want to focus on schools either as organisational units or as institutions but in the former case, we need to be cautious to not take as a given the notion of 'effectiveness', since this can only be studied empirically once the goals of these practices are made explicit. In other words, we need to ask: 'effective for what, for whom and to what end?'

## Understanding the chronosystem

In the case studies mentioned earlier, the historical reasons and conditions that mediate a school's trajectory towards a culture of research engagement are explained (Godfrey, 2016b), see Figure 1.1. Through the accounts of staff at eight secondary schools in England, the extent of each school's research engagement was examined in surveys and then explored in detailed interviews. Four developmental stages were identified in the surveys, from schools that were *emerging, establishing, established* and *embedded*.

This analysis shows an expansive spiral of development in research engagement at the case study schools. As the school leadership introduced research, this had tightly constrained improvement aims, in some cases aligned with the school's external inspection reports and self-evaluation. Despite this instrumental focus for the research, the professional learning environment improved; building collaboration and trust and in turn enabling more research activity to take place. This new activity started to generate a new language through which school practices were understood. In the more established research-engaged schools, this new language of research became a part of daily school life. This led to the demand for new structures and processes through which to work in a collaborative and enquiry mode and to learn from research and development activities. This in turn expanded professional learning, sometimes across subject teams and transgressing hierarchy,

| Professional learning community | Expansive learning cycles | Research engagement characteristics |
|---|---|---|
| • School learning community becomes more inclusive. Educational criteria evolving through research |  | • Multiple structures and spaces for learning. Research engagement embedded across senior leadership. Access to academic research expertise. Density of internal researching capacity increases |
| • School begins to work across subject disciplines, connecting research learning to decision-making and leadership | | • Increase in structures and spaces for learning through research/enquiry |
| • Professional learning culture mediated by research language/academic discussion | | • Research activity increases and diversifies |
| • Professional learning culture changed by collaborative nature of research and flat leadership structure | | • Research with clear improvement aims/tightly directed by senior leadership |

**FIGURE 1.1** Developmental trajectory of a research-engaged school (Adapted from p. 282, Godfrey, 2016b)

as teachers led initiatives at whole school level. Schools with embedded cultures of research were often able to call readily on external and internal expertise, generating new and enhanced research activity. These research-engaged schools became learning organisations that encompassed staff, students and other stakeholders in the community. They were able to set their own success criteria and to engage in ongoing cycles of evaluation to test how well they had met them. Furthermore, the enquiry stance taken by staff also led to reflection and learning and the renewal of their educational aims.

This spiral of development and expansive learning illustrates the way that new characteristics of the professional learning environment were afforded through the introduction of research-related activities and structures. However, the converse was also true, that the nature and extent of the research depended on the characteristics of the school as a professional learning community (PLC). This reciprocal relationship illustrates the kind of analysis needed to research ecosystems.

## Hostile and nourishing ecological conditions for research-engaged schools

While Figure 1.1 gives a representation of the development of research-engaged cultures in case study schools, we should be cautious in presenting this as a predictive model of what would occur in any other school or school system. Indeed, with the quickly changing context of the English school system, such a trajectory cannot be taken for granted as it depends very much on the will and ability of school leaders to strive towards this aim. Outside of England, the outcome is also likely to vary according to different times, contexts, people or school structures. Nevertheless, the study of the ecological conditions can help us test and build theories about particular types of ecosystems; in particular an ecosystem that affords research engagement and enquiry approaches to learning and improvement.

Such conditions are explored in the professional learning of teachers through enquiry in Chapter 10, where the concept of ecological agency is explored; here, agency is viewed as an emergent phenomenon that is achieved rather than as something that people have. In line with ideas about distributed intelligence, the point is made that the resources available in the environment (such as concepts or tools from research) 'are loaded with intelligence which enhances our action' (Edwards, 2007, p. 4). Edwards also emphasises that such agency occurs when the context allows for it, and this can occur in both formal and informal settings. Priestley and Drew's chapter also gives us a methodology for the study of this agency.

Applying this thinking to the macro context of English schools, we argue that there are a number of ecological conditions that encourage research-informed practice, while others act antagonistically towards this aim (Godfrey and Brown, 2018). This study looked at the capacity of schools to engage in research and development, the extent to which impact is being measured and the alignment between the external accountability environment and the aim to self-evaluate and learn through research and enquiry. On the plus side there was evidence of plentiful discussion, collaboration and will to engage in and with academic research, and increasing understanding of how to engage in research activity to improve school practices. However, it was also concluded that an effective ecosystem at present is hindered by a number of structures, cultures and incentives that bridge the research–practice divide, and by accountability arrangements that lead to defensive responses from schools rather than leading to genuine learning through enquiry and self-evaluation.

Exploring further theoretical and methodological approaches, Brown, in Chapter 11, introduces the concepts of Optimal Rationality and Optimal Rational Positions in the context of a research-engaged school in England. His chapter examines why research-informed practice does or does not occur in schools based on a semiotic analysis of how teachers interpret and respond to signals in their environment, such as the current 'push' for research-informed practice.

## What kind of research engagement?

Elsewhere, one of us has argued, through an analysis of English policy, that the emphasis on evidence-based policy and practice in schools may hide a narrative that disempowers and de-professionalises teachers and school leaders (Godfrey, 2017). A 'what works' model of evidence supports the idea of a hierarchy of knowledge and is in danger of downplaying the role of teacher professional judgement, and of favouring research that is proven to increase academic attainment on standardised tests. In Chapter 12, Wisby and Whitty argue for a broad and inclusive model of research-to-practice and to remain vigilant against creating an ecosystem that narrows and prohibits the use of certain kinds of research and professionally created knowledge.

After such an ambitious undertaking, we then draw together some of the key learning in Chapter 13 in order to stimulate further discussion about how policy makers, school practitioners, academics and other stakeholders can work together to create a healthy and sustainable research-engaged school system. We also offer an expanded conceptual framework of such an ecosystem and finally, point to some potential further lines of enquiry.

## Conclusions

In this chapter we have outlined our conception of the ecosystem of schools based on Bronfenbrenner's ecological model. We have applied this specifically to describe the elements of a research-engaged school mesosystem and some of the ecological conditions that enable such a system to survive, grow and flourish. Following this, we have raised some potential theoretical approaches and issues in the study of this ecosystem. Finally, we have cautioned that the nature of such an ecosystem must be made explicit so that the proposed relationship between research and practice is not disempowering for practitioners in particular.

In the chapters that follow, several distinguished authors working from their different perspectives have added their thinking, their evidence and some of their solutions to create an effective research-informed school ecosystem. We hope that you the reader will gain a sense of how a well-nurtured ecosystem could exceed the sum total of its elements.

## Implications for the research-informed ecosystem

- We can frame the school ecosystem according to the macrosystem, exosystem, mesosystem, microsystem and the chronosystem.
- A research-engaged school is a multifaceted concept, promoting research-informed practice, schools as learning organisations and connectivity to the wider system.
- Ecosystems often require 'non-linear' forms of analysis and research to account for the richness and complexity of interconnected elements.

## Note

1 www.bera.ac.uk/project/close-to-practice-research-project.

## References

Arhar, J., Niesz, T., Brossman, J., Koebly, S., O'Brien, K., Loe, D. and Black, F. (2013). Creating a third space in the context of a university-school partnership: supporting teacher action research and the research preparation of doctoral students. *Educational Action Research*, 21(2), 218–236.

Ball, S. (2008). *The Education Debate*. Bristol: Policy Press.

Barber, M. and Mourshed, M. (2007). *How the World's Best-Performing School Systems Come Out On Top*. New York: McKinsey & Company.

Berkemeyer, N., Bos, W., Manitius, V. and Müthing, K. (2008). 'Schulen im Team': Einblicke in netzwerkbasierte Unterrichtsentwicklung. In N. Berkemeyer, W. Bos, V. Manitius and K. Müthing (Eds.), *Unterrichtsentwicklung in Netzwerken: Konzeptionen, Befunde, Perspektiven*. Münster: Waxmann, pp. 19–70.

Berkemeyer, N., Järvinen, H. and Bos, W. (2011). Unterricht gemeinsam entwickeln. Eine Bilanz nach vier Jahren schulischer Netzwerkarbeit, *Pädagogik*, 11(11), 46–51.

Biesta, G. (2007). Why what works won't work: evidence based practice and the democratic deficit in educational research. *Educational Theory*, 57(1), 1–22.

Blackler, F. (2007). Knowledge and the theory of organizations as activity systems and the reframing of management. *Journal of Management Studies*, 30(6), 863–884.

Bronfenbrenner, U. (1992). *Ecological Systems Theory*. London: Jessica Kingsley Publishers.

Brown, C. (2017). How to establish research learning communities. *Professional Development Today*, 19(2).

Brown, C. (2015). *Leading the Use of Research and Evidence in Schools*. London: IOE Press.

Bryk, A. S. and Gomez, L. (2008). Reinventing a research and development capacity. In F. M. Hess (Ed.), *The Future of Educational Entrepreneurship: Possibilities For School Reform*. Cambridge, MA: Harvard Educational Press, pp. 181–206.

Darling-Hammond, L. (2010). *The Flat World and Education: How America's Commitment to Equity Will Determine Our Future.* New York: Teachers College Press.

Dimmock, C. (2014). Conceptualising the research–practice–professional development nexus: mobilising schools as 'research-engaged' professional learning communities. *Professional Development in Education*, 1–18.

Durrant, J. (2014). Children see differently from us – a fresh perspective on school improvement. *Professional Development Today*, 16(2).

Dyson, A. (2001). *Building Research Capacity. Sub-group Report chaired by Alan Dyson.* National Education Research Forum.

Edwards, A. (2007). Relational agency in professional practice: A CHAT analysis. *Action: An International Journal of Human Activity Theory*, 1, 1–17.

Engeström, Y. (1996). Interobjectivity, ideality, and dialectics. *Mind, Culture, and Activity*, 3(4), 259–265.

Frost, D. (2000). *Teacher-Led School Improvement.* London: Routledge

Furlong, J. (2014). *Research and the Teaching Profession: Building Capacity for a Self-Improving Education System.* Final report of the BERA-RSA Inquiry into the role of research in the teaching profession, BERA.

Glatter, R. (2015). Are schools and colleges institutions? *Management in Education*, 29(3), 100–104.

Godfrey, D. (2017). What is the proposed role of research evidence in England's 'self-improving' school system? *Oxford Review of Education*, 43(4), 433–446.

Godfrey, D. (2016a). Leadership of schools as research-led organisations in the English educational environment: cultivating a research-engaged school culture. *Educational Management Administration & Leadership*, 44(2), 301–321.

Godfrey, D. (2016b). *Exploring Cultures of Research Engagement at Eight English Secondary Schools.* PhD Thesis. Institute of Education, University College London.

Godfrey, D. and Brown, C. (2018). How effective is the research and development ecosystem for England's schools? *London Review of Education*, 16(1), January.

Greany, T. and Higham, R. (2018). *Hierarchy, Markets and Networks: Analysing the 'Self-Improving School-Led System' Agenda in England and the Implications for Schools.* London: IOE Press. Accessed online on 20 July 2018 at: https://camdenlearning.org.uk/wpcontent/uploads/2018/07/Hierarchy-Markets-and-Networks.pdf.

Handscomb, G. (2012). Collaborate, connect and learn. *Professional Development Today*, 14(4).

Handscomb, G. and MacBeath, J. (2003). *The Research-Engaged School.* Essex: Essex County Council, FLARE.

Handscomb, G. and Ramsey, D. (2008). *Meaningful Self-Evaluation: Using Reflection for Self-Evaluation and the SEF.* Essex: Essex County Council, FLARE.

Handscomb, G., Gu, Q. and Varley, M. (2014). *School-University Partnerships: Fulfilling the Potential. Literature Review.* Institute of Education, London Centre for Leadership and Learning, University of Nottingham, Nottingham Trent University. National Coordinating centre for Public Engagement. Accessed online at: www.publicengagement.ac.uk/sites/default/files/publication/supi_literature_review.pdf.

Hargreaves, D. H. (1998). A new partnership of stakeholders and a national strategy for research induction. In: (Harris, 2002, p. 58).

Harris, A. (2002). *School Improvement: What's In It for Schools?* London: RoutledgeFalmer.

Matthews, P., Higham, R., Stoll L., Brennan, J. and Riley, K. (2011). *Prepared to Lead. How Schools, Federations and Chains Grow Education Leaders.* National College.

McLaughlin, C., Black-Hawkins, K., Brindley, S., McIntyre, D. and Taber, K. (2007). *Researching Schools.* London: Routledge.

Muijs, D. and Rumyantseva, N. (2014). Coopetition in education: collaborating in a competitive environment. *Journal of Educational Change*, 15(1), 1–18.

Robinson, V. (2011). *Student-Centered Leadership* (Vol. 15). John Wiley & Sons.

Rubin, B. C. and Jones, M. (2007). Student action research: reaping the benefits for students and school leaders. *NASSP Bulletin*, 91(4), 363–378.

Sachs, J. (2011). Skilling or emancipating? Metaphors for continuing professional development. In N. Mockler and J. Sachs (Eds.), *Rethinking Educational Practice Through Reflexive Inquiry: Essays in Honour of Susan Groundwater-Smith* (Vol. 7). Dordrecht: Springer.

Sahlberg, P. (2011). *Finnish Lessons: What Can the World Learn from Educational Change in Finland*. New York: Teachers College Press.

Sharp, C., Eames, A., Sanders, D. and Tomlinson, K. (2006). *Leading a Research-Engaged School*. Nottingham: National College for School Leadership.

Sharp, C., Eames, A., Sanders, D. and Tomlinson, K. (2005). *Postcards From Research-Engaged Schools*. Slough: National Foundation for Educational Research.

Sharp, C. and Handscomb, G. (2007). *Making Research Make a Difference. Teacher Research: A Small-Scale Study to Look at Impact*. Essex: Essex County Council, FLARE in partnership with NFER, and DCSF.

Stoll, L. (2015a). Using evidence, learning and the role of professional learning communities. In Brown, C. (Ed.), *Leading the Use of Research and Evidence in Schools*. London: IOE Press.

Stoll, L. (2015b). *Three Greats for a Self-Improving School System – Pedagogy, Professional Development and Leadership Teaching Schools R&D Network National Themes Project 2012–14*. Research Report. Spring 2015. National College for School Leadership.

Van Holt, N., Berkemeyer, N. and Bos, W. (2015). Netzwerkarbeit und schülerleistungen. In N. Berkemeyer, W. Bos, H. Järvinen, V. Manitius and N. van Holt (Eds.), *Netzwerkbasierte Unterrichtsentwicklung. Ergebnisse der wissenschaftlichen Begleitforschung zum Projekt "Schulen im Team"*. Münster: Waxmann, pp. 119–152.

Whitchurch, Celia (2009). The rise of the blended professional in higher education: a comparison between the United Kingdom, Australia and the United States. *Higher Education*, 58 (3), 407–418.

Wilkins, R. (2011). *Research Engagement for School Development*. London: Institute of Education.

# 2

# DEVELOPING A SYSTEM FOR KNOWLEDGE MOBILISATION

## The case of the Knowledge Network for Applied Education Research (KNAER) as a middle tier

*Katina Pollock, Carol Campbell, Doris McWhorter, Kelly Bairos and Erica van Roosmalen*

## Aims of the chapter

- To argue that the middle tier of a research-informed ecosystem serves a much more crucial function than policy makers and practitioners typically consider.
- To demonstrate, via the case study of the Knowledge Network for Applied Education Research in Ontario, Canada that (a) a research-informed ecosystem requires dynamic, connected, structured and sustainable initiatives and organisations at middle level that strategically connect the macro- and micro-level of the system; (b) these initiatives require resources and strategies – such as multi-year funding and networks – that can be dedicated to building capacity for knowledge mobilisation and evidence use in schools; and (c) knowledge mobilisation initiatives at the middle level can build upon existing structures and information communications technology to extend reach in all directions: down into the classroom, up to decision-making at the policy level, and out beyond the existing ecosystem.

## Introduction

In any ecosystem, the exosystem's role is most difficult to define. Often described as the middle tier, the middle level and the meso-level, this tier/system has the integral role of connecting the macro- and the micro-levels: *Without the middle, there would be limited to no connection or interplay between the system levels.* In an education ecosystem, the macro and the micro can be conceptualised in several ways. For example, the formal education system can be understood, on the one hand, as education policy, regulation and governance; on the other, learning environments in classrooms and schools. The issue of research use brings the functioning of educational ecosystems into sharp focus: How can co-constructed evidence and research generated at higher education institutions – at the macro-level – be shared, maintained, sustained and in some cases co-created in micro-level educators' practice within a publicly funded school system? In this chapter, we argue that organisations, structures, and initiatives at the middle level play a crucial role in this process; we do so by examining one of these middle-level initiatives from Ontario, Canada.

School systems are complex and the middle tier is no exception. In education systems throughout the world, multiple organisations, structures and initiatives nourish the overall ecosystem from the middle tier. In Ontario, there are many structures (e.g. district school boards) and initiatives (e.g. KNAER, The Teacher Learning and Leadership Program [TLLP], Managing Information for Student Achievement: Professional Network Communities [MISA-PNCs], etc.) at the middle level of the education ecosystem. Although there are many bodies at the middle level of education in Ontario, we focus on the Knowledge Network for Applied Education Research (KNAER) because it exemplifies how using a systems approach to knowledge mobilisation within an educational ecosystem can promote research-engaged schools.

The Ontario Ministry of Education created KNAER as part of its larger provincial strategy to advance evidence-based and research-informed policies, programmes and practices across the education system. Since its inception, KNAER has functioned within the middle tier: The network has been tasked with building strong relationships between the Ontario provincial government and local universities; building capacity within Ontario's publicly funded education systems for knowledge mobilisation and evidence use; fostering research to practice partnerships among a wide range of education, health, professional and community organisations; and acting as a knowledge broker through cross-sector provincial networks. To accomplish its mandate, KNAER has evolved over the past seven years to embrace its unique, structurally important and often difficult to define role in the public education ecosystem.

We begin by briefly outlining the creation of KNAER and its first two phases. We then define our conceptualisation of knowledge mobilisation, the use of evidence and research and systems to understand complex organisations or entities. We then focus in on a specific component of a particular systems theory – the ecological systems theory, coined by developmental psychologist Urie Bronfenbrenner in 1979 – to challenge policy makers, knowledge mobilisation experts, and encourage researchers to think more deeply about the necessary meso-level structures and processes that can bridge and facilitate evidence use between the various levels of influence. We then consider KNAER's evolving role in a research-engaged ecosystem to argue for the crucial importance of cultivating dynamic, structured, sustainable and connected initiatives and organisations at middle level.

## The creation and evolution of the Knowledge Network for Applied Education Research (KNAER)

In 2010, the Ontario Ministry of Education created the KNAER as part of its larger strategy to advance evidence-based and research-informed policies, programmes and practices across the education system. The KNAER, established through a tripartite agreement with the University of Toronto and Western University, is unique in its focus on building strong relationships between government and universities, building capacity for knowledge mobilisation and evidence use, and fostering research/policy/practice partnerships among a wide range of education, health, professional and community organisations.

## KNAER Phase I

From 2010 to 2014, KNAER funded 44 projects involving more than 150 partner organisations. These projects were categorised under four KMb themes: (a) effective exploitation of available research, (b) building or extending networks, (c) strengthening research brokering work and/or (d) visits by world-leading researchers. Projects in the first category designed KMb strategies that made existing research accessible in practice and policy. *Building or Extending Networks* projects focused on extending networks to further disseminate existing research; these projects determined priority areas and identified how to leverage existing KMb capacities through the use of networks. Projects funded in the third category were responsible for connecting researchers and organisations with shared research interests to expand impact by using existing resources and expert knowledge. Lastly, the projects in *Visiting World Experts* category invited internationally renowned scholars to Ontario to share their knowledge with various stakeholder groups and with the larger education sector.

## KNAER Phase II

In 2014, based on an evaluation of KNAER – along with KMb literature, interviews with KMb experts and strategic planning sessions with Ontario educators and researchers – the KNAER co-directors developed recommendations for a renewed KNAER. A key recommendation for the next phase was to continue building on its successes and identified challenges, while evolving towards a systems approach to KMb. In Phase I, KNAER did not have an official secretariat, even though there were two co-directors and two project managers who engaged in behind-the-scenes leadership. A crucial shift from KNAER Phase I to KNAER Phase II was the establishment of a dedicated KNAER Secretariat to provide expert leadership, oversight and coordination for the overall KNAER system. Phase II also included a restructuring of KNAER to include four thematic networks: These networks enabled (and continue to enable) KNAER to scale-up and build capacity within Ontario's education system. KNAER's organisational structure now includes several different components (see Figure 2.2). From 2015 to 2020, KNAER II has and continues to support thematic knowledge networks to enhance knowledge mobilisation on clear and specific priority themes.

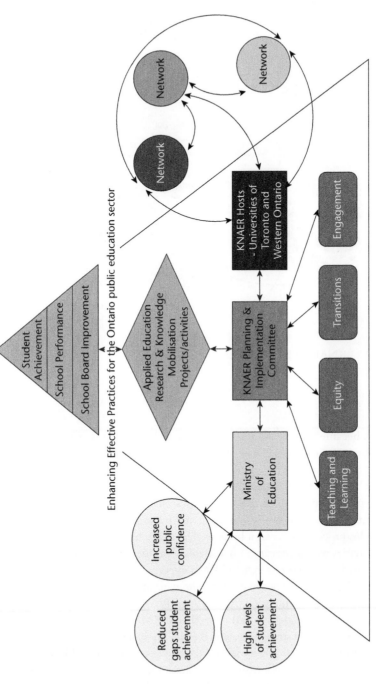

**FIGURE 2.1** Original KNAER model

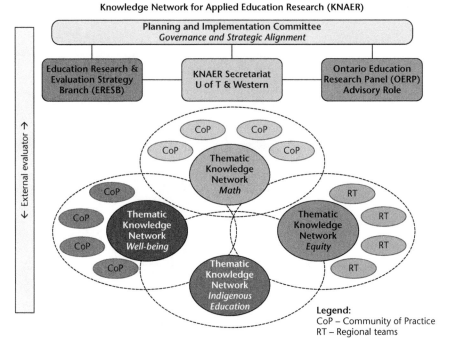

Knowledge Network for Applied Education Research (KNAER)

**FIGURE 2.2**  KNAER Phase II model (2015–2020)

*Source*: ERESB, 2017

What became evident in transition to Phase II of KNAER was the crucial role initiatives at the meso-level can play within the Ontario educational ecosystem. The meso-level work of the university partners during KNAER I initially concentrated on much of the managerial work to support 44 disparate projects throughout the province. Some of these managerial tasks included focusing or setting up project contracts, ensuring timely reporting and messaging the purpose of KNAER. During this process however, it became clear that while these operational management activities were necessary, other strategic practices were also required, such as strategic leadership and research and KMb expertise (Campbell et al., 2014).

Although some of the necessary structures were already in place at the meso-level for operational management (i.e. OERP and PIC) in KNAER I, in KNAER II, intentional strategic leadership and research and KMb expertise were further developed to maximise the strategic potential of the meso-level. Specifically, the formal creation of the KNAER Secretariat and the addition of the KNAER Coordinating Committee to connect with Ministry of Education stakeholders enhanced strategic leadership. The Ontario Education Research Panel (OERP) also took on an advisory role to KNAER to enable access to additional research and KMb expertise (which is described in more detail in a subsequent section). Moreover, four thematic networks were created to address some of the challenges identified in KNAER I, enabling multi-year networks and communities of practice focused on government education priorities (i.e. mathematics, student well-being, equity and indigenous education), rather many smaller or short-term KMb projects.

At the time of this publication, KNAER II just completed its third year of a five-year funding cycle (2015–2020). With varying start dates, all four thematic networks and their communities of practice were established in 2016–2017. In addition, the developmental evaluators for KNAER were in place; although the initial stages of this process have begun, this part of the approach has not been developed to a point where it would be usefully reported in this chapter.

In the next section, we apply Bronfenbrenner's ecological systems theory to argue, why, in a system, organisations and initiatives at middle tier or level are vital for a research-engaged educational ecosystem. This is followed by an explanation of how the KNAER Secretariat supports knowledge mobilisation and why this is a structurally essential component to mobilise evidence in any educational ecosystem.

## Knowledge mobilisation and use of research evidence

Before we explain KNAER's role in more depth, we must first explain what we mean by 'evidence-based practice' and 'knowledge mobilisation'. The concepts of evidence-informed practice, research-engaged schools and schools-as-learning-organisations have been widely debated in the education sphere for many years. Multiple education jurisdictions have created policies and programmes designed to enhance the quality, accessibility and use of evidence to improve outcomes for all students. There is growing consensus that evidence includes multiple sources of knowledge, including practitioner knowledge and judgement as well as data and research. Mobilising evidence requires collaboration among researchers, decision-makers and practitioners to ensure the creation, sharing and use of evidence. We use Sharples' (2013, p. 10) definition of 'evidence', encompasses – but is also broader than – research. It is part of a process of inquiry, judgement and adaptation – not a simple insertion of evidence *into* practice.

In our work at KNAER, we use the term 'knowledge mobilisation' to conceptualise 'the active and dynamic process whereby stakeholders (e.g. researchers, practitioners, policy makers and community members) share, create and use research evidence to inform programming, policy, decision-making and practice' (Malik, 2016, p. 11). 'Mobilisation' implies social interaction and iterative processes of co-creating knowledge through collaboration between and among researchers, decision-makers and practitioners (Phipps and Morton, 2013). This activity can take place individually, in groups, through networks and at the system level to inform decisions and practices with the ultimate goal of improving educational outcomes (Briscoe et al., 2015; Campbell et al., 2014). To promote research-engaged schools in a healthy educational ecosystem, it is highly important to actively mobilise – through a range of processes of communication, collaboration and interaction – multiple forms of evidence, including research.

## A systems approach

By system, we refer to an entity that is made up of interrelated and interdependent parts (von Bertalanffy, 1968). Systems theories were originally reserved for the pure and applied sciences, but were eventually adapted to organisational theory and the social sciences. Drawing on work in the health sector, Best and Holmes (2010) have helpfully identified three key developments in models of knowledge-to-action processes:

- Linear models in which research is produced and then made available for users in a mainly one-way relationship;
- Relationship models (such as network and partnership models), which build on linear models but focus on enhancing relationships between and among researchers and practitioners to facilitate the development and mobilisation of research and practice connections; and
- Systems models which move away from linear processes and involve a more complex process involving interaction, co-creation and implementation of evidence throughout all levels of a system, plus identifying and addressing barriers to mobilising research and practice knowledge for evidence use.

Early – and continuing – approaches to research dissemination and 'knowledge transfer' through the production and publication of research materials is a key feature of linear models. In recognition of the limitations of such processes for actively engaging educators (and other professionals) in and with research, there has been a shift from the traditional relationship models towards new models that are more interactive and value partnerships and networks. Although this is a positive move, it is becoming increasingly recognised that there needs also to be attention to the wider ecosystem in which research and evidence are part of a culture and infrastructure of co-development, critical inquiry, genuine collaboration and attending to existing structural challenges in accessing, adapting and applying research in and for education. For this reason, a deliberate systems approach to knowledge mobilisation was eventually initiated in the second iteration of KNAER. Although KNAER I enhanced collaboration among participating higher education institutes and public education, developed new and expanded existing networks, and created substantial knowledge products, the reach was not province-wide.

## Bronfenbrenner's ecological systems theory

The notion of ecosystems was derived from efforts to explain connections within the natural environment and to better understand studies of such environments. Eventually the ecosystem theory was also applied to human interactions and used to describe complex organisations. In this chapter, we draw on Bronfenbrenner's (1979) ecological systems theory (Figure 2.3) to emphasise the degrees of influence throughout KNAER and demonstrates the middle tier's central role in connecting these components. The present figures of KNAER I and II demonstrates the structural makeup of the KNAER over the years but do not necessarily demonstrate the degrees or levels of influence or, in our case, the paths of knowledge mobilisation required to support evidence use in research-engaged schools.

Bronfenbrenner's ecological systems theory in human development focuses on levels or degrees of influence around an individual child. This theory can help explain KNAER's influence as it mobilises knowledge and, specifically, how KNAER's role in the middle level is vital to supporting knowledge mobilisation in an education ecosystem. Briefly, Bronfenbrenner's theory (1979) consisted of nested circles of different sizes that radiate out from the centre circle 'like a set of Russian dolls' (p. 3). The central circle is meant to represent the immediate environment or the specific child's development (in our case the student's learning). Each outer circle represents various structures that influence the child's development (such as the school, school district policy, local community and culture, provincial policy, provincial initiatives such as the TLLP, MISA-PNCs, etc.). One of Bronfenbrenner's arguments was to consider looking beyond single settings (in our case, the classroom) to consider the relationships within and between each circle and their influence on the child's development. The challenge with Bronfenbrenner's

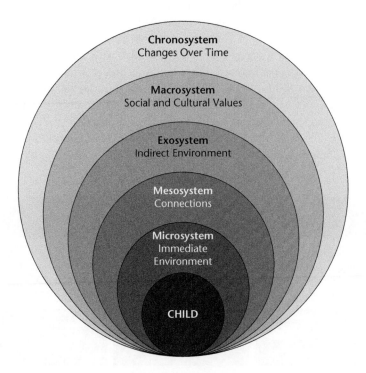

**FIGURE 2.3**  Bronfenbrenner's ecological systems theory

argument is that there are extensive influences on the child overall, and numerous middle-level initiatives and organisations that support the formal public education ecosystem. It is impossible to consider all of these within reasonable writing guidelines. As mentioned at the beginning of this chapter, we chose to focus on KNAER because it demonstrates the importance of taking a systems approach to knowledge mobilisation when cultivating a research-engaged ecosystem.

In his ecological systems theory, Bronfenbrenner separates the middle tier into the exosystem (indirect environment) and the mesosystem (connections). In its functions, *KNAER synthesises these two middle components to promote research-engaged schools and evidence-informed practice.* To promote and support research-engaged schools through knowledge mobilisation, the two middle components – the exosystem and the mesosystem – were connected, structured, well-resourced and aligned through communication and capacity building. KNAER structures and processes, collectively, can be considered functions within the public education exosystem, and the KNAER thematic networks can be conceptualised as functioning at the meso-level of the public education exosystem.

## Knowledge mobilisation in a research-engaged educational ecosystem: up, down and out

As an indirect knowledge mobilisation influencer that supports connections within the entire public education ecosystem, the KNAER Secretariat facilitates collaborating 'up' to the macro-level of government; 'down' to the micro-level of the local communities of practice, organisations and individuals within the education system; and 'out' to the wider community. This connection process would be severely limited if there were not an entity (KNAER Secretariat) dedicated to this function. As leading experts in KMb, the KNAER Secretariat provides strategic provincial leadership in network development and KMb in six areas (See Figure 2.4): facilitative capacity-building throughout the public education system; creating opportunities for information and knowledge exchange between the various levels within the

**FIGURE 2.4**   KNAER secretariat services

system; connecting, coordinating and expanding the KNAER networks throughout the macro-, meso- and micro-levels; providing access to tools and resources that support evidence use in practice; promoting KNAER networks and resources; and championing the 'KNAER Story' and KNAER KMb expertise.

## Up: collaborating with the Ministry of Education (use the existing structures)

In Ontario, the Ministry of Education is responsible for policy, regulation, governance and funding of the K-12 education system. The Ministry of Education, however, is not directly involved in the day-to-day education of students. For a systems approach to KMb to be effective, there needs to be a way for this governance structure to connect with the remaining levels within the system. The KNAER Secretariat is organised in such a way that it collaborates with and seeks to inform and influence the macro-level of government through three main mechanisms: partnership with the Education Research Evaluation and Strategy Branch (ERESB) of the Ontario Ministry of Education; governance and reporting through a Planning and Implementation Committee (PIC); and coordination and collaboration among KNAER and Ministry branches through a KNAER Coordinating Committee (CC).

The Education Research and Evaluation Strategy Branch (ERESB) is part of the System Planning, Research and Innovation Division of the Ontario Ministry of Education. Large knowledge mobilisation initiatives like KNAER require resources and funding. The ERESB is responsible for implementing the Education Research and Evaluation Strategy, including the establishment and funding of the KNAER. Because the KNAER is a publicly funded initiative, there is an expectation of public accountability, which KNAER achieves by formally working with funders and creating partnerships at the macro-level. For example, the KNAER Secretariat partners with the Ontario Education Research Panel and the PIC to ensure good governance, transparency and successful operation of the KNAER's four thematic networks by applying and implementing accountability frameworks and commissioning developmental evaluation.

The KNAER is governed through a Planning and Implementation Committee (PIC), composed of senior Ministry representatives, the university partners and the education sector. In the first phase of KNAER, the PIC provided overall governance and decision-making by developing an annual operational/strategic plan, approving KNAER funded projects, authorising calls for proposals, engaging external reviewers for proposals, and receiving/approving financial, interim and final reports. In Phase II, the PIC continues to provide strategic leadership and oversight, approve calls for proposals and champion the work of the KNAER with senior Ministry of Education leaders and relevant officials. The PIC structure is essential for several reasons. It provides an official governance structure that is accountable to the funder but also to the public education sector. It also provides an avenue for the KNAER Secretariat to update the Ministry on accomplishments, lessons learned and challenges posed, and for the various KNAER thematic networks to report progress and insights on structural processes back to funders.

Initiated in the fall of 2017, the purpose of the KNAER Coordinating Committee (CC) is to further coordinate KNAER's KMb efforts. This committee brokers connections and strengthens relationships between and among the four KNAER networks and those branches and divisions in the Ministry of Education that represent the Ministry priority areas. The 11 members represent the KNAER partners and programme areas in the Ontario Ministry of Education that are representative of the themes of the KNAER networks. Specifically, the KNAER CC connects communications from the networks to Ministry communication plans, champions a culture of KMb, supports research-to-practice and practice-to-research, and helps identify opportunities for collaboration and partnership to build system capacity for evidence use in support of furthering Ontario's education priority areas. The KNAER CC is essential because it expands the reach of the KNAER thematic networks' work upward and across other government branches and divisions – not just the branch exclusively responsible for the governance of KNAER.

## Down: using thematic networks to mobilise knowledge to the micro-level

The main purpose of KNAER is to mobilise research and knowledge to improve educational practices and student outcomes. KNAER champions thematic knowledge networks that focus on building connections and collaboration in their communities of practice. As Figure 2.2 demonstrates, there are four thematic networks within KNAER: The Mathematics Knowledge Network, the Knowledge Network for Student Well-Being, the Equity Knowledge Network and the Indigenous Education Network for Student Well-Being. Each thematic network includes a number of communities of practice. The thematic networks also overlap with each other to demonstrate efforts to cross-connect. The majority of these communities of practice are directly or closely connected to practitioners at the micro-level (i.e. schools or directly with individual students).

The KNAER is a network made up of networks for the purposes of knowledge mobilisation within a public education ecosystem. It is important to define what we mean by networks if we are to clearly illustrate how they function as connectors from between the macro-level and the micro-level within this ecosystem. Scholars have described 'networks' within the context of education as 'groups or systems of interconnected people and organisations (including schools) whose aims and purposes include the improvement of learning and aspects of well-being known to affect learning' (Hadfield et al., 2006, p. 5). Within this context, networks have the potential to change practice, as scholars have found they promote ongoing social interaction and contact (Gilchrist, 1995, 2000; Watson et al. 2002). It is also not uncommon for networks to occur within and across different levels of a sector (Borgatti and Foster, 2003), which is also a feature of KNAER that produces the multiple levels of influence in the education ecosystem (Briscoe et al., 2015). As we have argued elsewhere, social networks often exist to build partnerships (Briscoe et al., 2015). Scholars have shown that school-to-school networks and partnerships have the potential to improve education (Castells, 2001; Church et al., 2002). Moreover, using networks to partner researchers and practitioners can facilitate KMb and increase the use of researcher-generated evidence into educational practitioners' daily practice (Ainscow et al., 2006; Briscoe et al., 2015; Chapman and Fullan, 2007; Earl and Katz, 2006; Hargreaves, 2003; Hopkins, 2003). We also know that KMb can improve broader education systems by using the intricate social processes that involve interaction among groups or contexts; networks have been recognised as powerful mediums for sharing knowledge and effect change (Cooper, 2012; Daly, 2010; Degenne and Forsé, 1999; Kilduff and Tsai, 2003).

## KNAER thematic knowledge networks

The KNAER thematic networks function as connectors for knowledge mobilisation because of how they are strategically structured. For example, effective mobilisation of evidence or research occurs when there is an intentional effort for evidence, knowledge or research to be co-created with people who have expertise in research or evidence production and people who use the research or evidence. KNAER's thematic networks are structured to include diverse stakeholders, such as researchers, policy makers and practitioners. Because of these networks, macro-level knowledge, understanding, practices and programmes are connected with the micro-level – school sites.

Specifically, the four thematic networks are intended to establish and strengthen collaborative, evidence-based practice, and are aligned with the Ministry of Education's priority areas. They are designed to build capacity for evidence use and support meaningful KMb through co-learning collaboration, and connecting at both the micro- and macro-levels of the education system. Without the thematic network, there would be no coordinated structure or processes for sharing within and between the various networks and beyond to the larger education sector to effect large-scale change.

To further connect the macro- and micro-levels, each thematic knowledge network includes multiple communities of practice (CoPs). These CoPs consist of groups of people who share concerns, a set of problems, or a passion about a topic, and who deepen their knowledge and expertise in this area through committed and consistent interaction. The CoPs can also consist of members and groups who predominantly exist at both the meso-level (such as at the district school level) and the micro-level of influence on student learning. In some cases, CoPs take the form of a virtual community or informal group sponsored by an organisation to facilitate knowledge sharing or learning.

**TABLE 2.1** KNAER four thematic networks and communities of practice

| Network | Math Knowledge Network | Knowledge Network for Student Well-Being | Equity Knowledge Network | Indigenous Education Knowledge Network |
|---|---|---|---|---|
| Host | Fields Institute for Research in Mathematical Science | Hamilton-Wentworth District School Board, Offord Centre for Child Studies | University of Ottawa, Centre for Research on Educational and Community Services | Ontario Federation of Indigenous Friendship Centres |
| COPS | • Mathematics Leadership<br>• Critical Transitions in Student Mathematical Development<br>• Indigenous Knowledge and Mathematics Education<br>• Computational Thinking in Mathematics Education | • School Mental Health ASSIST<br>• The Social Planning Network of Ontario<br>• PREVNet<br>• The Ontario Healthy Schools Coalition | • Anti-Racist Education<br>• Refugee and Newcomer Education<br>• Inclusive Education for Students with Disabilities, Gender and Sexuality Education<br>• Minority Languages Education in Pluralist Contexts | |

## Out: repurposing existing mechanisms and using advances in ICT to mobilise information to the broader ecosystem

KNAER is also responsible for mobilising knowledge beyond its existing structure. Currently, there are two ways that the KNAER Secretariat reaches beyond KNAER network partners, the repurposing of the Ontario Education Research Panel (OERP) and the use of information communication technology (ICT).

### Ontario Education Research Panel (OERP)

Established in 2006 by the Ontario Ministry of Education, the Ontario Education Research Panel (OERP) supports and champions knowledge networks and partnerships for school–university research towards the advancement of education in Ontario. Panel membership is diverse, including university researchers, school board researchers, and school and system leaders from all regions of the province. Membership was recently expanded to include classroom teachers and students. Members are all external to the Ministry and appointed as individuals based on their contributions to education and/or education-related research.

The OERP promotes research, KMb networks and partnerships among multiple stakeholders; acts as an advisory body to the KNAER; provides expert advice to the Ministry of Education's Research and Evaluation Strategy; and identifies opportunities for collaboration to build system capacity for evidence use to support Ontario's renewed vision for education, 'Achieving Excellence'. In KNAER Phase II, the OERP provides advice to the KNAER on how the thematic networks and communities of practice can effectively inform and influence education practice. The OERP is also an important structure at the middle level: Its membership includes academic scholars who either co-create or conduct research and evidence that informs practice in schools and school district researchers who help to connect evidence and research to local school practice. The OERP provides an opportunity for the KNAER Secretariat to communicate the work of the Secretariat, the four thematic networks and their communities of practice to education research leaders. The OERP can, in a constructive and safe environment, provide collaborative expertise in the form of a 'critical friend' to KNAER. The critical friend approach is useful because it allows the Secretariat to keep in touch with recent developments in education research, practice and policy.

### Information communication technology (ICT)

As well as engaging in partnerships through governance arrangements at the macro-level and facilitating connections to micro-level actions in and through thematic networks and communities of practice, the KNAER Secretariat uses its structure and functions within the middle level to make connections within and outside the KNAER network, throughout the public education ecosystem and beyond. It does this by reaching out through communications, social media and interpersonal connections to mobilise knowledge and engage with a wider community of researchers, policy makers and practitioners and the public in Ontario, nationally in Canada, and internationally. The Secretariat does so by strategically (and crucially) employing both a social media and communications coordinator and a knowledge mobilisation facilitator. Below, we highlight some of the knowledge mobilisation mechanisms KNAER has used to indirectly influence and connect proponents working at the micro-level with key informants at the macro-level (and vice versa) such as the KNAER website and Knowledge Hub, *The KNAERative* and Listserv, and various social media platforms. Given that the KNAER Secretariat is not responsible for the daily working of the thematic networks, it can dedicate more time and resources to extending the KNAER reach beyond those directly involved the initiative: This is a feature unique to the meso-level within an ecosystems approach to education.

## KNAER website

In September 2017, in an effort to increase reach not only across the province of Ontario but also beyond, the redesigned KNAER website (www.knaer-recrae.ca) was launched with the purpose of making information more accessible and easy to navigate. The website is open access and does not require a username and password. Each thematic network has its own profile page, which was created in collaboration with each network and includes the most pertinent information about who they are and what they aim to do. These pages are regularly updated to reflect the evolving nature of the networks (e.g. growth in network partners, change in logo, change of guiding principles) and includes the network's most popular resources from the Education Resources section of the Knowledge Hub, and regular updates of the work that the networks and their communities of practice and/or Regional Teams have been doing. The website also includes the KNAER Twitter and Facebook feed, as well as blog posts and an events calendar.

## The Knowledge Hub

The Knowledge Hub is an open-access repository that holds an increasing range of resources easily accessible to Ontario educators and the broader sector. It has four components: Research & Evidence, Education Resources, KMb Resources and KMb Blog. Research & Evidence provides resources to help educators find and assess evidence, helping them become teacher-researchers. These resources are prescreened to ensure practicality, and come in the form of lesson plans, activities, presentations, videos, research summaries, teaching tips and more. There are currently 135 resources (English and French) and this number is consistently growing as each network produces more resources for educators to support Ontario students. The KMb resources provide tips and tools for knowledge mobilisation that the KNAER team have assembled to help not only the Ontario education sector, but also anyone interested in learning about best practices for mobilising knowledge in their field. The final section of the Knowledge Hub is the KMb Blog, which has become a resource for experts all over the world to share their knowledge and wisdom on effective ways to mobilise knowledge, as well as their experiences with knowledge mobilisation. We share a new KMb blog post every month featuring contributors from both inside and outside of Ontario, and inside and outside of the education sector. These posts are geared towards the general public with the intention that everyone can learn something from each post, regardless of whether they are just starting to learn about knowledge mobilisation or are currently experts in the field.

## The KNAERative and Listserv

The e-newsletter for KNAER is called the 'The KNAERative'. The KNAERative is distributed to subscribed readers through the constantly growing KNAER Listserv. Each e-newsletter provides an update from the KNAER co-directors and the ERESB. It also provides a space for each network to update the broader sector about its work over the last quarter and what is to come in the next quarter. In addition to informing network members and the broader sector about these updates, we also include links to Featured Resources (the Educational Resources section of our website), Upcoming Events (the Events Calendar on our website), KNAER News (on our website), and KMb Blogs (on our website), allowing subscribers to easily access the various ways in which we disseminate knowledge in one newsletter that goes straight to their inbox.

## Social media

The use of social media as a tool for making connections from the middle has proven to be essential for knowledge mobilisation between and among researchers and public educators. Although KNAER has engaged with multiple social media platforms (i.e. Facebook and LinkedIn), Twitter has proven to be its most valuable social media tool. The KNAER Secretariat has used Twitter to increase awareness of network activities and events by disseminating knowledge mobilisation information, news and event information, KNAER project outputs, KNAER thematic network resources and Ontario Education Research Exchange (OERE) summaries. With the development of Twitter accounts for the Math, Well-Being, and Equity Networks in the past year, it has also provided a platform for cross-network collaboration. The social media coordinator and knowledge mobilisation facilitator have played a vital role in enabling the continued cross-network collaboration and outward push.

## Conclusions

What can KNAER teach us about the importance of initiatives at the middle tier of an educational ecosystem? First, a research-informed ecosystem requires dynamic, connected, structured and sustainable organisations and initiatives at middle level that strategically connect the macro- and micro-level of the system. Second, these organisations and initiatives require resources and strategies – such as multi-year funding and networks – that can be dedicated to building capacity for knowledge mobilisation and evidence use in schools. Third, they can build upon existing structures to extend reach in all directions: down into the classroom, up to decision-making at the policy level, and out beyond the existing ecosystem.

A systems approach to knowledge mobilisation that consists of communities of practice nested within thematic networks – which themselves are nested within a larger provincial network – is mapped onto an existing school ecosystem. In this case, KNAER's position at the meso-level facilitates intersectional and inter-disciplinary communication between and among the various levels of influence found within the KNAER, and specifically enables the mobilisation of research and knowledge from the macro-level to the school level.

We at the KNAER Secretariat often describe our role as being the glue that holds everything together. Through the openness of the ERESB at the Ministry of Education and trial and error around processes and practices, we believe that our intentional development of an initiative at the middle tier for knowledge mobili-sation has allowed the KNAER to strengthen relationships between the Ontario provincial government and local universities, build capacity within Ontario's pub-licly funded education systems for knowledge mobilisation and evidence use; foster research to practice partnerships among a wide range of education, health, pro-fessional and community organisations; and act as a knowledge broker through cross-sector provincial networks. Organisations at the middle tier often have the unique ability to see both broadly and deeply, and as such are able to facilitate con-nections that may have otherwise been overlooked. In this capacity, the middle tier is crucially important to the functioning and interconnectedness of research-engaged educational ecosystems.

## Implications for the research-informed ecosystem

- A research-informed ecosystem requires dynamic, connected, structured and well-resourced initiatives and organisations at middle-level that strategically connect the macro- and micro-levels of the system – in the KNAER case, this is achieved through knowledge mobilisation networks;
- Initiatives and organisations at the middle level can build on existing structures to extend reach in all directions: down into the classroom, up to decision-making at the policy level and beyond the existing ecosystem;
- Resources that support connected and sustainable middle-level initiatives include multi-year funding, and dedicated communications staff;
- Organisations and bodies at the middle tier are able to facilitate connections that may have otherwise been overlooked because they are uniquely posi-tioned to see both broadly and deeply, and;
- Information communications technology – especially social media platforms – has a large role to play in research-engaged ecosystems. Those considering an ecosystems approach may want to dedicate resources and time to investigate how they can strategically use social media as a means to mobilise knowledge, research and evidence.

# References

Ainscow, M., Muijs, D. and West, M. (2006). Collaboration as a strategy for improving schools in challenging circumstances. *Improving Schools*, 9(3), 192–202.

Best, A. and Holmes, B. (2010). Systems thinking, knowledge and action: towards better models and methods. *Evidence & Policy: A Journal of Research, Debate and Practice*, 6(2), 145–159.

Borgatti, S. and Foster, P. (2003). The network paradigm in organizational research: A review and typology. *Journal of Management*, 29, 991–1013.

Briscoe, P., Pollock, K., Campbell, C. and Carr-Harris, S. (2015). Finding the sweet spot: Network structures and processes for increased knowledge mobilisation. *Brock Education Journal*, 25(1) 20–34.

Bronfenbrenner, U. (1979). *The Ecology of Human Development: Experiments by Nature and Design*. Cambridge, MA: Harvard University Press.

Campbell, C., Pollock, K., Carr-Harris, S. and Briscoe, P. (with Bairos, K. and Malik, S.). (2014). *Knowledge Network for Applied Education Research (KNAER)*. Final Report. Ontario Institute for Studies in Education, University of Toronto, and Western University. Retrieved 6 January 2019 from: www.knaer-recrae.ca/about/reports.

Castells, M .(2001). *The Internet Galaxy: Reflections on the Internet, Business and Society*. Oxford: Oxford University Press.

Chapman, C. and Fullan, M. (2007). Collaboration and partnership for equitable improvement: towards a networked learning system? *School Leadership and Management*, 27(3), 207–211, doi:10.1080/13632430701379354.

Church, M., Bitel, M., Armstrong, K., Fernando, P., Gould, H., Joss, S. Marwaha-Diedrich, M., De La Torre, A-L. and Vouhe, C. (2002). *Participation, Relationships and Dynamic Change: New Thinking on Evaluating the Work of International Networks*. London: University College London.

Cooper, A. (2012). *Knowledge Mobilisation Intermediaries in Education: A Cross-Case Analysis of 44 Canadian Organisations*. Unpublished doctoral dissertation, Ontario Institute for Studies in Education, Toronto, ON.

Daly, A. J., Moolenaar, N. M., Bolivar, J. M. and Burke, P. (2010). Relationships in reform: the role of teachers' social networks. *Journal of Educational Administration*, 48(3), 359–391.

Degenne, A. and Forsé, M. (1999). *Introducing Social Networks* (A. Borges, Trans.). London, UK: SAGE Publications Ltd.

Earl, L. and Katz, S. (2006). *Leading in a Data Rich World: Harnessing Data for School Improvement*. Thousand Oaks, CA: Corwin.

Education Research and Evaluation Strategy Branch (ERESB). (2017). Internal and unpublished government report.

Gilchrist, A. (1995). *Community Development and Networking*. London, UK: Community Development Foundation.

Hadfield, M., Jopling, M., Noden, C., O'Leary, D. and Stott, A. (2006). What does the existing knowledge base tell us about the impact of networking and collaboration? *A Review of Network-Based Innovations in Education in the UK*. Nottingham, UK: National College for School Leadership.

Hargreaves, A. (2003). *Teaching in the Knowledge Society: Education in the Age of Insecurity*. New York, NY: Teachers College Press.

Hopkins, D. (2003). Understanding networks for innovation in policy and practice. In OECD (Ed.) *Networks of Innovation: Towards New Models for Managing Schools and Systems*. Paris: OECD Publishing, pp. 153–163.

Kilduff, M. and Tsai, W. (2003). *Social Networks and Organizations.* London: SAGE.

Malik, S. (2016). *Knowledge Mobilisation in Ontario: A Multi-Case Study of Education Organisations.* Doctoral thesis, Ontario Institute for Studies in Education, University of Toronto. Retrieved 6 January 2019 from: www.knaer-recrae.ca/about/reports.

Nelson, J. and Campbell, C. (2017). Evidence-informed practice in education: meanings and applications. *Educational Research*, 59(2), 127–135, doi: 10.1080/00131881.2017.1314115.

Nutley, S. and Davies, H. T. O. (2014). What counts as good evidence? [Part B: Discussion]. RURU, University of St Andrews. Video retrieved 6 January 2019 from: www.ruru.ac.uk/newsevents.html.

Nutley, S., Walter, I. and Davies, H. T. O. (2007). *Using Evidence: How Research Can Inform Public Services.* Bristol: The Policy Press.

Ontario Ministry of Education. (2014a). *Achieving Excellence: A Renewed Vision for Education in Ontario.* Retrieved 6 January 2019 from: www.edu.gov.on.ca/eng/about/renewed Vision.pdf.

Phipps, D. and Morton, S. (2013). Qualities of knowledge brokers: reflections from practice. *Evidence & Policy: A Journal of Research, Debate and Practice*, 9(2), 255–265, doi: 10.1332/174426413X667784.

Sharples, J. (2013). Evidence for the frontline: a report for the Alliance for Useful Evidence. London, UK: The Alliance for Useful Evidence. Retrieved 6 January 2019 from: www.alliance4usefulevidence.org/assets/EVIDENCE-FOR-THE-FRONTLINE-FINAL-5-June-2013.pdf.

von Bertalanffy, L. (1968). *Teoria General de Sistemas.* Mexico D.P., Mexico: Fondo de Cultura Economica.

Watson, D., Townsley, R. and Abbott, D. (2002). Exploring multi-agency working in services to disabled children with complex healthcare needs and their families. *Journal of Clinical Nursing*, 11(3), 367–375.

# 3

# ACCOUNTABILITY STRUCTURES THAT SUPPORT SCHOOL SELF-EVALUATION, ENQUIRY AND LEARNING

*Melanie Ehren*

## Aims of the chapter

- To explain how current top-down, standardised accountability systems shape the ecosystem in which schools are working, narrow teaching and learning, and prevent schools from developing a culture of professional learning.
- To present an alternative model of 'intelligent accountability' which supports schools to become enquiring and learning organisations.

## Introduction

This chapter will first explain how current standardised accountability systems, such as high-stakes testing and school inspections, have standardised aspects of a school's organisation. DiMaggio and Powell's (1983) work on isomorphism is used to understand how formal and informal pressure, uncertainty and professional networks and norms lead to high levels of standardisation of schools' cultures and structures which are narrowly organised around the standards in accountability frameworks. The conclusion of this chapter draws on work of Alkin (2013) to present an alternative, more localised and subjective model of evaluation which would support schools in using research evidence to improve their practice, and develop a research-engaged organisational culture.

### External top-down accountability to standardise educational practices

Much has been written about how external accountability, such as school inspections or high-stakes testing, reshape schools' organisational structures and processes and the ecosystem of which they are part. Prior studies for example show how school inspections may have effects on schools in terms of whether, when and how teachers and head teachers reflect on school/teaching quality when responding to inspection feedback or preparing for a visit. Chapman (2001) for example talks about how, in England, 'issues became re-emphasised' when the inspection team endorsed needed improvements in certain areas, where the inspection process was seen to encourage reflection on practices, particularly ones that led to better achievement. In Flanders, Penninckx et al. (2015) refer to 'conceptual effects' where school staff reflect on the quality of lessons and general quality of education before the inspection and where some members of staff became more aware of the value of their profession or of policy matters in their own school.

Many studies indicate that such reflections also lead to actual changes in school improvement planning, in school self-evaluation and in how teachers and head teachers organise their work and teaching. Particularly schools who expect to fail their upcoming inspection, or who are placed in a failing category would feel the pressure to improve. Improvement activities in these schools would be informed by the inspection standards and particularly the standards those schools are failing on, or expect to be failing on. In England, such changes would, given the performance-based nature of school inspections, often focus on the introduction of improvement of assessments, and the use of assessment data to improve student outcomes. Hardy (2012) for example explains how Ofsted influenced target setting processes in schools, so that highly aspirational targets were set for student attainment. Other studies (Whitby, 2010; NfER, 2009) report similar practices, such as: 'Headteachers and governors making use of data to alert staff to students at risk of under-achieving. Headteachers focused on eliminating "in-school variation", for example through middle- leader support and training', (Whitby, 2010) or inspections that led to improved assessment practices and the quality of teaching and attainment.

School inspections also have a profound effect on how schools evaluate their own quality and the criteria they use to develop their curriculum, assessment, teaching and school leadership, particularly when Inspectorates of Education assess those school-internal evaluation practices or request school-evaluation outcomes as part of their inspection data collection. Matthews and Ehren (2017) explain how the validation of self-evaluations by school inspectors has incentivised schools to become proficient in gauging their own effectiveness, but how most schools choose to base their self-evaluation on the aspects covered by inspection, even though they are encouraged to set their own standards. The strong link between inspection and self-evaluation is felt on various levels of the school system, not just in single schools, but also by their boards or governing bodies. Recent work in the Netherlands and England (Ehren et al., 2017) for example highlight how Dutch school boards and Multi-Academy Trusts in England introduce strong internal quality control and reporting requirements for schools in an attempt to respond to external inspections and ensure they are in charge of school quality improvement and prepared for external inspections scrutinising the quality of their leadership and support of schools. Ofsted's inspection standards are often used by CEOs of Multi-Academy Trusts in the performance management of head teachers, school governors use these standards to understand performance and quality of schools, parents tend to choose a school with a 'good' or 'outstanding' Ofsted grade, and head teachers use Ofsted-inspired protocols to observe their teacher's lessons (Ehren and Godfrey, 2017).

The high stakes nature of inspections and standardised assessments, and their key role in informing school improvement and education system reform has had a profound effect on how people and organisations in education hold each other accountable, and how 'quality of schools' is understood throughout the system. Several studies explain how schools' organisational structures and processes have become standardised as and when those working with and in schools use external accountability measures to inform their work and decision-making.

Ehren et al. (2015), Gustafsson et al. (2015) for example found that accountability frameworks change our understanding of educational quality (through processes of normalisation or institutionalisation), which is reinforced and informed by the performance feedback provided to schools in inspection visits, reports or league tables, and when external actors (such as parents) use such information to select schools (in systems with free school choice), or try to enact change through participation in school council meetings. The many examples of 'how to become inspection-ready' indicate how an entire industry is making money out of selling services and products that are supposed to help schools get a good inspection grade. Box 3.1 provides an example of an advertisement from the *Times Educational Supplement* (5 January 2018) in England.

---

## Box 3.1   Becoming inspection-ready for Ofsted

*Conquer inspections and observations with confidence by exploring these helpful tips and hand-picked resources*

Ofsted: probably every teacher's least favourite two-syllable word. Up and down the country, staff are united by the fact that when that dreaded call comes in, it brings with it stress, sleepless nights and heightened emotions for already over-worked teachers. Quite simply, it creates panic.

While no one can control when Ofsted will come knocking, we can offer support, and a few carefully selected resources, to make the process less painful. After all, regardless of who is walking in to your classroom, there is still a lesson to teach. And, while teachers are no longer graded on individual lessons, we know the team-player within you will be keen to shine.

Remember, you know your students and what works well

*(continued)*

*(continued)*

Let's be realistic – this isn't the time to try out a completely different lesson style with a class that is usually productive. While there is no need to share any planning with Ofsted, it can be a good idea to have a copy out in the room. By displaying something like this simple sheet, the inspectors have access to the order of activities and development of learning beyond the short time that they are with the class. For a confidence boost, this easy-to-digest guide gives a quick overview of how to plan and teach a lesson that is being observed.

Source: www.tes.com/teaching-resources/blog/becoming-inspection-ready-ofsted (accessed 6 January 2019).

The example indicates how the external environment of schools supports the integration of accountability standards and measures into schools' organisational structures and classroom practices. The consequences schools face for their performance on the standards shifts the functioning of these standards from measurement to setting norms about what good teaching and a good school looks like. In addition to schools, other actors in the education system, such as support services working with schools, textbook and test developers, and teacher training colleges use the standards to coordinate and align their activities.

These processes of institutionalisation where schools become 'self-inspecting' are 'fired' when principals and schools feel pressure to respond to inspection prompts and improve the education in their school. Ehren (2016), using DiMaggio and Powell's (1983) notions of coercive, mimetic and normative isomorphism, explains how changes in the organisation and daily practices in schools emerge out of the structuration of organisational fields, such as the education and evaluation system in which schools function. These organisational fields provide a context in which the efforts of individual schools to organise their teaching and learning are constrained and lead to some homogeneity in structure, culture and output, typically in how mathematics and literacy is taught and organised as these subjects are generally at the forefront of external accountability.

### *Coercive isomorphism*[1]

Schools are part of an exosystem in which they interact with other schools, local community organisations, parents, and suppliers of services and resources (e.g. suppliers of textbooks). These organisations and stakeholders exert pressure on schools (both formal and informally), particularly when schools are dependent on these organisations. Equally, cultural expectations of how schools are expected to function (e.g. having grades, classroom settings) equally pressure schools into conforming to a predefined standard. Such formal and informal pressures exerted on organisations by other organisations upon which they are dependent and by cultural expectations in the society within which organisations function is referred to as 'coercive isomorphism'. Pressures may be felt as force, as persuasion, or as invitations to join in 'collusion' (DiMaggio and Powell, 1983, p. 150). Coercive pressures have an impact on the behaviour of those working in and with schools and lead to schools becoming similar over time.

Inspections play an important role in creating such coercive pressures and in defining how schools are expected to be structured and formed. Inspectorates' assessments of schools against legal and technical requirements of the state, and the consequences for failing schools will pressurise schools to adopt certain pro-tocols, roles, programmes or structures to meet these requirements. Teachers and head teachers will try to confirm to inspection standards because they fear punishment from inspections. Fear of repercussions is enhanced when inspec-tion assessments and reports are disseminated to the wider public and schools imagine and anticipate potential negative reactions of school authorities, boards of education or parents.

Particularly clear and detailed standards seem to produce real conformity as it's easier for schools to understand ways in which they can align themselves to these standards; something that is more difficult when more open norms are used to evaluate schools. The clarity and detail of standards also allows a school's stake-holders to impose financial fines on schools who fail to meet these standards, or impose other types of sanctions and pressures, motivating schools to model them-selves after these standards and after schools who are considered to be successful in responding to the standards. External pressures become absorbed, negotiated and embodied within schools and change how teachers and head teachers make decisions, do their jobs and think about their schools, particularly when external stakeholders have power and use rankings and assessments to inform their choice of, or funding of, schools and when schools face legitimacy threats (see Sauder and Espeland, 2009).

Westhorp et al. (2014) describe this as an *anticipatory* mechanism: it operates because those who are observed fear a sanction if they are caught (or desire the reward for good performance) and change their own behaviour *before* the sanction or incentive is applied. This requires, according to Westhorp et al. (2014) a belief, on the part of the observed actor, that the observation will happen and will lead to the enactment of sanctions. Schools will try to conform to inspection stand-ards when they believe inspectors are capable of detecting corrupt or undesirable behaviour, when they believe that inspectors will report their observations to those with the authority to implement sanctions, when those authorities will enforce the sanctions and when the sanction constitutes a greater cost than the actor is will-ing to bear. A similar logic applies to potential rewards and the potential to detect desirable behaviour and outstanding quality.

The types of alignment to accountability standards varies according to what the standards measure. Typical examples are provided by DiMaggio and Powell (1983) who describe how schools promulgate curricula that confirm with state standards, creating new formal roles which have responsibility to interact with and represent the school to outside authorities and have responsibility to ensure compliance with external standards and meeting external benchmarks. New roles are typically maths and literacy coaches who are tasked with improving student performance in these inspected subject areas, quality assurance managers who are responsible for the implementation of school self-evaluation systems and with the collection of information requested by Inspectorates of Education.

Such institutional conformity in response to inspection standards is often broader than what schools are legally required to do. Brandsen et al. (2006) for example point out how guidelines (such as letters, handbooks, manuals, websites and meetings organised by professional associations) that have no formal status take on the character of formal regulation when schools suspect they cannot choose alternative courses of action without sanction. These guidelines are particularly forceful when the organisations issuing them (e.g. teacher unions or national lobby organisations or consultancy firms) are (perceived as) connected with the regulating body or inspection agency are considered legitimate experts in the area. When conforming to standards is a complex task, which calls for a high level of expertise, adopting such guidelines is often the easiest way in which to ensure alignment and compliance, and something schools would do out of uncertainty or inexperience. The line between formal regulation and unofficial guidelines becomes very thin when both are interpreted as rules to be obeyed.

## Mimetic isomorphism

'Mimetic processes' refers to organisations modelling themselves after similar organisations in their field that they perceive to be more legitimate or successful (DiMaggio and Powell, 1983, p. 152). Modelling and imitation is, again, caused by uncertainty; not just uncertainty about how to meet inspection standards but also uncertainty about how to best organise school-internal processes and teaching to meet high-stakes performance targets around student outcomes. The complexity of teaching and learning an often diverse student population qualifies the field of education as one that is prone to mimetic isomorphism. Given the lack of clarity over which types of activities lead to high student performance, schools would be inclined to copy models they perceive to be successful, particularly when their search for potential effective practices leads them onto seemingly viable solutions that can be implemented with little expense.

Inspections have an important role in augmenting such processes. Their publication of good practices, league tables of high performing and failing schools and benchmarking schools on common indicators of 'good educational practices' and outcomes allows schools to copy protocols, structures and good practices from schools considered to be high performing and provides legitimacy to such practices. Questions of whether such practices are fit for purpose for the specific context they are transported to are often ignored and schools simply copy the practices from the schools who have passed their inspection. Figure 3.1 provides an example from

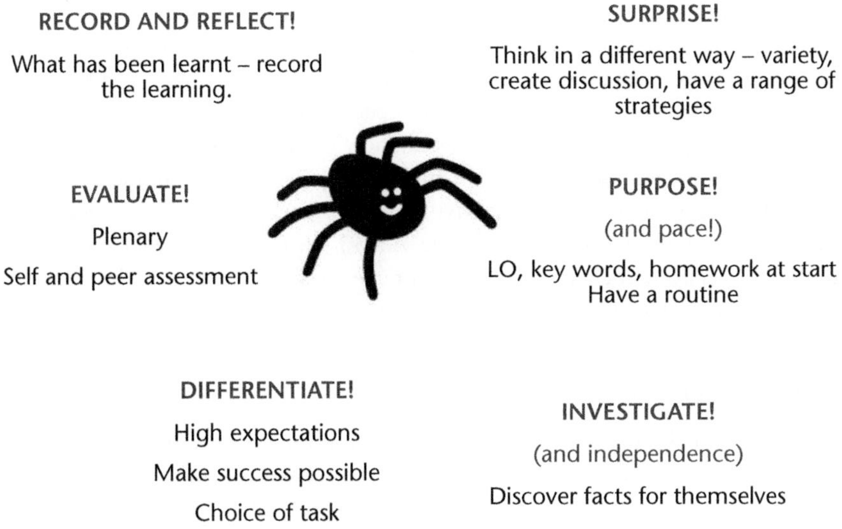

**RECORD AND REFLECT!**

What has been learnt – record the learning.

**EVALUATE!**

Plenary

Self and peer assessment

**SURPRISE!**

Think in a different way – variety, create discussion, have a range of strategies

**PURPOSE!**

(and pace!)

LO, key words, homework at start
Have a routine

**DIFFERENTIATE!**

High expectations

Make success possible

Choice of task

**INVESTIGATE!**

(and independence)

Discover facts for themselves

**FIGURE 3.1**   Ofsted six part lesson

*Source*: M. McCarthy and J. Beere (2011). The perfect (OFSTED) lesson (www.tes.com/teaching-resource/planning-and-teaching-the-perfect-ofsted-lesson-6113548, accessed 6 January 2019).

England where teachers share resources online that have helped them prepare for Ofsted inspections. Sharing of these practices has led to a common understanding of the structure of a good lesson as one that has a beginning, a starter (stimulate curiosity and open mindedness and prepare the brain for learning), a specific lesson objective that is challenging but differentiated for children with different ability levels, a main body which meets the criteria in the below 'spider's diagram', and a review of what was learnt throughout the lesson.

Schmidt (2013) similarly explains how, in the German federal state of Saxony, schools unpick high scores of other schools on specific inspection standards and copy the practices underlying those standards. A school which was rated highly in terms of personnel management would for example receive requests to share documentation about its on-the-job training programme.

Schools use their connections with other schools and local networks to inform them about successful practices and to duplicate such practices, creating new reference frames to categorise each other and communicate strategically to meet performance norms which are set through school inspection. Other examples of such mimicking were found in studies of Gärtner (2011), Gärtner and Wurster (2009) where principals reported in a survey to implement procedures and protocols specifically to meet inspection criteria. Examples include 'inspection-approved' curricula and textbooks, and publishers selling 'inspection-conform' self-evaluation tools that allow schools to benchmark themselves against the inspection framework. The educational field of textbook developers, support organisations etc. typically reinforces this process by selling and marketing products that are 'inspection-approved' and aligning their products to inspection frameworks.

Interestingly, in England the dissemination of such 'good practices' is now actively discouraged by Ofsted in an attempt to prevent the resulting narrowing of teaching and learning. In their 'Myth busting campaign', Ofsted actively communicates (though tweets and YouTube videos) what it does NOT expect to see in their inspections, such as a lesson plan for every lesson or a school self-evaluation which incorporates Ofsted's inspection standards.

## Normative pressures

A third and final source of isomorphic change is normative pressure, according to DiMaggio and Powell (1983). Normative pressure stems primarily from professionalisation where members of an occupation collectively define the conditions and methods of their work, how people enter the occupation (e.g. setting requirements on qualification for new entrants), and to establish a cognitive base and legitimation for their occupational autonomy. Particularly the formal education of teachers, and the growth and elaboration of professional networks that span organisations are important sources of isomorphism, such as when teacher training institutions shape the development and conveying of organisational norms and set common expectations among professionals (Greenwood and Suddaby, 2006). Professionals from the same training centres and networks tend to view problems in a similar fashion, see the same policies, procedures and structures as normatively sanctioned and legitimated and approach decisions in much the same way, according to these authors. Current trends of schools collaborating in networks to share good practices, or engaging in peer reviews provide additional opportunities to share examples of teaching and leadership which are considered good practice.

The external inspection framework again, provides an important benchmark to understand the practices that are considered to be 'good' and successful and some Inspectorates of Education actively encourage the teaching profession to understand and use inspection standards in their work. In England, head teachers and teachers have the opportunity to participate in inspections of other schools and to be trained in using the framework to evaluate their, and other schools. Under Part 2 to Schedule 12 of the Education and Inspections Act 2006 Her Majesty's Chief Inspector can delegate any of his/her functions to HMI or to 'any additional inspector', which are mainly serving or recent practitioners directly contracted by Ofsted and are commonly referred to as 'Ofsted inspectors'; www.legislation.gov.uk/ukpga/2006/40/schedule/12 (see Box 3.2). These (head) teachers are trained to inspect schools as a secondary activity to their headship, creating a new framework across the country for what successful leaders should be able to do, and who successful heads are. Training head teachers to be school inspectors reinforces the dissemination of 'inspection-approved' practices to their school and to other schools as they become knowledgeable about how to interpret inspection categories and the kind of practices an inspector would want to see.

---

### Box 3.2 Ofsted's inspection workforce from September 2015

Frequently Asked Questions

Q5. What are the benefits of having more serving practitioners on inspection teams?

By having an increased proportion of education professionals on our teams, we're enabling more people from the sectors to get involved in the inspection process. Their familiarity of contemporary education practice will continuously refresh Ofsted's working knowledge and ensure that our inspections are of the quality that parents, learners and colleagues across the sectors rightly expect. This will increase the credibility and value of inspection with those we inspect.

The serving practitioners who inspect will gain first-hand insight into inspection, continuous professional development and closer working links with HMI. They'll be able to take the experience and lessons learnt from training and inspection back to the settings they lead, building capacity and expertise in the sector.

We're investing more time and resources in high-quality ongoing training and development so that all our inspectors are well equipped to conduct inspections – this training is free for OIs when they commit to a minimum number of days inspecting.

Those OIs who are serving practitioners will also be invaluable in helping us shape up inspection by drawing on their expertise of what works and what doesn't work in inspection from the point of view of providers.

Source: https://assets.publishing.service.gov.uk/government/uploads/system/uploads/attachment_data/file/465626/Ofsteds_inspection_workforce_from_September_2015.pdf, accessed 6 January 2019.

---

The ease of having a national legitimate classification system in place to understand the quality of schools has great appeal for those working in, and with schools to reinterpret their practices and internalise new self-conceptions around these categories. By copying these models, teachers and head teachers are able to quickly establish legitimacy without having to build a repertoire of practices which can be time-consuming without necessarily leading to any tangible outcomes. Such external measures often also inform a school's internal quality control as incorporating the measures in head teacher performance management systems, school self-evaluation or peer review, allow schools to prepare for inspections and prevent any unpleasant surprises of a failing inspection outcome. In England alone, there are many examples of how school performance management systems to evaluate head teachers and teachers reference inspection standards, classroom observations protocols to evaluate their teachers are copied from inspection lesson observations forms, and the internet is replete with teachers and representatives of teacher unions providing examples of what an 'outstanding' lesson would look like.

This culture of 'self-inspection' or performativity is reinforced over time when new teachers do not question the existing system and take Ofsted's expectations of 'professionalism' and teaching for granted. Wilkins (2011), Dougill et al. (2011) and Berry (2012) explain how new young teachers in England will themselves have been educated in a system in which pupils were frequently tested and schools were required to meet externally imposed standards and are regularly inspected. According to Berry (2012, p. 402) 'it is all they have known so they don't imagine it can be different'; new teachers have a 'post-performative' identity (Wilkins, 2011). Teachers who express different views of the importance of individual teacher autonomy are now even considered out of date or incompetent. Inspection categories, and rankings of schools along those categories clearly create new meanings of how the profession is viewed, the roles people are expected to fulfil in schools and the types of interventions and knowledge appropriate for those roles. After a while, these roles and practices become the norm and redefine the status of the teaching profession and what is considered high quality teaching.

### Towards a more holistic understanding of school quality

The previous sections highlighted how external accountability measures, such as school inspections, have shaped the actions and interactions of school staff, the professional learning and organisational culture and structure in the school. Our exploration of coercive, normative and mimetic isomorphism allowed us to understand how a school's interaction with its environment creates similarity in those structures and cultures, often in a very narrow manner as external accountability standards prioritise performance in a small number of academic subjects, on a limited number of standardised tests and inspection measures.

As Godfrey and Brown (2018) explain, an effective research and development ecosystem however needs to have accountability arrangements which support (honest and open) school self-evaluation and enquiry, where schools are motivated to become learning organisations and use research to inform decision-making. The current high-stakes and top-down nature of external accountability however oftentimes restricts schools in setting its own improvement agenda in a way most appropriate to its context. The anxiety around ensuring a good inspection outcome creates a culture of fear in schools where school staff are predominantly focused on external performance targets, diminishing a culture of professional learning, and breaking down trust between teachers and head teachers. How can we create more 'intelligent accountability' that allows schools to become research-engaged and develop effective ways of using research evidence to inform their practice?

Ehren et al. (2017) have used Alkin's (2013) framework of evaluation theories to describe an alternative model of inspection which captures the mechanisms and conditions that explain the functioning and performance of an intervention, programme or organisation and motivate school staff to use research evidence to inform their practice. Such an approach would:

- include multiple levels of analysis (individual, interpersonal and collective) at which influence occurs, and
- use constructivist approaches to develop and test theories of 'how something works'.

The model of Ehren et al. (2017) describe the use of a set of evaluation methods to validate local and context-specific approaches to shaping educational quality and in using research evidence to improve school-based practices, such as through 'developmental evaluation' or 'participatory evaluation'. In Ehren et al. (2017) proposed model, Inspectorates of Education facilitate evaluations which are goal-free, flexible and specific to context and information needs of (network of) schools and stakeholders. School staff and their stakeholders are involved in all the phases of the accountability exercise, from developing the standards and methods for evaluation, to deciding on how to define failure and success, and how to improve the quality and performance of the school and potential consequences for failure.

School staff and a school's stakeholders engage in judging the types of behaviour considered effective and appropriate, thinking about the settings in which specific practices are effective, allowing for the development of a deep understanding of how schools operate and are effective in solving local problems. The role of the Inspectorate shifts from making judgements on a centralised framework, towards the facilitation of evaluation and inspection. School self-evaluation and enquiry, and a discussion of why certain practices are considered effective in a particular context given the available wider research evidence and school-level data and evidence, is at the heart of the inspection.

There are currently no inspection models which use this particular type of approach to evaluate schools as most Inspectorates of Education or accountability agencies in general, are required by law to use a standardised framework to assess school quality, where the general public generally favours relatively simple benchmarks and league tables to understand and compare school quality. However, the below example of 'place-based scrutiny' in East Perthshire, Scotland provides an idea of a goal-free evaluation and how such an evaluation would allow for a more localised assessment (see Box 3.3).

---

**Box 3.3  Place-based scrutiny in Scotland**

Education Scotland, responsible for inspection of Scottish schools, led the place-based scrutiny exercise which included a number of Inspectorates over-seeing services within that area (the Care Inspectorate, the Scottish Housing Regulator, Audit Scotland, Healthcare Improvement Scotland, HMICS, the Fire Inspectorate and the Academic Advisor), as well as a number of representatives from the local community (the environment and consumer services, Housing and Community Care, Children and Families' Services, Scottish Fire and Rescue Service, Police Scotland, Senior Community Capacity Worker and the National Health Service). The 'place-based scrutiny' occurred in 2015 with a scoping exercise in February and fieldwork during a week in March. The scrutiny led to a report which focused on the answering the following questions:

1.  What is it like to live in this community?
2.  How well are services collaborating to improve outcomes for people living there?
3.  Is our collective activity addressing/tackling inequalities?

The exercise aimed to identify issues that need to be addressed to improve the lives of the people living in the area. For more information: www.schoolinspections.eu.

---

## Conclusions

This chapter explained how high-stakes external accountability shapes the eco-system in which schools are working through informal and formal pressures, exerted by stakeholders in the environment of the school, professional networks and norms, and the distribution and legitimisation of 'good practices' which are adopted by schools in an attempt to reduce the uncertainty inherent in teaching and learning. The examples from England indicated how the anxiety of school staff to do well on the Ofsted framework prevents schools from developing a culture of professional learning, and narrows teaching and learning. An alternative model of 'intelligent accountability' was presented that could support schools in becoming enquiring and learning organisations. Such a model uses a more localised and flexible approach to evaluation and intervention, where evaluation criteria are designed around how schools engage in research and use research evidence to inform their practice. A school's own objectives act as reference points for performance indicators, requiring school staff to be clear about their intentions, standards and created expectations. This will in turn enhance informal control within schools and in anchoring partnerships with other stakeholders, and will inform how other actors in the system engage with schools.

## Implications for the research-informed ecosystem

- For schools to become research-informed, the external accountability system needs to support them in becoming enquiring and learning organisations.
- Such a system needs to move away from current high-stakes, top-down, standardised approaches which create a culture of fear and anxiety where schools and their environment are focused on complying with inspection standards.
- Instead, more localised and 'intelligent accountability' is needed, building on existing goal-free and constructivist models of evaluation.
- Such models start with a set of open questions on how schools engage with research, the objectives they have to improve their education and the evidence they have that this is improving children's learning and well-being and the school's professional community overall.

## Note

1  The section on coercive, mimetic and normative isomorphism was adapted from Ehren (2016).

## References

Au, W. (2007). High-stakes testing and curricular control: a qualitative metasynthesis. *Educational Researcher*, 36(5), 258–267.

Alkin, M. C. (Ed.). (2013). *Evaluation Roots: A Wider Perspective of Theorists' Views and Influences*. Thousand Oaks: Sage Publications.

Berry, J. (2012). Teachers' professional autonomy in England: are neo-liberal approaches incontestable? *FORUM: for promoting 3-19 comprehensive education*, 54(3), 397–409.

Brandsen, T., Boogers, M. and Tops, P. (2006). Soft governance, hard consequences: the ambiguous status of unofficial guidelines. *Public Administration Review*, 66(4), 546–553.

Chapman, C. (2001). Changing classrooms through inspection. *School Leadership and Management*, 21(1), 59–73.

DiMaggio, P. J. and Powell, W. W. (1983). The iron cage revisited: institutional isomorphism and collective rationality in organizational fields. *American Sociological Review*, 48(1), 147–160.

Dougill, P., Raleigh, M., Blatchford, R., Fryer, L., Robinson, C. and Richmond, J. (2011). *To the Next Level: Good Schools Becoming Outstanding*. Reading: CfBT Education Trust.

Ehren, M. C., Gustafsson, J. E., Altrichter, H., Skedsmo, G., Kemethofer, D. and Huber, S. G. (2015). Comparing effects and side effects of different school inspection systems across Europe. *Comparative Education*, 51(3), 375–400.

Ehren, M. C. M. (Eds.) (2016). *Methods and Modalities of Effective School Inspections*. Dordrecht: Springer.

Ehren, M. C. and Godfrey, D. (2017). External accountability of collaborative arrangements; a case study of a multi academy trust in England. *Educational Assessment, Evaluation and Accountability*, 29(4), 339–362.

Ehren, M. C. M., Janssens, F. J. G., Brown, M., McNamara, G., O'Hara, J. and Shevlin, P. (2017). Evaluation and decentralised governance: examples of inspections in polycentric education systems. *Journal of Educational Change*, 18(3), 365–383.

Gärtner, H. (2011). Die wirkung von schulinspektion auf schulentwicklung. Eine quasi-experimentelle feldstudie. In C. Quesel, V. Husfeldt, N. Landwehr and P. Steiner (Eds.), *Wirkungen und Wirksamkeit der externen Schulevaluation* (pp. 145–161). Bern: Hep.

Gärtner, H. and Wurster, S. (2009). *Befragung zur Wirkung von Schulvisitation in Brandenburg: Ergebnisbericht.* Berlin. Retrieved 6 January 2019 from: www.isq-bb.de/uploads/media/ ISQ_Ergebnisbericht_Schulvisitation_Brandenburg_final.pdf.

Godfrey, D. and Brown, C. (2018). How effective is the research and development ecosystem for England's schools? *London Review of Education*, 16(1), 137–153.

Godfrey, D. (2016). Leadership of schools as research-led organisations in the English educational environment: cultivating a research-engaged school culture. *Educational Management Administration & Leadership*, 44(2), 301–321.

Greenwood, R. and Suddaby, R. (2006). Institutional entrepreneurship in mature fields: the big five accounting firms. *Academy of Management Journal*, 49(1), 27–48.

Gustafsson, J.-E., Ehren, M. C. M., Conyngham, G., McNamara, G., Altrichter, H. and O'Hara, J. (2015). From inspection to quality: ways in which school inspection influences change in schools. *Studies in Educational Evaluation*.

Hamilton, L. S. and Koretz, D. M. (2002). Tests and their use in test-based accountability systems. In L. S. Hamilton, B. M. Stecher and S. P. Klein (Eds.), *Making sense of Test-based Accountability in Education*. Santa Monica: Rand Corporation. Retrieved 6 January 2019 from: www.rand.org/pubs/monograph_reports/MR1554/.

Hardy, I. (2012). 'Managing' managerialism: the impact of educational auditing on an academic 'specialist' school. *European Educational Research Journal*, 11(2), 274–289.

Holbombe, R. W., Jennings, J. L. and Koretz, D. (2012). The roots of score inflation: an examination of opportunities in two states' tests. In G. Sunderman (Ed.), *Charting Reform, Achieving Equity in a Diverse Nation*. Greenwich, CT: Information Age Publishing.

Matthews, P. and Ehren, M. C. M. (2017). Chapter 4. Accountability and improvement in a self-improving system. *School Leadership and Education System Reform*. London: Bloomsbury Academic.

McCarthy, M. and Beere, J. (2011). The perfect (OFSTED) lesson. Retrieved 6 January 2019 from: www.tes.com/teaching-resource/planning-and-teaching-the-perfect-ofsted-lesson-6113548.

NfER (2009). *Parents' perceptions of Ofsted's work – a report of the NFER for Ofsted*. London: Ofsted.

Penninckx, M. (2015). *Inspecting School Inspections*. Doctoral dissertation. University of Antwerp.

Penninckx, M., Vanhoof, J., De Maeyer, S. and Van Petegem, P. (2014). Exploring and explaining the effects of being inspected. *Educational Studies*, 40, 456–472.

Sauder, M. and Espeland, W. N. (2009). The discipline of rankings: tight coupling and organizational change. *American Sociological Review*, 74(1), 63–82.

Schmidt, M. (2013). Schulleitungen im prozess der externen evaluation. In B. Drinck, D. Flagmeyer, D. Diegmann, M. Schmidt, J. Keitel, R. Schubert and K. Herzog (Eds.), *RuN-Studie. Rezeption und Nutzung von Ergebnissen der Externen Evaluation an sächsischen Grundschulen, Mittelschulen und Gymnasien* (pp. 27–45). Radebeul: Sächsisches Bildungsinstitut.

Stecher, B. M. (2002). Consequences of large-scale, high-stakes testing on school and classroom practices). Tests and their use in test-based accountability systems. In L. S. Hamilton, B. M. Stecher and S. P. Klein (Eds.), *Making Sense of Test-based Accountability in Education*. Santa Monica: Rand Corporation. Retrieved 6 January 2019 from: www.rand.org/pubs/monograph_reports/MR1554/.

*Times Educational Supplement.* (2018). "Becoming inspection ready". 5 January. Retrieved 6 January 2019 from: www.tes.com/teaching-resources/blog/becoming-inspection-ready-ofsted.

Westhorp, G., Walker, B., Rogers, P., Overbeeke, N., Ball, D. and Brice, G. (2014). Enhancing community accountability, empowerment and education outcomes in low and middle-income countries: A realist review.

Whitby, K. (2010). *School Inspections: Recent Experiences in High Performing Education Systems.* Reading, England: CfBT Education Trust.

Wilkins, C. (2011). Professionalism and the post-performative teacher: new teachers reflect on autonomy and accountability in the English school system. *Professional Development in Education*, 37(3), 389–409.

# 4

# LEADING RESEARCH-INFORMED PRACTICE IN SCHOOLS

*Clive Dimmock*

## Aims of the chapter

This chapter has three main aims reflected in addressing the following questions:

- What is a research-engaged school and what is its rationale? What is the significance of leadership to the research-engaged school?
- How does leadership promote scaled-up and sustained research-informed practice in schools?
- What role does leadership play in overcoming the barriers to research engagement?

## Introduction

The purpose of research-informed practice in schools is improved decision making regarding core practices such as teaching and learning, student welfare and counselling. However, it is well acknowledged that teacher decision making has been, and still is in many schools, too reliant on sources other than research and evidence (Teh et al., 2013). Teachers, it is argued, have traditionally over-relied on customary practice, expedience and tacit knowledge. Critics of this failure to embrace research- and evidence-informed practices argue that the quality and equity of teaching and learning suffer as a consequence, as do teachers' levels of professionalism (Dimmock, 2012).

While the case for more informed practices might be self-evident, there are reasons why schools have been slow to adopt evidenced informed practices. Resistance has been grounded in the pragmatic and harsh realities of school life, such as lack of resources (money, time, human capital and skills), and an obsession with assessment and examination agendas – emphasising accountability – that prioritise curriculum coverage and test results, rather than investment in the quality of the processes that lead to improved learning outcomes (Godfrey, 2016). It might also be said that leaders themselves are not often strong champions of basing their leadership practices, let alone teaching and learning, on an evidenced-based, 'what works' footing. However, the presence of leadership that both advocates and adopts evidence-informed practices is an essential feature of research-engaged schools.

Consideration of both issues above – that is, understanding and appreciating the potential benefits of research-informed practices on the one hand, and overcoming the many sources of resistance to them on the other, place leadership at the very heart of research-engagement. Leadership is an integral part of efforts to create schools as champions of research-engagement, to scale-up and sustain such practices, and overcome the barriers that may block their adoption and implementation (Dimmock, 2012; Godfrey, 2016).

Ideas and argument guiding the chapter are primarily derived from, and applicable to, Anglo-American settings, although, given the increasing globalisation of education policy trends, much of the chapter is relevant to school systems in other parts of the world. To this end, an example from Singapore is included later in the chapter.

## What is a research-engaged school and what is its rationale? What is the significance of leadership to the research-engaged school?

The rationale for such evidence-informed practices in schools is compelling. Dimmock (2016) discusses the persistent problems in education systems created by the so-called 'gaps' between policy, research and practice. These disconnects between government policy – what Godfrey (2016) terms the macro- and exo-systems that are mainly concerned with policy making, the world of research in the universities (the mesosystem) and the world of practice in schools (the microsystem) – have undeniably handicapped the professionalisation of schools and school improvement in the past, and continue to do so. As Dimmock (2016) argues, the profound consequence is weak knowledge mobility through and across the different levels of the education ecosystem.

Specifically, much of the educational research undertaken to date – particularly in universities, but increasingly in other agencies, too – is criticised for its lack of relevance to improving teaching and learning, and to closing the equity gaps (Teh et al., 2013). This separation of functions – universities do the research (knowledge production), schools do the practice (knowledge utilisation), with insufficient knowledge mobilisation and transfer between the two – has resulted in teachers and schools over-relying on tacit knowledge (that is, accumulated practical experience) in their decision making and practice (Dimmock, 2016). Consequently, the idea of bridging the two has emerged, where schools become the sites for research as well teaching and learning (Handscomb and MacBeath, 2003, Teh et al., 2013). Handscomb and MacBeath (2003) go on to outline the features of a research-engaged school as having a:

- Research–rich pedagogy
- Research orientation
- Research community
- Culture that puts research at the heart of school policy and practice.

These four features were developed further by Godfrey (2016, p. 305) who after extensive study, listed the characteristics of research-engaged schools that differentiated them from other schools; these are:

- Promoting practitioner research among their staff
- Encouraging their staff to read and respond to published research
- Welcoming (as a learning opportunity as well as a responsibility to the wider educational community) being the subject of research by outside organisations
- Using research to inform their decision making at every level
- Having an outward-looking orientation (Wilkins, 2011), including research-based links with other schools and universities.

The above clarification of the concept of the research-engaged school, is helpful in answering why is leadership significantly relevant to it? Definitions of leadership abound, but for the purposes of this chapter, leadership is – a social influence process guided by moral purpose, with the *aim of building capacity* by making the best use of available resources to achieve shared goals (Dimmock, 2012). Generalised statements like this, however, need qualifying. *First*, 'leadership' implies more than just 'management' in that it adds value – it improves and transforms, rather than just maintains, present levels of performance. *Second*, is what is meant by 'capacity'? And how do leaders develop it? In the sociology literature, capacity is akin to capital, hence by developing capital, one is also developing capacity, as argued below.

A conception of leadership seen as building 'capital' is echoed in the reasoning of Hargreaves (2003), who re-conceptualises the work of schools as organisations. Hargreaves argues that there is an increasing need for teachers and leaders with *intellectual capital* (knowledge, skills, values, and dispositions), *social capital* (trust and respect built around collegiality and collaboration), and the *leverage capacity* to convert 'inputs' to schools to more highly performing and equitable outputs. But there is also the need, argues Hargreaves, for a third form, namely, *organisational capital*, which he sees as the use of leadership knowledge and skill to change and redesign the school by making better use of its intellectual and social capital to produce high-leverage strategies of teaching and learning (Dimmock, 2012). Hence, a salient task of leaders is to devise new and effective forms of organisational capital to enable improvement in intellectual and social capital. Hargreaves (2003, p. 6) states:

> on the one hand, leaders have to devise a knowledge management strategy, without which none of these assets can be realized; and on the other, leaders have to stimulate and support communities of practice, without which the social and intellectual capital lies under-used.

This exercise of organisational capital is at the heart of leadership in its championing of research-engagement in schools, as argued later in this chapter.

Leadership thus focuses on developing human resources in a school – students, teachers and leaders – aimed at enhancing students' learning, through developing better teaching and leadership. Good management of financial and physical resources assists in the development of human resources, but essentially leaders build capacity in schools by focusing on the human resources and their working conditions (Dimmock, 2012).

Further support for this perspective, is provided by Leithwood et al. (2008) who claim that leaders build capacity through four main tasks:

- Setting directions – motivating staff, setting high expectations, visioning and goal-setting
- Developing people – building the knowledge and skills that teachers and leaders need to accomplish the organisation's goals; and by fostering individual and collective intellectual and social capital
- Managing the curriculum, teaching and learning programme – creating productive working conditions for colleagues by fostering, supporting and monitoring efficacious teaching and learning practices
- Redesigning schools as organisations – allowing leaders, teachers and students to perform at the highest levels; this includes building collaborative cultures, restructuring (and re-culturing) the organisation and forming networks and close relationships with the ecosystem, especially other schools and parents.

*Third*, how do these central capacity building tasks of leadership connect with research-engaged schools? This is achieved mainly by leadership in its role of organisational capital developing the school's intellectual and social capital by firstly, ensuring that teachers apply informed practices of learning, teaching and leadership to enable all to learn successfully; and secondly, by nurturing and sustaining leader and teacher talent. In these two respects, leadership connects directly with research-engagement. For four decades, leadership research has focused on instructional (learning-centred) leadership (Dimmock, 2000; Hallinger and Heck, 2011), emphasising leaders' responsibilities to improve curriculum, teaching and learning in their schools. Yet, there is little in this body of research that explicitly connects leadership with evidence- and research-informed practice. However, conceptions of school redesign defined by Dimmock (2000) and Leithwood et al. (2008) remind us that leaders have responsibilities for intentionally engineering schools to make them fit for their environments. In this regard, schools need to be seen as innovative learning environments fit for the 21st century. A key feature of such contemporary learning environments has to be research- and evidence-informed practices.

## How does leadership promote, scale-up and sustain research-informed practice in schools?

Senior school leaders – especially head teachers and their deputies – have responsibility for designing the organisational and human infrastructure to create 21st century innovative learning environments. Research-engagement is central to this responsibility; it entails more than simply participating in research, rather, it signals a willingness and capability on the part of schools to install a *research-into-practice* mentality and set of institutional procedures. When teachers, leaders and schools become 'research-engaged' in the sense of research-into-practice, they generate and mobilise professional knowledge, value both academic and tacit knowledge, and empower the professionalism of teachers and leaders (Dimmock, 2012).

In creating a research-into-practice environment, leaders need first to encourage teachers at the individual level to be reflective practitioners and to value the contribution that evidence- and research-based approaches can make to improvement in their teaching and student learning. Second, they need to build a school culture whereby expectations across all staff in the organisation are that teaching, learning and leadership practice are improved when they are informed by evidence and research. Third, and most important, senior leaders need to establish an organisational structure and set of processes that embed expected ways of working, and at the same time, help scale-up and sustain research-into-practice approaches, in their schools. This third dimension of leadership enables the first two, and hence justifies emphasis below.

In establishing an organisational structure and set of institutionalised processes for research-engagement, the following are key leadership considerations (Dimmock, 2016):

- Teachers need knowledge and skills related to research and evaluation; indeed, research capacity should become part of teachers' job descriptions, henceforth
- Professional development of teachers to impart the skills to seek, interpret and apply research, and awareness of how evidence can be translated into practice
- Networked and collaborative links to universities, research institutions and other schools
- A whole-school approach to a methodology of data collection and analysis that promotes teacher collaboration is necessary; collaborative action research and design research appear to be appropriate tools and techniques
- Formal roles that recognise the importance of research-informed approach will need to be established in schools, such as a research coordinator, and even a research section, with recognised physical space and a budget.

As the above considerations imply, senior school leaders, in particular, need to articulate that there are at least least five ways in which research-engaged schools can source research information and evidence to underpin improvements in practice. They are:

1. Academic research – codified, theory-driven, formalised, and found in magazines, journals, and books; also presented at conferences
2. Tacit knowledge – the accumulated and aggregated knowledge of teachers and leaders gained from practical experience in situ

3.  School records and similar data that schools currently possesses for other purposes, such as student performance data, parent and staff information
4.  School-generated projects on particular topics, such as action research projects undertaken by staff
5.  Collaborative (i.e. school-school, school-university) school-wide, school-deep coordinated intervention projects intended to be sustainable and scalable.

School data from the first three sources already exists in most cases; the main challenge for teacher-researchers is to access them, and to interpret their significance in the specific context of their schools. The fourth and fifth sources require schools to be proactive in generating new data *in situ*, the main difference between them being scale. In the case of the fifth, research on a larger scale involves the whole school (or partnership networks) and external collaborators, such as universities.

In reality, more than one of the sources of information/data listed are likely to be used simultaneously. For example, teachers' and leaders' tacit knowledge are invariably relevant as a source of valuable data alongside other forms of research information generated from within and outside the school. Likewise, data generated from within the school might be compared with academic research data from other case schools sampled or surveyed.

## *Translating research into practice*

In establishing the research-into-practice culture of the school, senior leaders take responsibility for establishing the definitions of what constitutes research, evidence and knowledge. This is important in two respects. First, they transmit a culture that values both academic (coded) knowledge and tacit knowledge, that is, knowledge gained by teachers through practical experience. To over-rely on one or other is unwise, since it is teachers' ability to mediate and make sense of evidence and research, before adapting it to their particular contexts, that makes for successful implementation of new practice. Second, leaders shoulder responsibility for persuading teachers that some evidence may not be research-based, but is still worthy of consideration, and that research itself takes many forms, including the whole gamut of quantitative to qualitative paradigms and methods. Teachers can be reassured that much of the research that they might undertake is applied and evaluative and does not call for advanced statistical skills, for example.

Changing and improving practice is the ultimate purpose of schools becoming *research-engaged*. There is little justification for the research-engaged school if research that is judged to improve teaching and learning, fails to translate into practice. Senior school leaders have a key role to play here, in that leadership is centrally about achieving goals and getting things done. Setting a culture of expectations that the school is focused on implementing (rather than just talking about) improvements to practice, given the support of compelling evidence, is a key function of leadership. This is not to claim, however, that all research evidence should be implemented, especially where after considerable analysis and reflection teachers remain unconvinced that it would improve learning in their contexts. Nonetheless, history is littered with teachers failing to adopt and implement new practices, even where there is convincing evidence that improvement in teaching and learning is likely. Indeed, this final step of putting research into practice is traditionally the Achilles heel of all change and reform initiatives.

How and why are *research-engaged* schools more likely than other schools to be successful in putting research into practice? As suggested earlier, appropriate organisational structures and processes need to be institutionalised and formalised – a task and responsibility for senior leadership. Policies, roles and structures all need to deliver research–into-practice, and as explained below, the embedding of research into the social context of the school is all-important for success.

Experience over the past two decades has shown that the school as a *professional learning community* (PLC) is a most effective way – potentially – to achieve these aims. In these ways, and especially through establishing the school as a PLC, research-into-practice is both scaled-up (across the whole school and even beyond, into collaborative networks of schools), and sustained, because the structures and processes are embedded in the daily working routines of teachers and leaders.

### Schools as professional learning communities

The professional learning community provides compelling institutional conditions to expect and reinforce implementation of research- and evidence-informed practice. However, as the following suggests, there is still a lot we don't know about what makes PLCs effective vehicles for research-engagement in specific contexts (Brown and Poortman, 2017). Additionally, this section outlines the importance of effective leadership in building, scaling-up and sustaining PLCs.

Various definitions of what is meant by professional learning community (PLC) are to be found (see Darling-Hammond, 1996; DuFour, 2004, DuFour and Eaker 1998; Hord, 1997). However, Hord's (1997, p. 1) well accepted definition of a 'professional community of learners' is one:

> in which the teachers in a school and its administrators continuously seek and share learning, and act on their learning. The goal of their actions is to enhance their effectiveness as professionals for the students' benefit; . . . this arrangement may also be termed communities of continuous inquiry and improvement. The notion, therefore, draws attention to the potential for a range of people, based inside and outside a school, to mutually enhance each other's and pupils' learning as well as school development.

Other advocates of PLCs (e.g. Bolam et al., 2005) list the following attributes regarding their effectiveness:

- Shared values and vision generated
- Collective responsibility for pupils' learning;

- Collaboration focused on learning;
- Individual and collective professional learning;
- Reflective professional enquiry;
- Openness, networks and partnerships;
- Inclusive membership
- Mutual trust, respect and support.

Many claim positive relationships (admittedly often on the basis of flimsy empirical evidence) between professional learning communities and student learning outcomes (DuFour & Eaker, 1998; Bolam et al., 2005; Vescio et al., 2007; Hord & Sommers, 2008), arguing that student achievement is attained when teachers make collaborative pedagogical decisions adding value to student learning (Thompson, Gregg, & Niska, 2004). PLCs allegedly have an intermediate positive impact, too, on teachers' professional learning, performance and morale, which ultimately – it is argued – transfers to a positive impact on student achievement (Bolam et al., 2005).

Advocates also emphasise the vital role of principals' supportive leadership in PLC success (Louis & Kruse, 1995). Bolam et al. (2005) argue that the principal is responsible for optimising resources, promoting individual and collective learning, promoting and sustaining PLCs, and leading and managing them. PLCs, it is claimed, promote professional collaboration between teachers and principals, sharing of authority, encouragement of teacher participation, and the adoption of leadership styles that focus on the goal of developing people, including themselves, as 'lead teachers and lead learners, and stewards of the learning process as a whole' (Senge, 2000, p. 15). Through PLCs, principals can develop teacher leaders, promoting the notion of teachers as change agents (Thompson, Gregg & Niska, 2004; Wells, 2008). As Fullan (1997) claims, 'principals can make even more long-lasting contributions, by broadening the base of leadership of those with whom they work' (p. 46), including teachers. This broadening of the base of leadership implies distributive leadership, and notions of re-culturing of schools in order to successfully implement PLCs (Fullan, 2001). In this regard, emphasis is therefore not on adopting a PLC 'program' but changing the culture of the school that values the principles of PLCs (Fullan, 2006).

### PLCs as vehicles for expansive leadership in the school

The model of PLC advocated in this chapter not only promotes improved practices in curriculum and pedagogy, but also develops leadership opportunities at middle and teacher-levels through a school-wide involvement of all staff. Teacher leadership in particular is afforded opportunity through collaborative action research in school learning teams, and between-school collaboration on joint projects. In this regard, not only is good leadership essential to the establishing and sustaining of PLCs, but also the PLCs themselves foster school-wide and school-deep development of leadership. When research-engagement is formalised in the school, and when it is school-wide, involving leadership at all levels – senior, middle and teacher – it is more likely to be sustained. That is, it is less dependent on one or two enthusiastic staff members, who – were they to leave the school – would herald the end of research–engagement.

There are few sobering or cautionary voices among the many strong advocates espousing PLCs. But what is the research evidence that PLCs come anywhere near to meeting and delivering on all these expectations? As yet, there appears to be a lack of robust evidence that this form of professional learning benefits students and impacts on student outcomes (Bolam et al., 2005). However, studies by Robinson and Timperley (2007) find large leadership effects on student outcomes through teacher development, emphasising the worth of PLCs as vehicles for professional development.

In summarising the present knowledge base on PLCs, more attention needs to be given to the centrality of research evidence on effective teaching for student learning in the agendas of PLCs – so that teachers have hard data and evidence of 'what works' – as well as their individual and collective experience (tacit knowledge) – on which to rely. Two further questions on PLCs posed by Firestone and Riehl (2005) are:

- How does the organisation of teacher communities and teacher interaction affect teacher learning?
- How do leaders contribute to the organisation of teacher communities, and which leaders matter for which purposes?

This is not to decry the PLC concept, which has strong appeal. However, like most 'good ideas', whether it actually achieves its purpose has more to do with how it is set up, implemented, led and managed, than the concept itself. In this respect, there is a need for more empirical studies of different PLC models and how they function in different cultural contexts.

### PLCs take advantage of the strong social capital in school group norms

A strong argument for schools to become PLCs is that the PLC concept recognises that teacher behaviour in schools is grounded in social behaviour and the influence and values of colleagues and leaders; personal norms are adjusted to fit group norms. As Levin (2004) insightfully claims, school leaders and teachers rely more on tacit knowledge (gained from experience and practical intuition and wisdom) than on research knowledge. They are more influenced by workshops and in-service publications than they are by academic books and papers. They are also more persuaded by colleagues than by governments and academic researchers. While practice based on tacit knowledge draws much support (for example, it is usually strongly contextualised), there are nonetheless problems with too heavy reliance on it. As Levin (2008) argues, people are not necessarily skilled at using experience to make sound decisions or exercise judgements about what is good practice. Personal judgement, he claims, is not always a good substitute for evidence. A similar and related point is championed by Kahneman (2011) whose poignant message is that human reason left to its own devices is apt to engage in a number of fallacies and systematic errors, so if we want to make better decisions in our personal and occupational lives, and as a society, we need to be aware of these biases and seek workarounds. Placed in the present context of teacher professional practice, Kahneman's thesis would be that there are dangers in over-reliance on individual teachers' experience as the basis of practice, especially tacit knowledge, and that teachers as a community, with an increased capacity to use evidence-informed practice, provide safeguards against 'errors' or, in Kahneman's terms, 'workarounds'.

It is clear that we need to take greater cognisance of the school as a social organisation in how it influences teacher values and behaviours. Here, leadership and management play a crucial role in what Levin (2008) refers to as 'knowledge mobilisation'. In short, for knowledge mobilisation to underpin the research-engaged school, organisational factors appear to exert greater influence than individual factors. More focus needs to be put on how organisations mobilise knowledge and convert it to practice. Hemsley-Brown and Sharp (2004, p. 462) put it succinctly thus:

> the conclusions from empirical research, in both education and nursing, con-firm that the main barriers to knowledge use in the public sector are not at the level of individual resistance but originate in an institutional culture that does not foster learning.

The logical conclusion from the above argument is not just that schools must become learning organisations, but that we need to appreciate the ways in which organisations affect how practitioners think and work within them. Levin (2004) is right when he claims we need to boost organisational supports and incentives – and especially consider the part that school leaders and districts can play in fostering research in schools and its take-up in practice. But at present most social service organisations have low capacities for research absorption because managers have weak research backgrounds and are too busy to reflect on how research can boost teaching and learning performance in their schools.

## An example of PLCs in Singapore schools

In 2010–2011, after piloting PLCs in 51 schools, the Singapore Ministry of Education (MOE) made it policy for all of its schools to become PLCs (Hairon and Dimmock, 2012). All teachers in every school were expected to be active members of their PLCs. The MOE circulated to all schools its PLC framework and a Starter Kit. Each school was viewed as a PLC, consisting of groups of teachers, called *Learning Teams*, with the purpose of improving instructional practice through development in subject content knowledge and pedagogy. Learning Teams have the choice of adopting various collaborative methods, such as Learning Circles,

Action Research and Lesson Study. They were also to adopt a 'cyclical process of continuous improvement' which includes the following: use of data to identify student needs; study and analysis of own and peer research; engagement in rigorous reflection; use of research and professional wisdom to make good choices; collaborative experiment with new teaching practices; monitoring and assessment of implementation; and communication of information to other stakeholders. Learning Teams are directed and supported by a *Coalition Team* comprising the school principal and middle managers, whose role is to provide both the direction of the Learning Teams in tandem with the school's vision, mission and values, and the appropriate structures, processes and resources for the building of a learning culture in the school. The overall objectives are improvement of student outcomes and achievement of the school's overall goals. The MOE document outlining the model ends with the conclusion that the success of schools as PLCs is dependent on three factors derived from Fullan's 'Triangle of Success' namely – school leadership, 'system-ness', and deep pedagogy (Dimmock, 2012).

In presenting its PLC model for system-wide implementation, the MOE focused on key structural and outcome elements, including the major justification of improved student learning outcomes. It has provided extra funding, created an additional weekly hour of professional development time and the position of School Staff Developer (SSD) in every school, and disseminated a framework and tools and templates to enable the establishment of PLCs at school level. Importantly, MOE sees the means of achieving effective PLCs and their outcomes to be through improved instructional practices and the building of a learning culture in schools – both of which are the prime responsibility of school leaders and teacher leaders (Hairon and Dimmock, 2012). Consequently, charged with responsibilities of implementation, principals and teachers must overcome cultural and workplace realities, deeply embedded ways of working, and the complexities of teachers' professional lives in a hitherto centralised top-down system. School leaders themselves will need professional development to enable them to meet these major new challenges. According to evidence from the feedback evaluations of the 51 pilot schools, time and resource constraints at teacher and school level will prove major impediments for leaders and others to overcome.

The PLC Starter Kit outlines several roles for school leaders including – prioritising staff professional development; developing and communicating a shared vision on PLCs; building staff commitment (fostering trust, collaboration and ownership; building a learning culture; handling resistance; balancing creativity and autonomy within parameters and boundaries); role modelling commitment to PLCs; optimising existing organisational structures and processes; leveraging existing structures; providing training, resources, tools and templates; mentoring; recognising, affirming and celebrating PLC activities; and leveraging on the notion of PLC to enhance professional development as a whole.

Successful implementation of PLCs is predicated on three co-related and interdependent models of school leadership – transformational, distributed and instructional. Transformational leadership (Leithwood, 1994; Bass and Avolio, 1993, 1994) builds staff commitment to PLCs and focuses on the commitments and capacities of teachers, and the potential to increase performance and productivity. Influence is based on school leaders' ability to inspire commitment to collective aspirations, and for personal and collective mastery over the capacities needed to accomplish such aspirations. The key features of distributed leadership centre on the empowerment of middle level and teacher leaders across schools (Leithwood et al., 2004; Harris, 2004) and are consistent with the roles of leaders described in the MOE's discourse of PLC. Finally, the PLC policy initiative requires school leaders to become instructional leaders, engaging in activities directly and indirectly influencing the learning and growth of students (Hallinger and Heck, 2011). 'Direct' leadership influence includes advising, mentoring and coaching teachers on pedagogy, while 'indirect' involves setting broad policy directions for teachers, and building a learning-centred school culture (Dimmock, 2000).

In reality, given the context of Singapore and other strong hierarchical social and work structures in Asian countries, the notion of PLCs and their influence is likely to be confined to pedagogical practices, subject expertise and student learning. This is a more restricted connotation of teacher professionalism and PLC than pervades Anglo-American school systems, where discourse includes teacher agency, empowerment and autonomy.

## A suggested model for teacher research-into-practice within the PLC

Schools often express difficulty in knowing where to start the whole process of research into practice. Based on my experience of the Singapore school system the following sketches how a successful model might work. Brown (2017) reinforces many similar features of this model for an English context. A good start point is for the school community (including parents) to share data about the problem areas of school performance. For example, inspection reports and the school's own data may reveal a particular pedagogy in the school is poorly executed, or under-used, or a new curriculum emphasis is needed to support more equitable practices for low achievers. Other problems may relate to behavior and bullying. The school community, especially principals, teachers and parents, decide which priority (ies) the school should focus on over the following six or 12 months, or longer. Agreement and consensus is important, since all teachers need to buy-in to the priorities in a scaled-up and sustained way. Consensus and buy-in are more likely if the process is data driven. Teams of teachers then work collaboratively on researching, piloting, and evaluating the best practices to overcome the problems. The following paragraph explains the process.

Collaborative teams of teacher-researchers, for example, can mediate and internalise the research findings and evidence, plan together how to accommodate new curricula or pedagogies, think through the implications for new methods of teaching and learning, and then decide on a strategy to pilot or trial the new practice in a classroom. Following the collaborative action learning cycle (based on the Japanese lesson study), one of the team may trial the new practice, while other members of the team act as evaluators. After the first round of trials and evaluation, the team might decide to amend the practice, hold re-trials, and scale-up the practice in more than one teacher's classroom – thereby applying a form of evaluative data collection consistent with the action research cycle. In this way, research-into-practice becomes routine and institutionalised, always with the proviso that only those new research-based practices are implemented for which there is compelling evidence of improvements in learning.

## What role does leadership play in overcoming the barriers to research-engagement?

Embedding PLCs in schools may be seen as a process of bolting on yet more duties and tasks for teachers to perform. Policymakers and school leaders must be able to justify PLCs in order to subsequently convince teachers of the benefits that can potentially flow in transforming teacher practices and learning outcomes. Leadership knowledge and skills are crucial in convincing and motivating teachers that PLCs are key innovations around which their professional practices and their teaching lives can be made more efficacious and rewarding (Dimmock, 2012).

The status quo in many schools, however, may not be conducive to their transition to productive research environments. Good leadership addresses some of these obstacles. Teachers generally do not have the skills necessary to conduct rigorous research – hence the need for leaders to ensure relevant professional development opportunities afford them the time and opportunity to develop the necessary skills. Nor do they have the resources – time especially being at a premium. An advantage of the collaborative action approach is that many of the skills needed are blended in with the new practices being trialed and evaluated. In many cases, they may not have the motivation, seeing their prime function as teaching rather than researching. An advantage of the PLC in this respect is that it affords a whole school approach where colleagues work collaboratively – which can offer a more professionally enriched environment, and peer-to-peer learning. The absence of institutional rewards and motivators for teachers to undertake research is a further deterrent, especially in systems where accountability is focused on student learning outcomes. Teachers generally concentrate on achieving short-term goals, and may see any benefits from research as long term, and thus lacking priority. Evidence suggests (Cooper, Levin and Campbell, 2009) that teachers are interested in research, but spend little time on learning about research directly. Instead, they rely on third parties, intermediaries and on attending conferences, professional development activities, and in some cases, graduate study. Barriers to teacher uptake of research also include problems of access and understanding. It is commonplace for teachers to complain of lack of synthesis of research findings and inconsistency and unreliability of findings, as well as difficulties in clarifying the practical and contextual implications. In these respects, leaders need to establish good networks with universities and access to databases and libraries so that their teachers can obtain the materials they need.

Furthermore, teachers often distrust research – seeing it as irrelevant to practice, their lack of ability to interpret it, the complexity and ambiguity with which much research is presented, and above all, their predisposition and preference to rely on their own tacit knowledge – account for this perspective. Indeed, surveys conducted on the factors influencing teachers' choice and selection of teaching methods consistently place high rankings on practical issues such as curriculum coverage, formal summative assessment, and student ability, and very low ranking to research evidence of what works (Dimmock, 2012). To reverse all these, good leadership of PLCs to change school collective culture is a *sine qua non*.

## Conclusions

In all school systems – whether more devolved to school-based management or more centrally controlled, as in Singapore, the quality of school leadership at principal, middle- and teacher-levels assume major importance in establishing and sustaining PLCs. In schools and systems characterised by devolution to school-based management, schools are more likely to *become* PLCs. PLCs are then likely to be more transformative, with holistic school redesign changing values, relationships, patterns of power and influence, school organisation and professional practices – with school leadership playing a central part as change agent. In contrast, schools in centralised systems where school-based leadership is less developed, a more restricted model of PLCs may prevail, where professional development is confined to innovations in classroom teaching practices and subject knowledge. In such cases, PLCs are less likely to be seen as transformational or holistic in their ramifications; changes are largely confined to innovations in teaching and learning practices. Thus the PLC concept adapts to fit culture and context.

In both devolved and centralised systems, the quality of school leadership is bound to be tested by the challenge of implementing, scaling-up and sustaining PLCs. Changing teachers' pedagogical practices in the 'black box' of the classroom – without changing organisational structures – presents just as great a challenge to leadership as whole school redesign associated with more comprehensive and transformational notions of PLCs in more devolved systems (Dimmock, 2000). In both scenarios, leaders build community around professional practice and 'finesse' the boundaries between government control and school-based initiatives. The importance of site-based leadership in motivating teachers, managing hierarchies, adopting creative ways to combat teacher work overload, and clarifying understandings, goals and benefits of PLCs – assumes major significance in both centralised and devolved systems. Above all, principals and school leaders need to envision the PLC as a powerful vehicle to create the *research-engaged* school, the ultimate purpose of which is to enrich and improve student academic and non-academic learning.

## Implications for the research-informed ecosystem

- Leadership plays an essential part in establishing research-engaged practices in schools; in regard to the ecosystem, and particularly the micro and mesosystems, this is true for all levels of leadership – from head teacher, to middle and teacher leadership
- Leadership builds the social and organisational capital – and hence the school culture of the mesosystem for teaching and learning to be research-engaged
- Among the most important functions of leadership in research-engagement are building a school culture (mesosystem) that values research and evidence-based practice
- A key part played by leadership in creating, scaling-up and sustaining the microsystem geared to research into practice is the formalisation of values, organisational structures and processes as described below
- Potentially powerful tools and techniques for formalising research-engagement are built around the school as a professional learning community, involving all staff in researching and evaluating their practices in order to improve teaching, learning and leadership in the micro and mesosystems
- Formalisation also includes first, an agreed strategy for school-wide and school-deep research and evidence-based practice around agreed problems faced by the school community in its ecosystem (mesosystems and exosystems especially); and secondly, a methodology for teachers to apply – such as collaborative action learning
- Leadership is also instrumental in creating collaborative networks with other schools to undertake joint research (mesosystem), and in addressing obstacles and barriers to research-engagement.

## References

Bass, B. M. and Avolio, B. J. (1993). Transformational leadership: a response to critiques. In M. M. Chemers and R. Aymans (Eds.), *Leadership Theory and Research: Perspectives and Direction* (pp. 49–80). San Diego, CA: Academic Press.

Bolam, R., McMahon, A., Stoll, L., Thomas, S. and Wallace, M. (2005). *Creating and Sustaining Effective Professional Learning Communities*. Research Report No. 637. UK: Department for Education and Skills.

Brown, C. (2017). Research learning communities: how the RLC approach enables teachers to use research to improve their practice and the benefits for students that occur as a result. *Research for All*, 1(2), 387–405.

Brown, C. and Poortman, C. (Eds.). (2017). *Networks for Learning: Effective Collaboration for Teacher, School and System Improvement*. London: Routledge.

Cooper, A., Levin, B. and Campbell, C. (2009). The growing (but still limited) importance of evidence in education policy and practice. *Journal of Educational Change*, 10(2–3), 159–171.

Darling-Hammond, L. (1996). The quiet revolution: rethinking teacher development. *Educational Leadership*, 56(6), 4–10.

Dimmock, C. (2000). *Designing the Learning-Centred School*. London: Falmer Press.

Dimmock, C. (2012). *Leadership, Capacity Building and School Improvement*. London: Routledge.

Dimmock, C. (2016). Conceptualising the research-practice-professional development nexus: mobilising schools as 'research-engaged' professional learning communities. *Professional Development in Education*, 42(1), 36–53.

DuFour, R. (2004). What is a 'professional learning community'? *Educational Leadership*, 61(8), 6–11.

DuFour, R. and Eaker, R. (1998). *Professional Learning Communities at Work*. Bloomington, IN: National Education Service.

Firestone, W. A. and Riehl, C. (Eds.). (2005). *A New Agenda for Research in Educational Leadership*. New York: Teachers College Press.

Fullan, M. (1997). Broadening the concept of teacher leadership. In S. H. Caldwell (Ed.). Professional development in learning-centred schools (pp. 34–48). Oxford, OH: National Staff Development Council.

Fullan, M. (2001). *Leading in a Culture of Change*. San Francisco: Jossey-Bass.

Fullan, M. (2006). Leading professional learning: think 'system' and not 'individual school' if the goal is to fundamentally change the culture of schools. *School Administrator*, 63(10), 10–14.

Godfrey, D. (2016). Leadership of schools as research-led organisations in the English education environment: cultivating a research-engaged school culture. *Educational Management, Administration and Leadership*, 44(2), 301–321.

Hairon, S. and Dimmock, C. (2012). Singapore schools and professional learning communities: teacher professional development and school leadership in an Asian hierarchical system. *Educational Review, 64(4)*, 405–424.

Hallinger, P. and Heck, R. (2011). Conceptual and methodological issues in studying school leadership effects as a reciprocal process. *School Effectiveness and School Improvement*, 22(2), pp. 149–173.

Handscomb, G. and MacBeath, J. (2003). Professional development through teacher enquiry. In A. Lawson (Ed.). *Professional Development Today* (pp. 1–12). Slough: NFER.

Hargreaves, D. (2003, 5 January). From improvement to transformation. Lecture presented at the International Congress for School Effectiveness and School Improvement, Sydney, Australia. Retrieved 19 July 2011 from www.icsei.net/index.php/id=622.

Harris, A. (2004). Distributed leadership and school improvement. *Educational Management Administration and Leadership*, 32(1), 11–24.

Hemsley-Brown, J. V. and Sharp, C. (2004). The use of research to improve professional practice: a systematic review of the literature. *Oxford Review of Education*, 29(4), 449–470.

Hord, S. M. (1997). *Professional Learning Communities: Communities of Continuous Inquiry and Improvement*. Austin, TX: Southwest Educational Development Laboratory.

Hord, S. M. and Sommers, W. A. (2008). *Leading Professional Learning Communities: Voices from Research and Practice*. Thousand Oaks, CA: Corwin Press.

Kahneman, D. (2011) *Thinking, Fast and Slow*. New York: Farrar, Straus and Giroux.

Leithwood, K. (1994). Leadership for school restructuring. *Educational Administration Quarterly*, 30(4), 220–230.

Leithwood, K., Jantzi, D., Earl, L., Watson, N., Levin, B. and Fullan, M. (2004). Strategic leadership for large-scale reform: the case of England's national literacy and numeracy strategy. *School Leadership & Management*, 24(1), 57–79.

Leithwood, K., Harris, A. and Hopkins, D. (2008). Seven strong claims about successful school leadership. *School Leadership and Management*, 28(1), 27–42.

Levin, B. (2004). Making research matter more. *Education Policy Analysis*, 12(56), 1–20.

Levin, B. (2008). Thinking about knowledge mobilisation: a discussion paper for the Canadian Council on learning and the Social Sciences and Humanities Research Council. Retrieved 6 January 2019 from: http://webspace.oise.utoronto.ca/~levinben/thinking%20about%20KM%202008.pdf.

Louis, K. S. and Kruse, S. D. (1995). *Professionalism and Community: Perspectives from Urban Schools*. Thousand Oaks, CA: Corwin.

Robinson, V. M. J. and Timperley, H. S. (2007). The leadership of the improvement of teaching and learning: lessons from initiatives with positive outcomes for students. *Australian Journal of Education*, 51(3), 247–262.

Teh, L. W., Hogan, D. and Dimmock, C. (2013). Knowledge mobilization and utilization in the Singapore education system: the nexus between researchers, policy makers and practitioners. In B. Levin, J. Qi and H. Edelstein (Eds.), *The Impact of Research in Education: An International Perspective*. University of Bristol: Policy Press.

Thompson, S. C., Gregg, L. and Niska, J. M. (2004). Professional learning communities, leadership, and student learning. *Research in Middle Level Education Online*, 28(1), 1–15.

Vescio, V., Ross, D. and Adams, A. (2007). A review of research on the impact of professional learning communities on teaching practice and student learning. *Teaching and Teacher Education*, 24, 80–91.

Wells, C. (2008). A conceptual design for understanding professional learning community implementation. *Catalyst for Change*, 35(2), 25–37.

Wilkins, R. (2011). *Research Engagement for School Development*. London: Institute of Education.

# 5

# TEACHERS' PROFESSIONAL BODIES AND THE ROLE OF RESEARCH

*Gareth Mills and Lesley Saunders*

## Aims of the chapter

- To identify some current challenges to the use of research in schools.
- In particular, to note the changing status and role of teachers' professional organisations as sources of legitimate leadership.
- To restate the case for systemic 'research-engagement' and what this entails.
- To suggest what (more) teachers' professional bodies could do to support and sustain teachers' engagement in research.

## Introduction

There is widespread agreement nowadays about the need for teaching to draw on research and evidence to inform professional practice. In England, the Department for Education,[1] the main teacher unions and other organisations have all made a strong case for it. Two influential bodies, the British Educational Research Association and the Royal Society of Arts (BERA/RSA, 2014), conducted a joint in-depth enquiry into the role of research in teachers' initial and continuing education, which found that: 'teachers across the UK should be supported to become research literate. This should include being given frequent opportunities to read up on the latest findings, with every pupil entitled to lessons which are informed by the best evidence'.

However, there is less agreement across the educational community about what being an evidence-based, or – to use an alternative term – a research-informed, profession means. (We indicate the possible distinction between these terms in the section on research engagement below). There are different views about how it might be brought about and what the supporting roles of different agencies – particularly teachers' professional bodies – ought to be. The main issues we wish to explore in this context are:

- Where do the power, influence and leadership for engagement with evidence and research lie in an increasingly devolved (and, in some countries, increasingly fragmented) education system?
- Where does the legitimacy and authority for research-based knowledge come from? How can teachers evaluate the veracity of different pedagogic assertions that claim to be evidence-based?
- How far can teaching be led by research evidence in preference to policy and system pressures on the one hand and by espoused professional values on the other?

These issues lead us to explore the complex matter of how teachers' professional bodies can offer cohesive, critical and ethical thought-leadership, such that schools and teachers become fully 'research-engaged' and are able to sustain that engagement over time.

We discuss the definition and function of 'professional body' below; but first we want to say something about the changing ecology of the education system. The system with which we are most familiar is that of England, a landscape increasingly characterised by the fragmentation of both schooling and professional knowledge. We surmise that such epochal shifts are in the process of happening elsewhere too, so we hope our descriptive analysis of one system will be applicable to others.

## Shifting landscapes and influential narratives

The fragmentation to which we alluded is manifested on the one hand by the decentralisation and marketisation of schooling, which has resulted in a tendency for schools and trusts to brand themselves as if they were consumer services in competition with each other.[23] And, on the other hand, an increasing number of diverse and non-establishment organisations are seeking to influence policy and practice, and almost all of them claim to use evidence to legitimise their various positions. This phenomenon has been accompanied and enabled by a significant growth in the use of social media, particularly blogging and Twitter, as channels for communicating with schools, teachers and officials.

We can perceive, and indeed welcome, this widespread use of social media as a democratisation of communication, a positive shift in favour of giving voice to alternative perspectives beyond traditional elites and orthodoxies.[4]

Yet two problems have arisen as a consequence: first, the idea/ideal of a collective and shared body of professional knowledge is giving way to a marketplace of competing ideas for which there are no commonly agreed evaluation criteria. Moreover, such offerings often promote apparently definitive solutions based on 'common sense',[5] which stand in sharp contrast to the kind of scholarly knowledge that is accumulated through the processes of carefully designed and rigorously analysed research studies supported by a well-attested academic apparatus. Such scholarly approaches are sometimes devalued by government ministers. At a recent

ResearchED conference, for example, one minister asserted: 'The research histori-cally presented to teachers was monotone in content and it was seldom used.'[6] Indeed, doubt has continued to be cast on the legitimacy of 'academic' research, from Hargreaves (1996) to Bennett (2013, pp. 57–59), who wrote:

> there are few things that educational science has brought to the classroom that could not already have been discerned by a competent teacher intent on teaching well after a few years of practice. If that sounds like a sad indictment of educational research, it is . . . Here's what I believe; this informs every-thing I have learned in teaching after a decade: Experience trumps theory every time.

Secondly, some commentators[7] have begun to express serious concern about the quality of discourse on social media channels. There are also concerns about the use of social media channels to manipulate and distort the educational narrative for a variety of commercial, political and other non-educational ends. The 'discourse of derision, dichotomy, myth and meaninglessness', described by Alexander (2010), seems to have become the norm. This tribal mode of debate reduces complex mat-ters of curriculum and pedagogy to what he elsewhere (Alexander, 2017, pp. 28–29) castigates as grossly oversimplified alternatives:

> Such dualities have been profoundly unhelpful to the development of both effective teaching and the balanced debate upon which it depends. By reduc-ing classroom decision making to an almost Manichaean choice between polar opposites, those responsible have not only given comfort to journal-ists and politicians who believe that their credibility depends on successfully retailing of such simplistic nonsense, they have also grossly misrepresented the range of pedagogic possibilities which are available to every teacher.

An egregious example of this occurs in Young's (2014) paper, which claims:

> They [the educational establishment] all believe that skills like 'problem-solving' and 'critical thinking' are more important than subject knowledge; that education should be 'child-centred' rather than 'didactic' or 'teacher-led'; that 'group work' and 'independent learning' are superior to 'direct instruction.

This is such a misrepresentation of the situation – from the assumption that there is such a thing as an 'educational establishment' inherently opposed to reform, to the polarisation into 'either-or' of what most academics and teachers regard as the need to acquire and use a flexible repertoire – that it's hard to know where to start to dismantle it.

So it's beyond ironic to discover that many of the louder voices in this version of evidence-based educational innovation and reform have much in common: for example, sharing conference platforms, promoting each other's books and blogs, having close connections with the publishing industry, and being invited to serve on government commissions and as government advisors.

We would therefore argue that the way the environment currently functions – in its tendency to polarise and disparage alternative perspectives – has a deleterious effect on the status, dissemination and use of scholarly educational research. Moreover, it constitutes a major ecological challenge to developing a strategic narrative about teachers' use of evidence and their deeper engagement with research.

## Thought-leadership: an absence or a plethora of teachers' professional bodies?

At this point, therefore, we return to the concept of 'professional body'. It is a capacious term, covering the following main categories of organisation (though there is considerable overlap between them):[8]

- Regulatory bodies established by statute – these require practitioners possessing the relevant qualifications and employed in the public sector to be registered with them, and thus essentially confer a licence to practise;
- Professional associations – membership of these is voluntary, though they normally require members to possess a relevant qualification and thus confer a status on members; these include bodies like chartered institutes and some trade unions;
- Learned societies – membership of these may be open to all, or may require possession of some qualification, or may be an honour conferred by election.

All such organisations are concerned to safeguard the reputation and independence of the profession, occupation or disciplinary field, and to raise its standing in the eyes of government and the public; most are constituted as charitable bodies and run as not-for-profit organisations; they offer benefits and/or resources, and usually levy a membership fee. But otherwise we are dealing with a concept open to a certain degree of interpretation.

For the long-established professions, such as medicine, law, accountancy – a status to which teaching has long aspired – a professional body is understood to be the organisation which holds, through statute, the acknowledged authority to decide and institutionalise what is meant by 'professionalism' and 'professional practice' in any given profession. The means by which it accomplishes this include setting professional standards and articulating a code of professional conduct. In addition, such a body may maintain a register of practitioners, have a system for assuring the good standing of its registrants (through requiring registrants to undertake regular post-initial professional development), impose sanctions for professional misconduct or incompetence. It may also be charged with giving formal advice to government on matters relevant to the profession. This kind of regulatory body must be seen to be *independent* of government, trade unions and other organisations with particular vested interests. Most importantly, it must be seen to be acting in the *public interest* rather than mainly or solely in the interests of its members.

At present in England such a body – independent of government, but with a statutory responsibility for overseeing the teaching profession – does not exist. The situation is a little different in other parts of the UK, in that Northern Ireland and Scotland each have independent Teaching Councils whose powers and duties include supporting research-engaged practice.[9] The recently formed Chartered College of Teaching[10] may come in future to occupy a similar role in England, and we discuss below how the College is working specifically to promote teachers' use of research.

What does exist in England is a wide range of professional bodies in the second and third senses above and, in addition, several established groups and organisations that make bona fide research-based knowledge available and useable for teaching and learning, and/or provide guidance and advice for undertaking in-house research projects. They include (but are not limited to):[11]

## *Professional bodies*

- As mentioned above, the Chartered College for Teaching, which publishes the termly journal *Impact* and offers resources for research-informed practice on its pages https://chartered.college/research-access, https://chartered.college/research-practice-hub and https://chartered.college/evidence-engagement;
- Some teacher unions, for example, the National Education Union (formed through an amalgamation of the National Union of Teachers and the Association of Teachers and Lecturers in 2017): www.teachers.org.uk/edufacts, www.teachers.org.uk/expert-view and www.atl.org.uk/policy-and-campaigns/policy-posts/teacher-professionalism-0;
- Many of the subject associations, for example, the Association for Science Education www.ase.org.uk/resources/.

## *Academic bodies*

- The Institute for Effective Education (IEE https://the-iee.org.uk);
- The Centre for Evaluation and Monitoring (www.cem.org);
- The Evidence for Policy and Practice Information and Co-ordinating Centre (https://eppi.ioe.ac.uk/cms/);
- The National Foundation for Educational Research (www.nfer.ac.uk/schools/);
- Ongoing partnerships between individual university departments of education and local/national/international groups of schools, such as the UCLIoE Research and Development Network and Cambridge University's School-University Partnership for Educational Research.

## Charitable bodies and trusts

- The Centre for the Use of Research and Evidence in Education (www.curee. co.uk);
- The Education Endowment Foundation (EEF https://educationendowment foundation.org.uk), which in partnership with the IEE has established the Research Schools Network (https://educationendowmentfoundation.org. uk/scaling-up-evidence/research-schools/);[12]
- The Teacher Development Trust (http://tdtrust.org), which specialises in promoting teachers' professional development.

This range and variety might suggest that teaching is well-served and well-informed by these bodies and the resources for research which they provide – until we look at some of the numbers involved. In November 2017, the Chartered College for Teaching announced that it had reached the important milestone of 10,000 members (roughly 2 per cent of the active teaching population). Alongside the 20,000 followers on Twitter, this is an undoubted success for such a young organisation.

Nonetheless, it is instructive to set these figures alongside those of other sources of 'evidence' for teachers. Take the websites like Teacher Toolkit, one of the UK's most popular education blogs and Twitter accounts, which has more than 188,000 followers; or Edutopia, which has a large (though unquantified) international following; or the Learning Spy website, hosted by author and ex-teacher David Didau, who recorded in February 2017 that his site had had 2.5 million visitors. These and other popular edu-blogs and edu-tweets are clearly making an important contribution to the evolving eco-landscape: they are generating conversations about evidence and teaching to a degree unanticipated by earlier critics of educational research like Hargreaves (1996). However, in the growing marketplace of competing 'evidence-based' ideas it can be very hard for teachers to judge the provenance and trustworthiness of the many claims that are made – particularly those which advocate a standardised set of pedagogic approaches, or which promulgate controversial ideologies masquerading as fact.

At the same time, the growing phenomenon of school 'branding' noted above means that teachers are increasingly invited to see themselves as belonging[13] to a particular school or multi-academy trust, or even to a 'family' rather than to a unified profession. This has led to the proliferation of multiple sources of professional identity for teachers and to a concomitant decrease in the influence of national professional organisations.

In his presentation to the General Teaching Council for Northern Ireland, Whitty (2006, p. 9) could foresee the problems this proliferation of identities would bring and he proposed in its place the principle of a 'democratic professionalism' which 'encourages the development of collaborative cultures in the broadest sense, rather than exclusive ones'. We note that Whitty's proposition is not, and need not be, evidence-based. It is a statement of values, of an ethical position. The traction that a unified professional body exerts is as much on ethical values and practice as on evidence; as has been said many times 'what works' is not a value-free statement – the questions of what works for whom, in terms of which outcomes, with what unintended consequences, and with what financial and human investment, are ones that can properly be answered only with reference to the underlying questions of what education is for, whether it is a private or a public good, an entitlement or a responsibility, and where issues of democratic decision-making and social justice fit in (as Biesta, 2007, has so eloquently argued). Professional bodies have to make these and other ethical questions, and their provisional answers, explicit in order to articulate codes of professional values and practice that are acceptable to the public as well as binding on the profession. Bloggers do not.

So the environment that is arguably becoming inimical to scholarly research is also one that is inhibiting the capacity for professional bodies and organisations to be the thought-leaders for the profession. 'Biodiversity' might be a problematic analogy in an environment where 'letting a thousand flowers bloom' may result in as many weeds as roses. These newer species offer a serious challenge to those engaged in scholarly research and to professional organisations to redouble their efforts to enact and promote the kind of professional expertise, transparency and independence that opinion pieces, often with underlying commercial and political agendas, find more difficulty doing.

## Research engagement: thought-leadership in the classroom?

Leaving aside now this appraisal of the current landscape, we want to turn towards a potential future ecosystem, beginning with a restatement of the case for 'research engagement' as a genuine grass-roots movement. Sometimes we need to look over our shoulders and recall some compelling aspect of the cultural landscape from the past to help us envision the future. The engagement of teachers with research stretches back as far as the outstanding work of Lawrence Stenhouse, an educational scholar who during the 1970s and 80s was promoting teachers' active involvement in research and curriculum development, which he saw as intimately linked.[14] He proposed a model for the curriculum as an enquiry-based process, with school leaders, teachers and students working together to plan, evaluate and develop the content, learning experiences and outcomes of schooling so that it becomes a rich education with active learning for all those involved. One of Stenhouse's (1975) guiding principles was 'communication is less effective than community in the utilisation of knowledge.'

One of us has explored in a previous article (Saunders, 2015)[15] how the terms 'research-engaged', 'enquiry-led' and 'evidence-informed' are often used interchangeably, but since they may imply quite different understandings of the professional practice of teaching it seems more accurate to think of them as ranged on an epistemological spectrum, with 'evidence-based' at one end and 'research-engaged'/'enquiry-led' at the other. In brief:

evidence posits research as a kind of epistemic product, while 'enquiry' foregrounds the process of research as an activity . . . [T]he latter fits very well with the deliberative nature of pedagogy and the need to exercise nuanced professional judgement in deciding between courses of action . . . [T]he creation of expert professional knowledge is not a matter of 'applying' evidence designed and created elsewhere by others. It is a subtle combination of . . . individual and collaborative learning through experience and critical reflection, and immersion in scholarly knowledge.

*(Saunders, 2015, pp. 47–49)*

In other words, we need to go beyond the notion of being able to 'apply' the 'evidence' as if it were a pill or patch. Indeed we would argue that 'enquiry' and 'engagement with research' entail cultivating certain intellectual and ethical *dispositions*, which are integral to the development of extended professional expertise. In addition to the 'intellectual virtues' offered by Bridges (2016) (which include honesty, thoroughness, perseverance, careful attention to reasoned argument and evidence, open-mindedness, humility with regard to one's own knowledge, modesty about one's research and its claims, responsiveness to criticism and respect for the opinion of others), we could mention:

- A capacity and willingness to engage with theoretical ideas and concepts as well as empirical evidence; and to welcome the kinds of research that serve to deepen our insights and broaden our understanding as distinct from adding to our factual knowledge;
- A receptiveness to the idea that all knowledge is provisional, including our own, but some forms of knowledge are more reliable than others;
- An acceptance that straightforward cause and effect relationships are immensely hard to establish in education;
- An openness to the idea that 'what works' is relative – as noted above, it has meaning only in relation to specified educational ends or objectives, about which there may well be opposing views;
- A commitment to working alongside others – colleagues, students, academic researchers – as the best way of strengthening the reliability and relevance of any research enquiry.

Add to this that pedagogy is above all an ethical practice, an extended interchange between human beings for broader social purposes, and it is clear that the relationship between research and teaching is irreducibly, and excitingly, multifaceted. 'Research-rich' is the adjective used by John Furlong, chair of the BERA/RSA (2014) enquiry (mentioned at the start of this chapter) – it is a good one to describe the kind of environment we have in mind:

Teachers and students thrive in the kind of settings that we describe as research-rich, and research-rich schools and colleges are those that are likely to have the greatest capacity for self-evaluation and self-improvement.

## Thought-leadership in research: assuring the legitimacy of research-based knowledge?

We would accordingly like to replace the metaphor of a 'marketplace' of 'evidence' with a conception of research as a painstaking, collaborative and transparent approach to the creation of trustworthy knowledge and understanding (such as that exemplified by the Teaching and Learning Research Programme).

Teachers need to have the full picture about educational research, about the wide range of methods available to investigate different kinds of question, about how to tell a good study from a poor one, and how to judge whether inferences and conclusions have been correctly drawn from the data. They need to know at least a little about the false dichotomy of the 'paradigm wars' between quantitative and qualitative approaches; and to resist the notion that there is a single methodological 'gold standard' regardless of context. 'Research literacy' is the overall name for this critical understanding, and cultivating it is as essential a responsibility as making research findings accessible and useable. Some of the organisations listed above offer such support, but more needs to be done, especially in relation to the proliferation of evidence claims now circulating via social media.

The argument in favour of teachers' engagement with research – and the necessary components of it – seems to us incontrovertible. Even so, this may not be sufficient to bring about the kinds of positive change that the book is seeking to describe and promote. What else do we need to include in the environmental picture?

## Change-making: evidence plus ethics plus efficacy?

The principal motivation for teachers to engage with research is to make a positive difference to their students' learning: probably only a few teachers are driven primarily by the wish to become better researchers. However, a recent study by NFER for EEF (Lord et al., 2017) on the use of research in schools showed that teachers' access to and knowledge of research about literacy had little or no effect on pupils' Key Stage 2 English scores. The study concluded that 'simply communicating research evidence to schools is not enough to improve outcomes' and therefore 'schools may need more support in transforming such materials into actual change in the classroom' (p. 3).

Building on what is known from studies of effective continuing professional development (see, for example, Cordingley et al., 2014), we would go further and suggest that what schools need in addition to research knowledge is a deliberate and explicit strategy for change. There are so many demands emanating from system pressures as well as policy initiatives (particularly those resulting from the Programme for International Student Assessment [PISA])[16] that even compelling and accessible research can be overtaken in terms of what is at the forefront of teachers' minds on a daily basis as well as of how priorities are set at school-level. So school leaders and teachers need actively to question their assumptions about how and why research can make a difference in different classroom contexts; they need to work with a detailed understanding of how change happens, and what role organisational climate and culture play, in addition to knowledge.

Approaches to Change

+

| Susceptible to fads and fashion | Zone of Impact |
|---|---|
| Little, or uncritical, use is made of research evidence. Strategies for participation and implementation are well-developed. | Significant use of research evidence informs dialogue and planning. Strategies for participation, learning and change are well-developed. |
| For example: | For example: |
| *A strong focus on successful implementation – some successes.* | *A positive learning culture is established.* |
| *Activity can triggered by internal/external influences.* | *Activity focuses on genuine need – both student and teacher.* |
| *Resources for implementation are in place.* | *Activity is resourced and sustained over time.* |
| *Emphasis on delivery - less on learning/critical impact evaluation.* | *Strategies support collaborative enquiry, and impact evaluated.* |
| *Implementation is monitored and initiatives take root.* | *Proven successes are embedded into ongoing life of school.* |

Use of Evidence – ———————————————————————————————— +

| Wishful thinking | Pockets of success |
|---|---|
| Little, or uncritical, use is made of research evidence. Strategies for change are underdeveloped. | Good use of research evidence informs dialogue and planning. Strategies for participation and changes are less-developed. |
| For example: | For example: |
| *Many new initiatives are introduced - "Let's see what sticks"* | *Some groups are actively engaging with research and enquiry.* |
| *Insufficient time or resources are available.* | *Resources are available to groups – with supportive senior leadership.* |
| *Activity peters-out – sometimes overload or frustration.* | *Successful change is evident. Overall, knowledge is not well- mobilised in the absence of effective change strategies.* |
| *Senior leadership not always active or visible in activity.* | |

−

**FIGURE 5.1**  Research engagement and approaches to change: four scenarios

Figure 5.1 is an attempt to show the importance of enlisting a combination of research and change-theory to bring about improvements. Each quadrant represents a different combination of 'research evidence' and 'approach to change'. The upper right quadrant is the zone of greatest efficacy, where change is informed by both a knowledge of research and the intelligent deployment of strategies for change.

So teachers' collaborative in-depth engagement with research, underpinned by strong and explicit professional values and methodological integrity, needs to be supplemented with a commitment to, and an understanding of, systemic change. This will help teachers not only in engaging with research for a purpose as an integral aspect of their professional learning but also to be agents of change in their classrooms and schools.

## Conclusions

### Where do we go from here? An ethical compass for a research-engaged ecosystem

The question this chapter tasked itself with was, how can teachers' professional bodies better support schools and teachers in their engagement with research, and in sustaining that engagement over time? So far, we have looked at:

- The challenges to teachers' professionalism and professional knowledge in a fragmented system;

- The range of different groups and organisations – some of them classifiable as 'professional bodies' – that are providing support to teachers for accessing and using research;
- The proposition that teaching is a profession impelled by ethical as well as evidential issues, which needs to be made explicit in any discussion of evidence about 'what works';
- The consequent need for an expansive conceptualisation of 'research engagement' in 'research-rich' environments;
- The importance of 'theories of change' for using research and enquiry-led teaching to improve learning.

At this point we need to return to the question, 'Who holds "professionalism" in trust?' – which is not a trivial one, from either a profession's or the public's point of view; and the answer at present in teaching remains open-ended. As noted above, there exists a wide range of organisations with varying kinds of status and constitution that can claim to be supporting teachers' professional practice through the provision of 'evidence' or 'research', and/or through guidance and advice for the processes of in-house research and enquiry projects. Without wishing to suggest that progress towards a coherent, interdependent ecosystem of research-engaged practice will be easy or simple, we offer the following suggestions about how such bodies – and particularly for England the Chartered College of Teaching, whose role we explore in more detail below – can and should help to shape the agenda. We would urge that they develop a common *framework and strategy* for encouraging and resourcing research-engaged practice, and for countering some of the simplistic 'evidence-based' narratives that are in circulation. This would therefore comprise neither some kind of centrally imposed orthodoxy nor an epistemological free-for-all, but instead a commitment to the collaborative creation of knowledge that has integrity and trustworthiness, as well as relevance, for deepening the practice of teaching. It is what we mean by 'offering an ethical compass'.

The key components of such a strategy should include:

1. Acting as 'honest broker' for evidence claims, to assure their transparency and trustworthiness;
2. Creating strategic alliances to encourage research engagement as part of core professional standards and values in teaching;
3. Ensuring that programmes for teachers' initial and continuing education are informed by evidence on the one hand and structured around teachers' progressive engagement with research on the other;
4. Creating and supporting enquiry-based networks of teachers around key issues, building wherever possible on existing partnerships;
5. Providing/commissioning digests of high quality research findings on key themes of relevance to teaching and learning (noting where there are disagreements between different studies), supplementing these with school-based enquiry projects, and drawing out the implications for practice;
6. Acting as 'gatekeeper' and critic of policy pressures that are unsupported by research, whilst also nurturing teachers' own capacity for critical analysis.

The first of these raises the issue of how professional bodies can support teachers to evaluate the quality and relevance of research. A good starting point for discussion is the framework proposed by Furlong and Oancea (2005) over a decade ago. This was a comprehensive attempt to identify what 'quality' in practice-based educational research could and should look like; they devised four broad dimensions of quality, which we have summarised in Box 5.1.

---

**Box 5.1    Assessing 'quality' in practice-based educational research**

1.    *Methodological and theoretical robustness*

    Trustworthiness; contribution to knowledge; propriety; explicitness in designing and reporting; paradigm-dependent criteria (quantitative, qualitative, etc.).

2.    *Value for use*

    Salience/timeliness; purposivity; specificity and accessibility; concern for enabling impact; flexibility and operationalisability.

3.    *Capacity-building and value for people*

    Partnership, collaboration and engagement; plausibility; reflection and criticism; receptiveness; stimulating personal growth.

4.    *The economic dimension*

    Cost-effectiveness; marketability; auditability; feasibility; originality; value-efficiency.

---

We strongly suggest that this framework be revisited, and modified if necessary.

Of relevance to the third of our key activities is the BERA/RSA enquiry (2014), which shows the scale of the challenge of creating a *strategic* approach to research-informed teaching. Box 5.2 gives some brief extracts. The report identifies ten principles for self-improving and research-rich education systems, and 20 recommendations embracing both teacher education and teachers' professional development once in the job. These too should be revisited.

---

**Box 5.2    Research and the teaching profession: building the capacity for a self-improving education system**

The final report of the BERA/RSA enquiry into research and teacher education concludes that the UK 'lacks a coherent plan for teacher research and development'. The report goes on to say that teachers' experience of professional development in most parts of the UK is 'fragmented, occasional and insufficiently informed by research', in contrast to that of internationally well-regarded education systems such as Finland, Canada and Singapore.

England, Wales and Northern Ireland should follow the example of Scotland, which has set out a more systematic approach to helping teachers use the latest research to improve their lessons, although even there, there is room for improvement, the report said. It concluded that:

- In Scotland, 'it is now government policy to develop a systematic and coherent approach to [research-informed] career long professional learning', with universities given a prominent role, following the Donaldson Review for the Scottish government.
- However, across the rest of the UK there is a more fragmented and piecemeal approach to the use of research than that displayed by high-performing systems such as Finland and Canada.

There were some examples of good practice in England, such as the London Challenge initiative, which ran from 2003 to 2011, which had seen schools work together to share improvement strategies. But there is no 'co-ordinated strategy' to replicate its success across England.

The report acknowledged that pressures, including time pressures, facing teachers made this agenda challenging, but called for a cultural shift so that, over time, engaging in and with research becomes an everyday part of teachers' jobs: 'teachers across the UK should be supported to become research literate. This should include being given frequent opportunities to read up on the latest findings, with every pupil entitled to lessons which are informed by the best evidence'.

The enquiry laid down ten principles for self-improving and research-rich education systems, and 20 recommendations, embracing both teacher education and teachers' professional development once in the job.

This final report marked the end of an 18-month enquiry run jointly by BERA and the Royal Society for the Encouragement of the Arts, Manufacturing and Commerce (RSA) looking at the contribution research can make to improve the quality teaching.'

As promised, we now turn to the potential of the Chartered College of Teaching, still a relatively new organisation, to fulfil an overarching leadership role.[17] In conjunction with university and practitioner researchers, the College has already developed several research resources for its members; for ease of reference we list them again here:

- https://impact.chartered.college – *Impact* termly journal
- https://chartered.college/research–access – access to the EBSCO research database and to the University of Bristol's Document Summary Service

- https://chartered.college/research-practice-hub – 'a safe community where teachers can share practice, ideas and support'
- https://chartered.college/evidence-engagement – 'self-assessment toolkits for evidence-informed teaching'

– and more are in the planning stages, including a course on research literacy.

In terms of putting research engagement at the heart of professional practice, the Chartered Teacher programme (being piloted with an initial cohort of 140 teachers at the time of writing) is built around a progressive engagement with research evidence and research processes: see the pages under https://chartered.college/chartered-teacher for more details.

At a symbolic level, the chief executive of the College was one of the signatories in November 2017 of an evidence '*Magna Carta*', along with the heads of the UK professional bodies for medicine and policing. The Charter, reproduced in Box 5.3, signals their individual and joint commitment to evidence-based decision-making in their professions. This is intended to send a strong message to government as well as to the public and members of each profession about the importance they attach to research, and presumably represents the start of a valuable strategic alliance.

---

### Box 5.3  An 'evidence *Magna Carta*'

In November 2017 the heads of the UK professional bodies for medicine, policing and teaching signed and published an evidence '*Magna Carta*', to signal their commitment to evidence-based decision-making in their respective professions: https://chartered.college/medics-teachers-police-sign-adopt-professional-evidence. Their joint statement included a commitment to embed the principles with the strategic objectives of their own organisations.

The evidence declaration signing was hosted by the Alliance for Useful Evidence and Professor Jonathan Shepherd CBE, Royal College of Surgeons and Cardiff University, and chaired by Lord O'Donnell. Principal speakers included Professor Dame Alison Peacock, Chief Executive of the Chartered College of Teaching, Professor Carrie MacEwen, Chair of the Academy of Medical Royal Colleges and Chief Constable Ian Hopkins, of The College of Policing Board.

The declaration on evidence created by Professor Shepherd and agreed upon by the Colleges includes the following statement: 'Evidence of what works and what doesn't has become, through formal trial and error across all professions and public services, a foundation of professional practice. Equally, many untested interventions can do more harm than good and are wasteful of public and private resource . . . Therefore the Medical Royal Colleges, the College of Policing and the Chartered College of Teaching, as leaders of our professions, declare that our institutions expect all members to take full account of evidence and evidence informed guidance in their daily decisions and advice to individuals and organisations.'

Professor Jonathan Shepherd CBE, Royal College of Surgeons commented: 'Professional bodies are major influences on the daily practice of hundreds of thousands of professionals across the UK who are their members and fellows.'

Professor Dame Alison Peacock, Chief Executive of the Chartered College of Teaching, added: 'The Chartered College was formed earlier this year as a new professional body for teachers. We are working with eminent educational researchers both beyond and within schools and colleges to . . . connect theory and practice. We are establishing a rich variety of research networks across the country to foster dialogue throughout the teaching community in order that we can collectively enhance research-informed pedagogy.'

So our overarching conclusion must be that, for England, the most important factor in realising positive changes to the research ecosystem will be the future flourishing and growth in reach, status and authority of the Chartered College for Teaching, as the unified professional body for teaching. Other countries would need to assess how far their equivalent bodies can fulfil the kinds of role we have highlighted.

## Implications for the research-informed ecosystem

If the main challenges for establishing and nurturing a research-informed ecosystem are that:

- At present, there are too many organisations, bodies and structures to permit one single body to act, and to be seen to act, as the overarching professional body for teaching with authority for setting authoritative standards for research engagement;
- The education system in the UK currently operates with a model of knowledge creation which is based on 'a marketplace' of ideas, and communicated through social media in a way which is often detrimental to constructive and developmental dialogue;
- In any case, there are too many pressures on teachers that can detract or distract from the desire to engage with research;

– then the way forward for professional bodies will entail, among other things:

- Conserving the integrity and trustworthiness of research evidence about teaching and learning, by – for example – publishing and promoting evaluation criteria;
- Countering the polarised, adversarial and simplistic 'evidence-based' narratives that circulate through social media;

- Ensuring that programmes for teachers' initial and continuing professional education, as well as for Chartered Teacher status, have research literacy and engagement at their core;
- Creating more strategic alliances between different professional organisations around the production and dissemination of research, and research literacy, for teachers and other professionals;
- Developing all schools as enquiring, 'research-rich' (not merely 'evidence-based') environments;
- Promoting the wider educational values of equality, diversity and social justice by nurturing teachers' critical engagement with concepts and controversies as well as with different types of evidence.

## Notes

1  See, for example, www.gov.uk/government/publications/evidence-informed-teaching-evaluation-of-progress-in-england.
2  'The more we discussed what should be included on the website the more it reinforced that what we were discussing was establishing the school with a very clear brand.' www.inteta-uk.com/schools-and-academies-as-brands/. Downloaded 9 January 2018.
3  'Every school or colleges is a brand. Your brand is who you are, how others perceive you, how you operate and communicate and the image and reputation you build.' https://oysterdesign.co.uk/school-marketing/branding-and-design. Downloaded 9 January 2018.
4  See, for example, Hewitt et al. (2018), who argue that 'Web 2.0 has enabled a specific group of professionals to have some influence [on government] through their discourse.'
5  See, for example: Teacher Toolkit www.teachertoolkit.co.uk – 'the most influential blog on education in the UK', accessed 5 February 2018; or Edutopia www.edutopia.org, which reported that in 2010 its 'presence on social networks experience explosive audience growth', accessed 27 March 2018; or Learning Spy www.learningspy.co.uk 'one of the most influential education blogs in the UK', accessed 5 February 2018.
6  N. Gibb (2017). The importance of vibrant and open debate in education, www.gov.uk/government/speeches/nick-gibb-the-importance-of-vibrant-and-open-debate-in-education. Accessed 5 February 2018.
7  See, for example, an article in the *Times Educational Supplement*, 30 January 2018, Sir Kevan Collins calls for end of '*awful, polarised, adversarial*' Twitter debate. www.tes.com/news/school-news/breaking-news/research-chief-calls-education-twitterati-show-more-respect?amp&__twitter_impression=true. Accessed 5 February 2018.
8  The Wikipedia entry for 'professional association' gives this information: 'Many professional bodies are involved in the development and monitoring of professional educational programs, and the updating of skills, and thus perform professional certification to indicate that a person possesses qualifications in the subject area … Membership of a professional body, as a legal requirement, can in some professions form the primary formal basis for gaining entry to and setting up practice within the profession.' Retrieved 6 January 2019 from: https://en.wikipedia.org/wiki/Professional_association.
9  See, for example, www.gtcni.org.uk//index.cfm/area/information/page/competencere search and www.gtcs.org.uk/professional-update/research-practitioner-enquiry/research/current-academic-practitioner-research.aspx (accessed 6 January 2019).
10  https://chartered.college/.
11  All the websites in this list were accessed between October 2017 and February 2018.
12  The Research Schools Network is a collaboration between the EEF and the Institute for Effective Education (IEE), who are funding a network of schools 'which will support the use of evidence to improve teaching practice. Research Schools will become a

focal-point for evidence-based practice in their region, building affiliations with large numbers of schools, and supporting the use of evidence at scale.'

13 See, for example, www.harrisfederation.org.uk and http://mcsbrent.co.uk/so-you-want-to-work-at-michaela/. Both accessed 5 February 2018.

14 See, for example, Stenhouse, 1975.

15 See also Godfrey, 2017.

16 www.oecd.org/pisa/aboutpisa/.

17 Our warm thanks are due to Cat Scutt, Director of Education and Research at the Chartered College of Teaching, for generously agreeing to give her time to be interviewed for this chapter.

# References

Alexander, R. (2010). Speaking but not listening? Accountable talk in an unaccountable context? *Literacy*, 44(3), 103–111.

Alexander, R. (2017). *Towards Dialogic Teaching: Rethinking Classroom Talk*. York: Dialogos.

Bennett, T. (2013). *Teacher Proof*. London: Routledge.

BERA/RSA. (2014). *Research and the Teaching Profession: Building the Capacity for a Self-Improving Education System*. www.bera.ac.uk/wp-content/uploads/2013/12/BERA-RSA-Research-Teaching-Profession-FULL-REPORT-for-web.pdf. Downloaded 9 January 2018.

Biesta, G. (2007). Why 'what works' won't work: evidence-based practice and the democratic deficit in educational research. *Educational Theory*, 57(1), 1–22. See http://onlinelibrary.wiley.com/doi/10.1111/j.1741-5446.2006.00241.x/full. Downloaded 5 February 2018.

Bridges, D. (2016). *Philosophy in Educational Research: Epistemology, Ethics, Politics and Quality*. London: Springer.

Cordingley, P. et al. (2014). *Developing Great Teaching: Lessons from the International Reviews Into Effective Professional Development*. London: Teacher Development Trust. http://tdtrust.org/wp-content/uploads/2015/10/DGT-Summary.pdf. Downloaded 16 February 2018.

Furlong, J. and Oancea, A. (2005). *Assessing Quality in Applied and Practice-Based Educational Research: A Framework for Discussion*. Oxford: Oxford Department of Educational Studies. www.birmingham.ac.uk/Documents/college-social-sciences/education/projects/esrc-2005-seminarseries5.pdf. Downloaded 10 January 2018.

Gibb, N. (2017). The importance of vibrant and open debate in education. www.gov.uk/government/speeches/nick-gibb-the-importance-of-vibrant-and-open-debate-in-education. Accessed 5 February 2018.

Godfrey, D. (2017). What is the proposed role of research evidence in England's 'self-improving' school system?. *Oxford Review of Education*, 43(4), 433–446.

Hargreaves, D. (1996). *Teaching as a Research-based Profession: Possibilities and Prospects. Teacher Training Agency Annual Lecture*. London: Teacher Training Agency.

Hewitt, S., Tiropanis, T. and Bokhove, C. (2018). Discovering the content of the edu-blogosphere, paper on work-in-progress submitted to ACM Webscience Conference 2018. (Copy acquired by request of authors.)

Lord, P., Rabiasz, A. and Styles, B. (2017). *'Literacy Octopus' Dissemination Trial: Evaluation Report and Executive Summary*. Slough: NFER. www.nfer.ac.uk/publications/EEFA02/EEFA02.pdf. Downloaded 9 February 2018.

Saunders, L (2015). 'Evidence' and teaching: a question of trust? In C. Brown (Ed.), *Leading the Use of Research and Evidence in Schools*. London: Institute of Education Press.

Stenhouse, L. (1975). *An Introduction to Curriculum Research and Development.* London: Heinemann.

Whitty, G. (2006). Teacher professionalism in a new era, Paper presented at the first General Teaching Council for Northern Ireland Annual Lecture, *Belfast—see* www.gtcni.org.uk/pub lications/uploads/document/annual%20lecture%20paper.pdf. Downloaded 5 February 2018.

Young, T. (2014). Prisoners of The Blob: why most educational experts are wrong about almost everything. www.civitas.org.uk/pdf/PrisonersofTheBlob.pdf. Downloaded 5 February 2018.

# 6

# INNOVATIVE MODELS THAT BRIDGE THE RESEARCH–PRACTICE DIVIDE

## Research learning communities and research-informed peer review

*David Godfrey and Chris Brown*

### Aims of the chapter

- To identify the challenges of bridging the research–practice divide.
- To outline two innovative and trialled research-to-practice models.
- To explain the key principles of each approach and how the two models compare and contrast in terms of the principles underpinning them.
- To present evidence of the impact of these models at participating schools.

### Introduction

During a roundtable held at the 2018 *BELMAS* conference to discuss this book, we asked participants to think about some of the key elements that might sustain and encourage research use within an 'ecosystem' framework. Among the responses provided were the vital importance of trust, the role of learning environments, and the function, nature and capacity of leadership. All things, in fact, that underpin both the research learning community (RLC) approach and research-informed peer review (RiPR), pioneering approaches developed by Chris Brown (RLCs) and David Godfrey (RiPR). Below we outline these approaches in more detail, drawing out their key features and then compare them along their shared principles of action. Finally, we examine the impact these approaches have had in terms in terms of outcomes for both staff and children in the participating schools.

In England, the increased tendency of schools to work in networks or alliances, such as Multi-Academy Trusts or Teaching Schools Alliances has created a demand for robust and rigorous processes for schools to work together, based on established research-informed principles for improving learning and leading change. RLCs were first trialled as an EEF funded research project in 2014 and have now been used in a number of alliances and federations in the UK and abroad (see below). RiPR began in 2016, with a pilot study involving six primary schools. Its research-to-practice approach is introduced through the vehicle of school peer review; it is now commonplace for schools in England to be part of one or more peer reviews (e.g. Greany and Higham, 2018). These peer reviews can also provide the professional challenge needed to improve through collaboration (Matthews and Headon, 2015).

The exercise of bridging the gap between the two 'worlds' of academia and school practice has been characterised throughout this book and elsewhere, in terms of: creating a 'third space', mobilising knowledge, or in the encouragement of evidence or research-informed practice. It is not our intention to expand on these themes here, rather to present potential solutions to these challenges. Both models seek to enrich and enhance the work of schools, school leaders and practitioners working in collaboration; they do so by providing them with processes and practices to engage in and with academic research.

As academics, we have a shared interest in working alongside school leaders and practitioners to help improve their schools and to implement meaningful changes in the education of the young people who study in them. This type of work presents problems both for us as academics and the school staff who commit to these projects. High among these challenges is the perceived lack of time by teachers to engage in research activity and for academics to work in schools. In terms of the latter, much of this work can be seen as outside of the immediate remit of an academic to engage in funded research or to publish in academic journals. Then there is the question of the purpose of 'research', which for school staff may be viewed as needing to have an instrumental and fairly immediate aim of improving practice and student outcomes, while as researchers we may wish to urge caution about the data and what it shows before moving on to action (the analogy of the sign post vs. the lamp post). Further to these challenges is the potential for some academic research to be viewed in a hierarchy of knowledge that relegates practitioner knowledge to the lower echelons. We have both argued against such a view (e.g. Godfrey, 2017 and Brown, 2014) and both of us have respect and admiration for the challenges of working in schools and recognise how the accumulated knowledge of practitioners must have equal status (at least) to knowledge derived from research.

Below, we discuss some of the key principles we have employed to engage practitioners in collaborative research-informed improvement, comparing and contrasting the two models. First, we begin with a summary of each approach.

## Research learning communities

RLCs were developed from a programme of research that focuses on establishing effective ways of connecting research and practice (e.g. Brown, 2017; Brown and Zhang, 2016). The RLC approach thus represents a synthesis of this work and, as such, is grounded in three core (research-informed) ideas. The first of these is the fundamental notion that educational practitioners do not become research-informed simply by being presented with research evidence; instead that two things should occur. To begin with teachers need to engage in a process of learning and accommodation, directed towards helping them make explicit connections between research knowledge and their own assumptions and knowledge (Katz and Dack, 2013). The aim of this accommodation process is to help teachers create new understandings in relation to a given issue or problem. Following this period of learning, which typically culminates in the development of new ideas, concepts, practices, strategies (and so on), teachers then need to practice employing these 'innovations'. As they do so in a variety of situations and contexts, teachers will subsequently develop expertise in their application, as they begin to understand how, where and why their use is likely to be most effective.

The second of the core ideas underpinning the RLC approach is that the successful roll out of new practices or ideas is dependent on effective change leadership. In other words, initiating innovation represents the introduction of something new and potentially countercultural. As such, there is a risk that new innovations are rejected by those required to adopt them. Correspondingly, the effective scale-up of research-informed innovation will be dependent on there being 'the right people in the room': those most likely to make change happen in schools (e.g. those with the influence and authority to lead change). This means these 'right people' must be identified and selected to take part in research to practice activity: with their participation ensuring that the implementation of research-informed innovation is both prioritised and remains top of mind. Related, however (the third core idea), is that is if evidence-informed practices are to spread widely, then those involved in the research to practice activity, as well as having influence and authority, must also possess the *ability* to deliver effective change on the ground: that is, they must explicitly know both what is required to lead change effectively and also their own role in making long lasting change happen.

Each RLC typically comprises eight to 12 teachers from four to six schools. Participants are often senior or middle leaders as well as 'opinion formers' (see below). Over the course of a school year, the RLC process involves four whole day workshops, which lead participating teachers through a research-informed cycle of enquiry which moves from problem identification to the development and trial of new approaches to teaching and learning. Finally, these approaches are implemented across the whole school and their impact ascertained. In between workshops participants are expected to work with school colleagues to share research knowledge and understanding, and to roll out research-informed innovation.

## Research-informed peer review

While peer reviews can provide highly valued lateral challenge and support, there are three potential drawbacks to guard against. The first is for peer reviewers to mimic an external inspection. Where this happens it risks creating a defensive mentality among participants and limits the potential for learning. The second is the tendency to recirculate ineffective practices through a process of groupthink or by referring only to anecdotal evidence or individual school level data. The third is for the peer review to merely validate schools' existing self-evaluations without providing tools to challenge the thinking of school teams or to propose improvements. RiPR avoids these limitations by adopting an enquiry process that is very different in kind from the practices used to judge quality in external inspections. No reference is made to the standard inspection framework; rather, reviewers seek to deepen learning and to gather data in relation to a shared educational theme. Participants also adopt a process of evaluation through theory engagement (Robinson and Timperley, 2013) that is developmental rather than summative. Engagement with academic research enhances peer reviewers' knowledge beyond anecdote by reviewing the literature from academic research (such as effective feedback). Finally, improvements to school policies and practices are proposed in terms of current and alternative theories of action (especially Robinson, 2017).

Conceptually, the RiPR model falls within two fields of research: school internal evaluation (IE) and school improvement, most especially the idea of joint practice development (JPD). IE can be defined as: 'a process of purposive evaluation of school practices which provides insights into the educational experiences of students, as more than those measured by test data' (Simons, 2013, from Nelson et al., 2015, p. 3). Unlike external evaluations, the schools themselves (at least the schools' leadership teams) decide on whether they wish to take part and when, the focus of the review, the evaluation criteria and with whom they wish to share findings of their evaluations. Although IE may have a summative function when evaluation reports are used for external accountability, such as to feed into inspections (Nelson et al., 2015), they are often (as is the case for RiPR) formative when focused on assessing strengths and weaknesses to inform continuous improvement and school development.

The notion of joint practice development (JPD) (Fielding et al., 2005) is the essence of RiPR. That is to say, school teams engage in structured mutual development related to practice, each partner has something to offer and something to learn, and the development is research-informed. JPD has been shown to be effective in providing challenge and support for building capacity (Fielding et al., 2005). JPD also helps provide context-relevant knowledge that meets the local needs of schools (Hadfield et al., 2005).

In the RiPR model, schools work in clusters of three for reciprocal review visits during the school year and also attend three half-day workshops (sometimes shared with other clusters). Although any number of shared themes could be adopted in principle, so far the RiPR groups have focused on improving feedback and assessment. This theme has proved popular with school leaders, due to its potential to have a positive impact on student attainment and has enabled enquiry to be focused on teaching practices as well as involving leadership policies in relation to assessment. It has also been a popular theme, with the anticipation of impact on student attainment. RiPR members comprise one senior leader (usually the head teacher) plus at least one other teacher, middle or aspiring school leader, up to a maximum of four people per school. The workshops first introduces participants to the research, through a literature review, and encourage self-evaluation and reflection in relation to their own school context. The second workshop involves mutual scrutiny of school policies in relation to the issue and the co-construction of data collection tools (interviews, observation pro-forma and book scrutiny procedures) informed by the research evidence. Each school visit lasts one whole day and is conducted as a process of enquiry and mutual learning, facilitated by a university representative who is experienced in the process. After the three review visits, all schools attend the final workshop in which the learning is consolidated, the process is evaluated and school leaders are shown how to plan for ongoing implementation challenges based on the Concerns-Based Adoption Model (CBAM) (Hall and Hord, 2006). Schools are encouraged to continue to support each other and to build a cycle of feedback loops to inform future actions.

## Key principles of research learning communities and research-informed peer review

While each model has its unique solutions to bringing schools together in research-informed school improvement, they follow eight key principles. These are outlined below.

### 1. Schools engage in deep self-evaluation and enrich their understanding of their baseline in relation to a shared theme

Previous research suggests that systematic reflection and working towards *shared objectives* are key ingredients in the effectiveness of school IE (Vanhoof and Van Petegem, 2011). When school self-evaluation is accompanied by engagement with research (see principle 3), this can lead to enhanced professional learning (Fernandez, 2002) and to a more rigorous focus on the pedagogical practices likely to improve outcomes for students (Mincu, 2013). Both RLC and RiPR approaches stimulate learning by building upon academic knowledge and encourage deep self-evaluation in relation to this theme. By capturing an enhanced and more evidence-rich baseline, each school leadership team avoids acting on poor information and knowledge before proposing action.

A review of the school evaluation literature (Nelson et al., 2015) suggests that for IE to lead to school improvement, participating staff need to have high levels of evaluation literacy, access to appropriate resources and formal leaders who endorse and enable the process.

The participation of more than just senior leaders in the IE is important as this leads to a collective understanding and ownership of the issues the school needs to address. The external support provided by a university partner in both models, helps to increase the success of the IE by increasing evaluation literacy and by providing critical friendship.

## 2. Participants engage in reflective and collaborative professional learning and model this with their own staff

In order for research-informed practice to become a meaningful way of life, practitioners need to engage with research in an effective learning environment (Brown et al., 2016). Therefore, in both models, but in the RLC approach in particular, the building of rich Professional Learning Communities (PLCs) is emphasised. PLCS are most effective when they have a *shared vision and sense of purpose*; members of the PLC consistently taking collective responsibility for student learning; participants collaborating in ways that go beyond mere superficial exchanges of help or support; the promotion of group as well as individual learning; and participants engaging in reflective professional enquiry (Stoll et al., 2006).

As mentioned above, RiPR is a form of JPD; our understanding of this process has been particularly shaped through developing and researching 'triad' approaches to lesson study in London schools (Godfrey et al., 2018). In lesson study, the triads are teachers who plan and observe each other's lessons and develop their understanding of a shared pedagogical focal area. In RiPR, the triads are school leaders and teachers who host and take part in evaluation and data collection visits in each other's schools. As with lesson study triads, these reciprocal reviews lead to an ever more sophisticated and shared understanding of the issues that are shared and developed collaboratively. The analogy we share with school participants of this process is of 'digging deeper, digging together' (Fielding et al., 2005).

In both RLCs and RiPR, schools send more than one representative to participate in the programme, to ensure both formal and informal leadership dimensions of change are encouraged (see principle 4). The spaces for professional learning in the workshops and reviews are highly valued by these participants. However, we emphasise that it is important for those who take part to create the same opportunities for staff back at the school. Therefore, our workshops model approaches to professional learning that school leaders are encouraged to adopt or adapt for staff at their own schools.

## 3. Practice-based knowledge is combined with research-based knowledge to create new knowledge

There is increasing evidence to suggest that, when done well, the type of learning that PLC activity typically facilitates can lead to improvements in both teachers' practice and student outcomes (Stoll et al., 2006; Harris and Jones, 2012). The nature of this learning activity is encapsulated by the notion of knowledge 'creation', i.e. where practically useful and contextually pertinent knowledge results when the producers and users of formal knowledge, who are, simultaneously, also the users and holders of 'practical' knowledge, come together and share what each group know. To successfully create new knowledge, PLC participants need to take part in facilitated 'learning conversations' to help teachers make sense of various forms of evidence in order to drive real changes in student outcomes (Earl and Timperley, 2008, p. 2).

Neither the RLC or RiPR approach comes with an inherent focus on 'what works' outcomes, but rather are concerned with the use of research to improve a wide range of outcomes for children. Specifically, outcomes can range from holistic approaches to children's development, which value intellectual, social and cultural development equally and mutually reinforcing (in Germany this is known as *bildungsbegriff*), children's well-being, to more instrumental notions such as improving feedback to enhance children's learning and performance. Outcomes are improved through the development of new practices or curricula, but also through the development and sharing of new values, concepts and ideas in relation to the role and purposes of education. Both models begin with the introduction of a literature review around a particular shared theme or concern, such as the effective grouping of children by prior attainment. This knowledge becomes integrated with further enquiries and data from the schools themselves. This can be seen as a good example of 'evidence-informed practice' (EIP) (e.g. Godfrey, 2017; Brown and Zhang, 2016).

The processes of leadership of change, evaluation and implementation in RLCs and RiPR are also informed by extensive academic research (e.g. Robinson and Timperley, 2013; Robinson, 2017; Hall and Hord, 2016). Both the active stance by participants as 'enquirers', along with engagement in and with research *theory*, also give our approaches the hallmarks of 'research-informed practices' (RiP) (Godfrey, 2017).

## 4. Key people participate and lead change

School leadership is vital to school improvement (Earley, 2013), and there are a number of key characteristics identified as important in relation to what effective leadership is and involves. These characteristics are often divided into the 'transformational' aspects of leadership and 'pedagogic' or learning centred leadership (Day and Sammons, 2013). The former can be thought of as a process based on increasing the commitment of those in a school towards organisational goals, vision and direction, and has been shown to have positive impact in relation to the introduction of new initiatives or the remodelling or restructuring of school activity. The latter is seen to relate to the efforts of school leaders in improving teaching in their school and their focus on the relationships between teachers as well as the behaviour of teachers vis-à-vis their work with students (e.g. Timperley and Robertson, 2011).

The implications for leaders in RLCs and RiPR are two-fold. First, they should actively promote their vision for research use within their school, while simultaneously encouraging and facilitating their teachers to develop and adopt research-informed innovation. Second, and perhaps even more importantly, however, is that school leader engagement in RLC activity is also vital. This is because having first hand involvement and experience in developing research-informed innovation also enables school leaders to 'walk the talk': to both demonstrate their commitment as well as engage in instructional leadership practices such as 'modelling', 'monitoring' and 'mentoring and coaching' (dialogue). As a result school leaders are able to not only showcase but also actively support staff in the adoption of such practices, ensuring wider buy-in and take-up across the school (Earley, 2013).

Leadership, when considered a form of influence, can also be undertaken by more than just those possessing 'formal' responsibility. Spillane et al. (2010), argue that, perhaps more than formal leaders, it is informal leaders who determine the fate of new initiatives. In the case of the RLC approach, informal leaders, or 'research champions' are identified to take part in the programme, sometimes through a social network analysis (e.g. Daly and Finnigan, 2010). These champions are ones with high level of Practice-Based Social Capital (PBSC) (e.g. Baker-Doyle and Yoon, 2010). These opinion formers can act as conduits for both mobilising opinion and the adoption of innovation. Likewise, in RiPR the middle leaders and teachers who take part, form a bridge towards the pedagogical team that ensures the learning gained during the process is not confined to the head teacher.

## 5. Theories of action are made explicit when proposing improvements

Stoll and Brown (2015) observe that school leaders can often be frustrated in their attempts to roll out innovations to colleagues. In part, this frustration derives from a lack of understanding or even confidence in relation to leading change. But it also stems from the notion that those within organisations instinctively oppose change initiatives that are likely to disrupt current ways of getting things done (Battilana and Casicaro, 2013). As Fullan argues, there is thus a need 'to understand change in order to lead it better' (2001, p. 34).

As part of their work on an Economic and Social Research Council funded knowledge transfer project ('Middle leaders as catalysts for evidence-informed change'), Stoll and Brown (2015), helped participants to understanding and apply theories of change and they felt this was fundamental to the success of these participants in being able to roll out innovations more widely.

In both RLCs and RiPR, the understanding of theories of action is important to the change model. The theories of action (ToA) approach used by RLCs is outlined in detail in Brown and Flood (2018). For RiPR, this is summed up well by the concept of evaluation through theory engagement, which is represented visually in Figure 6.1 and is based on the work of Timperley and Robinson (2013).

The idea is based on an understanding of ToA (Argyris and Schon, 1974). In their model, ToAs are the values, beliefs and rationale behind the observed actions and which lead to intended and unintended consequences of those actions. 'Theory engagement is, in essence, a process of theory competition in which the relative merits of the existing and proposed theories of action are debated' (Robinson and Walker, 1999, in Robinson, 2017, p. 26). In evaluation through theory engagement, evaluators work within two theories simultaneously, Practitioner Theory (P-Theory) and Evaluator Theory (E-Theory). In the case of the former, these are the theories of action of the schools staff – especially

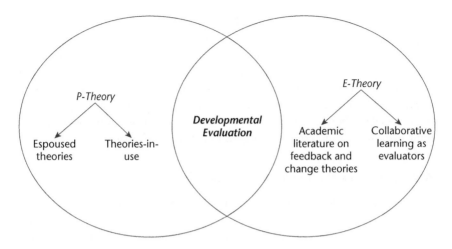

**FIGURE 6.1** Evaluation through theory engagement

the teachers and school leaders. The latter are the theories developed through engagement with the research literature, through analysis of data in the schools and in the workshop sessions. While it is expected that the E-Theory will add a new focus, this does not mean it is necessarily superior existing P-Theories, so it is through 'negotiation' between these competing theories that opportunities for development occur.

P-Theory contains both *espoused theories*, i.e. those that people report to be the basis of their actions and *theories-in-use*, and these are inferred from how people actually behave. To our peer reviewers in RiPR this corresponds to two questions (using the example of 'effective feedback' as the theme):

1. What is 'our' (the school's) espoused theory of action regarding the use of feedback? (the TALK)
2. What are we actually doing in terms of our feedback practices? (the WALK)

The first ToA can be seen in policy documents and what the school leaders and teachers say they are doing and why. Sometimes school posters or memes can also reveal the espoused ToA. The mutual scrutiny of policies on feedback and assessment forms part of the focus in workshop two. The theories-in-use (the TALK) are 'captured' by observational methods, especially through classroom observations and looking at examples of students' written work during the review visits.

Leading improvement by engaging with theories of action involves four phases: 1) agreeing on the problem to be solved; 2) revealing the relevant theory in action; 3) evaluating the relative merit of the current and alternative theories in action; and 4) implementing a new, sufficiently agreed theory of action (Robinson, 2017). By acknowledging the ToAs of teachers without judgement in constructive dialogue, the school leaders aim to build a rationale for a proposed improvement to the current policy and practices. In doing so, they avoid the so-called 'bypass' approach in which new ideas are simply imposed through persuasion or coercion. The bypass approach is more likely to lead to resistance by those who need to implement the change and thus less likely to lead to sustained improvement. This is especially true for changes in the day-to-day practices of many people, where these new practices require repeated effort and support to implement successfully, and where shifts in beliefs are ultimately required.

## 6. External facilitation plays a crucial role

Neither of our models are 'recipes' or simply 'protocols' to follow with an instruction manual; their success relies on skilled facilitation by people who can span academia and practice. Although both of us lead and facilitate RLCs and RiPR collaborations, we have also benefited by being able to count on other colleagues who are excellent facilitators, often with school leadership experience and who are well-versed in relevant academic research. These external facilitators provide the kind of critical friendship that can aid school development planning and improvement (Swaffield and MacBeath, 2005). As mentioned above, our processes are informed by research, the self-evaluations are based on a review of academic research and our evaluation and enquiry methods require the type of input and support that university staff are often better equipped to provide than those based in schools. The kind of impartiality and distance that an external person can provide can also help steer learning and ideas in useful ways, keeping participants 'honest' to the process and mindful to provide evidence for their assertions. Evidence from experimental research in a US context has shown that peer to peer working with external facilitation can lead to improvements in student achievement (Saunders et al., 2009). For both models to scale-up, the need to train and quality assure facilitators therefore becomes one of the utmost importance. Such facilitators may also be seen as system leaders who help schools work together and build knowledge that leads to continuous improvement in the network.

## 7. Change takes time and involves cycles of reflection and the development of knowledge and skills

In terms of the cyclical approaches to development, as stated above, RiPR follows the phases of theory engagement. As participants plan and implement their new theories of action, they begin to redefine the problem, often in a more nuanced and evidence-informed way. This can be understood in terms of Argyris and Schon's 'double-loop learning' (Argyris, 1976). As school leaders seek to implement their new approaches, they are also guided to understand how to evaluate the implementation, taking into account Hall and Hord's notion of the 'implementation bridge' (see Hall, 2013). This helps school leaders to understand how teachers become aware of and ready for change, how they develop their understanding of the innovation and finally their enactment in practice of these changes.

RLCs also propose a four workshop (Wx) cycle of enquiry approach. Here, in W1 participants focus on understanding both academic research and current teacher held knowledge concerning their teaching and learning issue. In W2 participants develop research-informed approaches to improving teaching practice and consider how these approaches might be trialed effectively through JPD. In W3 participants refine their approaches. The workshop is also used to introduce the idea of whole school change as well as change tools/approaches. Finally, W4 is used to examine impact and how to share knowledge of impact more widely.

As well as engaging meaningfully with research to develop innovations, practitioners also need to develop expertise in the 'use' of these innovations (even with concepts there is a need to see where these are applicable and require refinement etc.). Such expertise stems from the application of such innovations and, correspondingly, their ongoing trial and refinement. For example, with RLCs this practice is encouraged following W2.

## 8. Trust is essential and success is made more likely when schools support and challenge each other

Vital to the process of effective knowledge creation is that learning conversations are steeped in a culture of trust (Stoll et al., 2006), which reduces the 'transaction costs' of collaborating. For instance, high levels of trust are associated with a variety of reciprocal efforts, including where collaboration, learning, complex information sharing and problem solving, shared decision making and coordinated action are required (e.g. Bryk et al., 2010; Tschannen-Moran, 2004). In fact recent research by Brown et al. (2016) indicates that high levels of trust are three times more important than other factors in fostering research engagement by teachers. While trust may be to an extent a pre-existing factor that determines the success of RLCs and RiPR, both can also help to build such a culture of openness and sharing. This is made possible once participants begin to feel the benefits of a non-judgemental, enquiry-based school improvement process.

Further to this, research has shown that reciprocal support and challenge can help schools to implement the changes they wish to make, including beyond the duration of the initial collaboration of the RLC or RiPR cycle. Traditionally, PLCs have operated within individual schools and organisations. With the growing impetus for school-to-school support in many school systems, however, Networked Learning Communities (NLCs) have emerged as a means by which teachers, school leaders and other educationalists can move outside their day-to-day contexts to engage with a broader scope of ideas and possibilities as part of a cross-school or multi-school PLC (e.g. see Earl and Katz, 2006; Harris and Jones, 2012). In order to make 'network-level' changes, schools can also work together to share resources, to combine for professional learning and training, and can routinely interchange practices and policy ideas. As such, school collaborations of this nature can achieve more than the sum of its parts. Continued network activity, when built into the schools' annual cycles of self-evaluation and improvement planning, can also build network-level, laterally driven accountability that helps keep all partners on task and working towards their targets.

## The impact of the research learning communities approach

RLCs have been adopted by a range of school communities across England, as well as in Boise, Idaho, USA and in Malmo, Sweden. For example, over the past three years, the Chestnut Learning Federation, a family of three small church infant schools based in Hampshire, UK wanted to use the RLC model to develop research-informed interventions to improve the writing outcomes of their summer-born children (those born between 1 April and 31 August and who typically have lower educational attainment, as measured by standardised tests, than those born at the start of the year). The new research-informed practice resulting from the RLC activity appears to be responsible for a substantive increase in the federation's summer-born children's outcomes: in 2014–2015, 60 per cent of summer-born children in the federation achieved the expected level of the Early Learning Goal (ELG) for writing compared with 87.5 per cent of their autumn-born peers and 67.3 per cent of summer-borns in Hampshire. Following year one of the RLC (2016), 86 per cent of summer-born children met their ELG for writing: an improvement of 26 per cent. This improvement was also sustained in year two of the RLC (2017) with 82 per cent of summer-borns meeting their ELG for writing; in comparison, over the same period the federation average for all children achieving the ELG for writing remained at 83 per cent. Furthermore in year three, 85 per cent of summer-borns met their ELG for writing (in comparison to 84 per cent for all children).

There has also been an independent randomised control trial of the approach (see Rose et al., 2017). Here 119 primary schools were recruited, with half then randomly allocated by Rose's team to an intervention group and half to a control group. A team of colleagues at UCL Institute of Education then worked with the intervention group, taking them through the RLC approach for two years. As Rose et al.'s (2017) evaluation shows, the RLC approach did appear to increase instances of collaborative EIP at scale as well as a belief in the benefits of this type of approach.

## The impact of research-informed peer review

While RiPR started later than RLCs, with a pilot study in the 2016/2017 school year, we are seeing some early evidence of impact on staff and students. RiPR cycles have been completed with several schools in England and the approach has also been taught to a group of schools in Sofia, Bulgaria. In the summer of 2018, school networks over three regions in Chile started RiPR collaborations with the aim of improving the use of teacher feedback and assessment.

Participating head teachers in RiPR have described the experience as challenging and also leading to very deep thinking and awareness about their schools' policies and practices in relation to assessment and feedback. For example, at the end of the academic year 2017/2018, one primary school had rewritten its policy on feedback, having realised it was inadequate as a theory of action. A short extract can be seen in Box 6.1.

---

**Box 6.1   Primary School X rewritten policy on feedback**

Feedback should be MEANINGFUL, MANAGEABLE AND MOTIVATING. At X Primary we are aiming:

- to develop the self-regulation and independence of learners; taking ownership of their learning and making improvements
- to communicate effectively with all learners to enable them to make improvements, ensuring all learners understand their feedback in the context of the wider learning journey
- for all learners to take pride in their work
- to ensure all feedback is given that is needs driven and personalised
- to ensure that feedback is only given when useful. Constant feedback is less effective than targeted
- to raise self-esteem and motivate learners

---

At an earlier workshop, in December 2017, three schools had worked on modelling their current theories of action in relation to assessment and feedback. The participants from this school realised that they had a series of actions, but what was missing was a clear statement of beliefs and also of desired consequences – the elements of a theory of action. The information in Box 6.1 was rewritten in co-construction with the whole of the teaching staff. This was followed by a period in which teachers trialled approaches to meet these goals. The other element that was clear from this new policy was that it was now much more closely informed by academic research (e.g. the reference to the self-regulation aim of feedback, above). Measuring the long-term impact of these changes on teaching practice and pupil attainment forms the basis of our long-term research with this method.

## Conclusion

Research learning communities and research-informed peer review share eight key principles in the endeavour to enrich and improve educational practices in schools through bringing research into practice. Both involve developing a deep understanding of their baseline and then seek to move forward through a process of collaborative professional learning. The knowledge brought from academic research is combined with context-based professional knowledge and other evidence and key people are chosen to take part in the change to lead this development both formally and informally. In doing so, new ideas are presented as theories of action and phases of reflection and feedback are involved so that these proposals are not presented as one off initiatives but as part of a continuous improvement cycle. External facilitation helps guide all participants throughout and we have found that an academic lens can be a useful counterpoint to practitioners desire to move quickly to action. Often the kind of changes targeted by schools require the development of new knowledge and skills and this can take time and is helped considerably when schools work together to keep each other on track and to support each other to achieve their aims.

## Implications for the research-informed ecosystem

- An effective ecosystem would have many skilled facilitators and system leaders. While this capacity can be built from within the school system, there will always be a role for universities and other academic staff to provide critical friendship.
- Research–practice collaborations need to stick faithfully to their key principles; while there will be adaptations to fit context, these must not be cheated, as the effects of this JPD will become diluted.
- Improvement efforts by schools in a research-informed ecosystem should be seen as part of the natural improvement cycle and not as 'bolted-on' initiatives.
- High trust collaborations between locally based clusters are more likely to lead to network level cooperation that increases the chances of sustainable improvement in the local exosystem.

## References

Argyris, C. (1976). Single-loop and double-loop models in research on decision making. *Administrative Science Quarterly*, 21(3), 363–375.

Argyris, C. and Schon, D. A. (1974). *Theory in Practice: Increasing Professional Effectiveness*. San Francisco, CA: Jossey-Bass.

Baker-Doyle, K. and Yoon, S. A. (2010). Making expertise transparent: using technology to strengthen social networks in teacher professional development. In A. Daly (Ed.), *Social Network Theory and Educational Change*. Cambridge, MA: Harvard Education Press, pp.115–126.

Battilana, J. and Casicaro, T. (2013). The network secret of a great change agents. *Harvard Business Review*, July–August, 1–8.

Brown, C. (2014). *Evidence Informed Policy and Practice in Education: A Sociological Grounding*. London: Bloomsbury.

Brown, C. (2017). How to establish Research Learning Communities. *Professional Development Today*, 19(2), 30–55.

Brown, C., Daly, A. and Liou, Y.-H. (2016). Improving trust, improving schools: findings from a social network analysis of 43 primary schools in England. *Journal of Professional Capital and Community*, 1(1), 69–91.

Brown, C. and Flood, J. (2018). Lost in translation? Can the use of theories of action be effective in helping teachers develop and scale up research-informed practices? *Teaching and Teacher Education*, 72, May, 144–154.

Brown, C. and Zhang, D. (2016). How can school leaders establish evidence informed schools: an analysis of the effectiveness of potential school policy levers. *Educational Management and Leadership*, 45(3), 382–401.

Bryk, A., Sebring, P., Allensworth, E. and Luppescu, S. (2010). *Organizing Schools for Improvement: Lessons from Chicago*. Chicago, IL: University of Chicago Press.

Daly, A. (2010). Mapping the terrain: social network theory and educational change. In A. Daly (Ed.), *Social Network Theory and Educational Change*. Cambridge, MA: Harvard Education Press, pp. 1–16.

Daly, A. J. and Finnigan, K. S. (2010). A bridge between worlds: understanding network structure to understand change strategy. *Journal of Educational Change*, 11(2), 111–138.

Day, C. and Sammons, P. (2013). *Successful Leadership: A Review of the International Literature*. Reading: CfBT Education Trust.

Earley, P. (2013). *Exploring the School Leadership Landscape: Changing Demands, Changing Realities*. London: Bloomsbury.

Earl, L. M. and Katz, S. (2006). *Leading Schools in a Data-Rich World: Harnessing Data for School Improvement*. Thousand Oaks, CA: Corwin Press.

Earl, L. M. and Timperley, H. (2008). Understanding how evidence and learning conversations work. In L. M. Earl and H. Timperley (Eds.), *Professional Learning Conversations: Challenges in Using Evidence for Improvement*. Dordrecht: Springer, pp. 1–12.

Fernandez, C. (2002). Learning from Japanese approaches to professional development: The case of lesson study. *Journal of Teacher Education*, 3(5), 393–405.

Fielding, M., Bragg, S., Craig, J., Cunningham, I. A., Eraut, M., Gillinson, S., Horne, M., Robinson, C. and Thorp, J. (2005). Factors influencing the transfer of good practice. University of Sussex and Demos. Research Report RR615 Department for Education and Skills. Retrieved 6 January 2019 from: https://dera.ioe. ac.uk/21001/1/RR615.pdf.

Fullan, M. (2001). *The New Meaning of Educational Change*. 3rd ed. New York: Teachers College Press.

Godfrey, D., Seleznyov, S., Anders, J., Wollaston, N. and Barrera-Pedemonte, F. (2018). A developmental evaluation approach to lesson study: exploring the impact of lesson study in London schools. *Professional Development in Education*. DOI: 10.1080/19415257.2018.1474488.

Godfrey, D. (2017). What is the proposed role of research evidence in England's 'self-improving' school system? *Oxford Review of Education*, 43:4, 433–446.

Godfrey, D. (2016). Leadership of schools as research-led organisations in the English educational environment cultivating a research-engaged school culture. *Educational Management Administration & Leadership*, 44(2): 301–321.

Greany, T. and Higham, R. (2018). *Hierarchy, Markets and Networks – Analysing the 'Self-Improving School-Led System' Agenda in England and the Implications for Schools*. London: UCL IOE Press.

Hadfield, M., Kubiak, C. and O'Leary, D. (2005). *Network Building: A Review of the Formation Stage of Networks in the NLC Programme*. Nottingham: NCSL.

Hall, G. E. (2013). Evaluating change processes. *Journal of Educational Administration*, 51(3), 264–289.

Hall, G. E. and S. M. Hord (2006). *Implementing Change: Patterns, Principles, and Potholes.* Boston, MA: Allyn & Bacon

Hammersley-Fletcher, L. et al. (2015). Evidence-based teaching: advancing capability and capacity for enquiry in schools: interim report. NCTL.

Hargreaves, D. H. (2010). Creating a self-improving school system. Nottingham: National College.

Harris, A. and Jones, M. (2012). Connect to learn: learn to connect. *Professional Development Today*, 14(4), 13–19.

Katz, S. and Dack, L. A. (2013). *Intentional Interruption: Breaking Down Learning Barriers to Transform Professional Practice.* Thousand Oaks, CA: Corwin Press.

MacBeath, J. (2008). Leading learning in the self-evaluating school. *School Leadership and Management*, 28(4), 385–399.

MacBeath, J. et al. (2003). Self-evaluation: what's in it for schools? *Educational Research*, 45(2), 205–206.

Matthews, P. and Headon, M. (2015). *Multiple Gains: An Independent Evaluation of Challenge Partners' Peer Reviews of Schools.* London: IOE Press.

Mincu, M. (2013). Research and teacher education: the BERA-RSA inquiry: teacher quality and school improvement: what is the role of research? *Inquiry Paper*, 6.

Nelson, R., Ehren, M. and Godfrey, D. (2015). Literature review on internal evaluation. Retrieved 6 Jan 2019 from: http://schoolinspections.eu/wp-content/uploads/downloads/2015/09/Literature-review-internal-evaluation.pdf.

Ogawa, R. T. and Bossert, S. T. (1995) Leadership as an organizational quality. *Educational Administration Quarterly*, 31(2), 224–243.

Robinson, V. M. and Timperley, H. (2013). School improvement through theory engagement. In S. Kushner and M. Lei (Eds.), *A Developmental and Negotiated Approach to School Self-Evaluation.* Bingley: Emerald Group Publishing Limited, pp. 163–177.

Robinson, V. (2017). *Reduce Change to Increase Improvement.* Thousand Oaks, CA: Corwin.

Rose, J., Thomas, S., Zhang, L., Edwards, A., Augero, A. and Rooney, P. (2017). *Research Learning Communities: Evaluation Report and Executive Summary (December 2017).* Available at: https://educationendowmentfoundation.org.uk/public/files/Projects/EvaluationReports/ResearchLearningCommunities.pdf. Accessed 9 July 2018.

Saunders, W. M., Goldenberg, C. N. and Gallimore, R. (2009). Increasing achievement by focusing grade-level teams on improving classroom learning: a prospective, quasi-experimental study of Title I schools. *American Educational Research Journal*, 46(4), 1006–1033.

Simons, H. (2013). Enhancing the quality of education through school self-evaluation. In M. K. Lai and S. Kushner (Eds.), *A Developmental and Negotiated Approach to School Self-Evaluation. Advances in Program Evaluation Volume 14.* Bingley: Emerald Group Publishing, pp. 1–18.

Spillane, J., Healey, K. and Kim, C. (2010). Leading and managing instruction: formal and informal aspects of elementary school organization. In A. Daly (Ed.), *Social Network Theory and Educational Change.* Cambridge, MA: Harvard Education Press.

Stoll, L. and Brown, C. (2015). Middle leaders as catalysts for evidence-informed change. In C. Brown (Ed.), *Leading the Use of Research and Evidence in Schools.* London: Institute of Education Press, pp. 66–77.

Stoll, L., Bolam, R., McMahon, A., Wallace, M. and Thomas, S. (2006). Professional learning communities: A review of the literature. *Journal of Educational Change*, 7(4), 221–258.

Swaffield, S. and MacBeath, J. (2005). School self-evaluation and the role of a critical friend. *Cambridge Journal of Education*, 35(2), 239–252.

Tschannen-Moran, M. (2004). *Trust Matters: Leadership for Successful Schools*. San Francisco, CA: Jossey-Bass.

Timperley, H. and Robertson, J. (2011). Establishing platforms for leadership and learning. In J. Robertson and H. Timperley (Eds.), *Leadership and Learning*. London: SAGE Publications, pp. 3–12.

Vanhoof, J. and Van Petegem, P. (2011). Designing and evaluating the process of school self- evaluations. *Improving Schools*, 14(2), 200–212.

Vescio, V., Ross, D. and Adams, A. (2008). A review of research on the impact of professional learning communities on teaching practice and student learning. *Teaching and Teacher Education*, 24(1), 80–91.

# 7

# BROKERAGE FOR DATA USE IN SCHOOLS

## Potential, occurrence and facilitators

*Roos Van Gasse, Jan Vanhoof and Peter Van Petegem*

## Aims of the chapter

- Introducing the concept of 'brokerage' for building capacity for data use in schools.
- Describing and explaining current brokerage practices in primary and secondary schools.
- Identifying barriers and facilitators for data use in schools.

## Introduction

Worldwide, school leaders and teachers are expected to build policy and practice upon information rather than on intuition (OECD, 2013; Van Gasse et al., 2017). Such objective decision making has been proposed as a powerful way to improve schooling (Carlson, Borman and Robinson, 2011).

Decisions in schools can be informed by means of multiple sources of data, ranging from academic research results to various types of school-specific evidence. In this chapter, we will write about 'data'. *Data refers to everything that informs schools about core processes, as long as data are documented and their collection was goal oriented and systematic.* In this regard, *data use* starts from a common goal and is a systematic process to inform decisions and improve internal school processes (Schildkamp, Rekers-Mombargs and Harms, 2012). *As such, these definitions of 'data' and 'data use' are in line with conceptualisations of data-based decision making or evidence-informed practice* (Brown, Schildkamp and Hubers, 2017).

This chapter aims to introduce the concept of 'brokerage'. Central to the concept is the creation of data mobility to nourish a fit between data supplies and data needs. In this regard, *'brokerage' is a means to optimise the fit between the needs of data users (schools) and the supplies available in the wider ecosystem.* Knowledge brokering implies moving knowledge from one place or group of people to another and creating an environment that stimulates innovation (Canadian Health Services Research Foundation [CHSRF], 2003). Translated to schools, data brokerage is a way to ensure that school leaders and teachers get access to relevant data and, as such, support practical and policy related decision making. Therefore, *data brokers are people or organisations who facilitate data mobility in schools*. Data brokerage has the potential to cultivate human capital (e.g. practitioners' data use capabilities) and social capital (e.g. how the potential of teacher teams is used) in schools. As such, the concept can be a powerful way to understand how data use can be fostered.

## Problem statement

Literature suggests that successful data use depends strongly on the school's human and social capital to use data (Datnow and Hubbard, 2016; Van Gasse et al., 2016). However, research has not yet got to grips with how such human and social capital can be enhanced. The concept of brokerage is a way to address this lacuna as it addresses both the human and social capital dimensions of school data use. As such, this concept can be used to gain insight into how schools' capacity for data use can be increased by optimising the fit between needs within schools and supplies within the ecosystem.

Up to now, the concept of brokerage has gained little attention in the date use literature. Little is known about how data brokerage is manifested in schools. Given that limited support opportunities for data use are available in many educational systems, data brokers can be crucial for developing and improving the capacity for data and research use in schools.

Our main goal is to investigate the presence of data brokerage in schools and, more specifically, how data brokerage tasks are carried out. In order to support this in schools, additional insights are needed into facilitators of data brokerage. Therefore, our second goal addresses how data brokerage can be facilitated in schools. The aim of this study is to provide a rich description of data brokerage activities in schools and how these activities can be initiated and supported.

## Context of the study

The context of this study is Flanders, which is a specific context for the study of data use (activities). Compared to other countries, the Flemish government's perspective on data use is school improvement oriented. In Flanders there is an absence of accountability pressures on schools as standardised tests are not imposed on schools. This is in contrast to, for example, the Netherlands, where higher accountability pressures are perceived (Van Gasse, Vanhoof and De Vos, 2014). In Flanders, standards are defined at the end of primary education and at the end of the second and sixth grade of secondary education but schools are autonomous in how they achieve these standards (Penninckx, Vanhoof and Van Petegem, 2011). The responsibility for data use in Flanders lies with schools themselves. Schools need to define their own needs with regard to data use and apply the opportunities provided by the ecosystem to address those needs properly. This implies that the Flemish context is a powerful one to study data brokerage in. Given the great individual responsibility of schools in data use, brokerage activities are particularly needed to apply resources available within the ecosystem to support their data use maximally.

## Data brokerage

The potential impact of data use in schools strongly depends on its implementation by school leaders and teachers (Schildkamp, Poortman and Handelzalts, 2016). Generally, data brokerage has been described as a way to facilitate the use of data for practical and policy related decision making in schools (Dobbins et al., 2009). Data brokerage has the potential to build *human capital* for data use by creating a stimulating environment and adequately addressing resources available for data use in the wider ecosystem of schools. In addition, the concept implies building *social capital*; it is directed at creating data mobility by connecting data to people (Figure 7.1) (CHSRF, 2003).

From this point of view, data brokers are people or organisations that facilitate the creation of a data oriented environment and of data mobility. Data brokers connect data needs and data supplies and build bridges between data and potential data users. Therefore, the facilitating role of data brokers in data use can be found in collecting, sharing and using data (Sverrisson, 2001; van Kammen, de Savigny and Sewankambo et al., 2006). Data brokers are usually thought of as external people or organisations, for example, the government or a research institute. However, in theory, every individual within a school might take the role of data broker for him/herself or for others.

Data brokerage activities generally remain implicit or absent in schools (Vanhoof and Mahieu, 2013); brokerage activities are not systematically planned and data brokers are not purposefully appointed (CHSRF, 2003). Nevertheless, three core data brokerage activities can be distinguished: 1) collecting data and building knowledge, 2) connecting data supplies to data needs and 3) developing human capacity to use data (Sverrisson, 2001, van Kammen, de Savigny and Sewankambo, 2006).

**FIGURE 7.1** Data brokerage

## Collecting data and building knowledge

Collecting data and building knowledge is a two-in-one activity for data brokers, because merely collecting and communicating data does not automatically lead to data use within schools. A city, for instance, can take the initiative to collect data on neighbourhoods and subsequently process relevant aspects of that collection to the schools within its territory. In this case, it is not said that this data leads to data use within those schools. Next to collecting and managing data, building (new) knowledge upon this data is necessary with regard to policy and practice related decisions. However, most of the time school leaders' and teachers' data use gets stuck in the interpretation phase (Earl and Fullan, 2003; Vanhoof, 2007). Data brokers overcome interpretation problems by selecting suitable data for the users given the experience available in the group of users. In this context, activities, such as making available the necessary technological tools and expertise for knowledge building, can also be regarded as being part of the brokerage process.

## Connecting data supplies to data needs

An important step with regard to data use is connecting data supply to data needs. To prevent data getting stuck on the school leader's desk, it is necessary to develop strategies to ensure that data also reaches the appropriate other interested parties in the organisation (Hoy and Miskel, 2001). However, research shows strong differences between schools in terms of the extent to which they successfully connect data to the needs of the organisation. In some schools, data remain unused for the purposes of improvements to policy or practice. In other schools, information is currently not shared collectively, which means that data use remains the responsibility of individual school leaders or teachers (Van Petegem and Vanhoof, 2004; Verhaeghe et al., 2010; Weiss, 2001). Data brokers are crucial to overcome such problems since their focus is on making data available to people and on facilitating communication and data sharing among team members. In other words, the social capital for data use in the school is increased by data brokers. A knowledge broker therefore sets up processes of communication between the supply and demand sides of existing data by, *inter alia*, facilitating communication processes, making data accessible and exchanging knowledge. Activities for achieving these purposes range from: writing and sharing reports or booklets, working out websites, distributing newsletters, to the organisation of lectures, workshops and conferences. These activities can be carried out to reach targeted individuals, groups of people or a wide audience.

## Developing human capacity with regard to data use

The first important focus for the development of human capacity with regard to data use is stimulating a positive attitude towards data use and data brokerage among team members. Because school leaders' and teachers' data use largely depends on the extent to which this is perceived as valuable (Datnow and Hubbard, 2016; Vanhoof et al., 2014), data brokers aim at constantly demonstrating the contribution of data use for school improvement. Secondly, the development of human capacity with regard to data use comprises investment in team members' knowledge and skills through professional development and support initiatives. However, the impact of these initiatives increases if they are aligned to the specific school context and if the focus of these activities embodies a correct interpretation of the data as well as spelling out appropriate actions (Nevo, 1995; Schildkamp and Teddlie, 2008; Visscher, 2002).

## Method

With the aim of providing an in-depth description of data brokerage and exploring facilitators of data brokerage in schools, we used a qualitative research design including semi-structured interviews in six primary and six secondary Flemish schools (Guest, Bunce and Johnson, 2006; Morrow, 2005). Within each school, the school leader and a teacher were interviewed about their data use activities and data brokerage at the school to capture the specific school context and to triangulate perceptions of individual school leaders and teachers.

In order to answer the first research question (describing how data brokerage activities take place in schools), a mainly deductive coding process was followed using the theoretical framework as a starting point. General codes, such as 'data use' or 'data brokerage' were formulated and were specified through several sub-codes, such as 'collecting data and building knowledge' or 'connecting data supplies to data needs'. The analysis of the second research question, about facilitators of data brokerage in schools, was conducted more inductively, given its exploratory character, because of the limited indications in the literature.

A combination of an inductive and deductive approach was taken to deduce cross-case interview results (Miles and Huberman, 1994). Thereafter, we followed the principles of framework analysis (Maso and Smaling, 1998) and searched for general patterns of data brokerage in schools. Below, we present an overall view on how data brokerage is carried out in schools, and how these activities optimise the fit between needs in schools and supplies in their wider ecosystem.

## Findings

In this section, we describe the appearance of data brokerage activities in Flemish schools and how these activities are facilitated in the schools.

### Brokerage activities in Flemish schools

The results for data brokerage in Flemish schools are described following the three core activities of brokers: collecting data and building knowledge, connecting data supplies to data needs and developing human capacity with regard to data use.

## Collecting data and building knowledge

The interview data showed several initiatives with regard to collecting data and building knowledge. Sometimes, these initiatives are driven by stakeholders within the school. In other cases, external stakeholders take initiatives to collect information and build knowledge. Examples of brokerage activities within both categories can be found in Table 7.1.

Internal initiatives with regard to collecting data and building knowledge are primarily directed to improving the learning process of pupils, for example, school leaders and teachers collect data about new pupils' academic achievement by contacting the previous school. Additional information about pupils' social-emotional functioning is gathered through conversations with parents or by contacting the pupil counselling centre. Usually, particular teachers (for example personal tutors) are made responsible for collecting this information. Another type of information that is collected within schools is data about (improving) pupils' learning, for example, current data on pupils' learning outcomes or data on educative tools. Initiatives, with regard to collecting data and building knowledge within schools usually depend on individuals within the school rather than being the responsibility of the whole school team. These initiatives are perceived to be very time-consuming, and several school leaders' and teachers' report that data sources or data systems are poorly structured.

According to school leaders and teachers, a large amount of information is made available to them by external stakeholders. The Flemish government or the school's network provides, for example, data about policy decisions that are made. At a regional level, school communities provide financial data or information about the curriculum. These initiatives originate from external stakeholders with the aim of supporting the school's functioning. However, school leaders and teachers do not always perceive available information as supportive, and the combination of different data systems sometimes leads to overlapping messages from different stakeholders;

**TABLE 7.1** Examples of activities aimed at collecting data and building knowledge

| Internal activities | External activities |
| --- | --- |
| Use observation schemes | Schools providing results of former pupils |
| Fill in pupil dossiers | |
| Contact prior schools of pupils for additional information | School boards or network organisations sending newsletters |
| Analyse school inspection reports | |
| Talk to colleagues, parents and pupils about pupils' achievement | Policy documents provided by governmental bodies |
| | Visits of the school inspection |
| Invite experts (e.g. on certain subjects) | Research groups providing research feedback |

data about policy decisions reaching them several times through different external stakeholders, requiring school leaders to invest more time in selecting what is relevant. Furthermore, the plethora of information can lead to the attitude that 'if data is important to the school, it will be made available automatically'. This deters some school leaders from collecting data actively.

> I do not search for data myself, or very rarely, because so much data reaches us already
>
> *(School leader in primary education, primary school 2)*

## Connecting data supplies to data needs

By describing the connection of data supply to data needs in schools, we gain insight into how access to several types of information is facilitated within schools. From the interviews, we define four kinds of initiatives, situated on a continuum, ranging from making data unavailable to teachers, over initiatives that require no or little involvement, to initiatives that require a large amount of active involvement. In concrete, we distinguish:

- Deliberately or non-deliberately making data unavailable
- Making data available
- Exchanging data
- Knowledge creation.

The first finding is that, in some cases, data are – deliberately or non-deliberately – are not available to school leaders or teachers. While most of the time school leaders and teachers indicate that significant effort is invested in making information available within the school, some teachers report that not all available data, that might be relevant to them in some situations, reaches them. For example, teachers rarely have insight into data on results of pupils in higher education, into data of pupils whom they do not teach, or, in some cases, into data on their pupils' home background. According to several teachers, data are sometimes made unavailable for reasons known only to school leaders or due to the lack of information flow within the school. Restricted access to this information can lead to frustrations among teachers.

> It is very frustrating when you are at a class council and the school leader tells: 'We have data about this boy or girl and he or she is in a tricky situation.' If you tell A, just tell B. How tricky is this situation? Shed a light on it, so we can take it into account.
>
> *(Teacher in secondary education, secondary school 3)*

Initiatives to make information available are common in primary schools as well as in secondary schools, although the extent to which school leaders or teachers get involved in data use turns out to vary substantially at individual level. From the interviews, we learn that school leaders function as important data brokers by making data available through, *inter alia*, newsletters, emails to certain teachers or presentations at staff meetings. Another important way of making data accessible is through data systems. especially data about pupils' learning processes and outcomes or reports of staff meetings. Over time, such software systems have become integrated tools and important sources of support in schools.

> At school, we use a data system and most of the teachers know how to use it and put a lot of data in it.
>
> *(Teacher in secondary education, secondary school 5)*

Next, we distinguish exchanging data. Whereas making information available is often an individual process, exchanging data incorporates an interactive component. Data are exchanged through interaction. Therefore, the school leader or teacher who provides the information might add his or her own experiences or perception of it. From the interviews we learn that examples of exchanging data are of a formal as well as an informal nature. Some schools have elaborate formal structures for consultation. Some teachers, for example, indicate that pupil learning outcomes are exchanged and discussed at class councils or at meetings with pupil care teachers or specialists. Such meetings can serve to discuss pupils' progress and to formulate advice for future studies. Next to formal structures for consultation, teachers report the informal exchange of data. The staffroom, for example, is a place where informal exchanges about pupils' learning processes takes place.

> Usually, information on problematic situations is exchanged most quickly. To the responsible teacher in the first place. [. . .] And those things, depending on the seriousness of the situation, will eventually become the subject of for example a class council.
>
> *(Teacher in primary education, primary school 6)*

Lastly, we also find that initiatives with regard to knowledge creation take place within schools. Knowledge creation differs from exchanging data in the sense that interaction on data leads to new knowledge. New knowledge can take many forms, such as knowledge about school quality or school improvement or detecting (new) data needs. A remarkable finding is that, mainly school leaders and secondary school teachers, report knowledge creation. Knowledge creation may be established in work teams or at staff meetings by, for example, discussing pupils' learning outcomes or formulating conclusions on the basis of an external quality control report. In the following example, a teacher in primary education illustrates how the whole school team gets involved in thinking about improvement strategies for reading comprehension in the school. According to her, the blackboard she talks about stimulates discussions among teachers and mutual knowledge creation on strategies to cope with the weak reading results of pupils.

We put the staff meeting's blackboard in the staff room so it would be further completed. This way, those ideas keep living and the nice thing is that the more people are involved with this information, the more visions there are. And that is what we want to utilise.

*(Teacher in primary education, primary school 5)*

Knowledge creation also occurs at the cross-school level. Several school leaders indicate, for instance, that they had data-based discussions with school leaders from other districts and that such discussions do lead to the creation of new knowledge. More specifically, school leaders share experiences on strategies that (had not) worked in the past to cope with particular problems. As such, they mutually create knowledge on appropriate strategies for the educational problems they face. Also, at the teacher level, these cross-school interactions are reported.

## Developing human capacity with regard to data use

The last activity of data brokers is to develop human capacity to use data. This includes developing data use knowledge and skills and establishing a school culture that facilitates data use.

The first task of school leaders is to sensitise school staff to data use. This can be achieved by communicating the reasons for using data (e.g. creating an objective stance) and through modelling how they use data (e.g. explaining how certain information guided a decision). School leaders and teachers suggest that they want to establish an attitude towards data use that is sufficiently critical. Several interviewees noted the enthusiasm with which younger teachers talk about information on projects and new teaching methods. However, they were also concerned that these same teachers took uncritical interpretations of this information without fully considering the consequences of the new practices. Interviewees thus suggested the importance of critical friendship that questioned the potential improvements of these changes. School leaders also need to engender a positive attitude towards data use. This is not easy; one secondary school leader we interviewed talked about his personal disappointment when he noticed his teacher team was not really interested in listening to the researcher he had invited to explain the school's PISA results. Other evidence for modelling that we find in the interviews includes school leaders who communicate their data-based decision-making process around the use of new digital devices in class (e.g. iPad). For example, by discussing research that points at positive effects of the iPad on pupil learning.

I was surprised by some teachers' attitudes. That is because I always try to underpin the things I am saying, for example with scientific studies.

*(School leader in primary education, primary school 3)*

Another initiative with regard to developing human capacity is to delegate responsibilities among the school team. We found that, in about half of the schools we visited, data use is the responsibility of individuals. In most cases, those individuals are important brokers within the school, such as the school leader or teachers particularly responsible for pupil care. Within the other half of the schools we visited, certain responsibilities with regard to data use are delegated to individuals or work teams. In this way, a high density of data use is created within the school. School leaders and teachers indicate that these (formal) divisions of labour are a way to avail oneself of strengths within the school team.

In terms of making the school team more professional and skilled in the use of data, programmes, courses or coaching are usually not available in schools. Few opportunities, with the purpose of making the school team more literate, are reportedly taken up by a minority of individuals who follow formal training;. one school leader, for instance, took a course in 'data processing' with an external body. Overall, school leaders and teachers firmly indicate that learning how to use data comes with the experience of being a practitioner, with trial and error.

## How data brokerage is currently facilitated

Next to investigating brokerage activities in Flemish schools, our aim was to gain insight into how it can be facilitated in schools. We found evidence of two major conditions under which brokerage flourishes: the presence of structural support and the existence of a data use-oriented culture within schools.

## Structural support for data brokerage

According to Flemish school leaders and teachers, there is no such thing as pre-service training with regard to data use. Therefore, practitioners are mostly left to fend for themselves when it comes to learning how to use information properly. Brokerage can be a way to overcome this problem since it can build human and social capital for data use within the school. From the interviews we found several structural supports for brokerage in schools, such as scheduling time for brokerage activities and dedicating specific brokerage duties to individuals.

School leaders and teachers indicate that a lack of time is a problem; and that data use and data brokerage are not the core business within schools. However, school leaders and teachers indicate that brokerage can be facilitated by structuring it into the daily schedule of schools. This is a way to facilitate the connection of data supplies to data needs as well as to build supportive relationships among the team. Often, structuring brokerage into the daily schedule of the school was done for practical reasons and not with the aim of facilitating data brokerage. For example, a school leader mentioned that pupil care teachers had a 'free' Monday morning in their schedule so that they could discuss certain pupils. Other examples include structuring time for team meetings or delegating brokerage responsibilities to certain teachers, such as coaching or mentoring. A school leader in primary education, for example, reports that she divides teachers into work teams who are responsible for tackling certain problems within the school, such as the curriculum for world studies. She provides free Monday mornings in the schedule of teachers in this work group so that this responsibility is not experienced as an 'extra job'. While these work teams are not designed for brokerage as such, the school leader states that scheduling time for work teams might lead to a more thorough investigation of the curriculum on the basis of data. Therefore, the team setting provides opportunities to build human and social capital for data use.

An additional problem with regard to data use in schools is the lack of knowledge and skills to handle it. Therefore, school leaders and teachers search for external support. External brokers include, for example, educational counselling services or school groups. These are consulted to inform school leaders and teachers on how to select, interpret or analyse different types of information needed to make improvements within the school. From the interviews we find that the consultation of these external data brokers is demand-driven rather than routinely used.

## A data use-oriented culture: informal relationships and common goal setting

According to school leaders and teachers, it is vital for data brokerage that practitioners are able to broach certain problems they experience with regard to data use. This requires relevant school leaders and teachers be approachable. In addition, the presence of a lot of informal consultation at school results in data use 'living' at school, for example through the actions of teachers who discuss pupils' learning or ideas for tackling certain problems in the staff room.

> A lot lives in the hallways. How is this pupil doing? Do we need to think of something extra? Would it be good to take him/her out of class for an hour? It is always about the pupils.
>
> *(School leader in secondary education, secondary school 3)*

We find that participation in goal setting is an important characteristic for brokerage. Most of the school leaders and teachers frame the importance of goals and decisions that are supported by the school team. A pupil care teacher states that she and the school leader once had the idea of investigating curriculum gaps on the basis of standardised tests. Since teachers did not participate in this goal setting, there was no support for this goal among teachers. Therefore, no potential data brokers were available within the school team and it became impossible to set up this investigation. Thus, according to school leaders and teachers, it is important to let (certain members of the) school team participate in goal setting and decisions with regard to data use. In doing so, several team members can take up a role as data broker and share the lead with regard to the objectives for any proposed data use.

On the basis of the audit report, we chose in a co-operative team meeting to work on comprehensive reading first and afterwards on mathematics. It is really important that team members are involved in these decisions. Otherwise, such decisions will never be supported.

*(Teacher in primary education, primary school 5)*

## Discussion, limitations and future research

Whether and how data are used in schools largely depends on the alignment between supplies in data use (e.g. data, know-how or support) and the needs in schools (e.g. data, skills or support). Brokerage is vital to optimise this alignment. Moreover, activities such as collecting data and building knowledge, connecting data supplies to data needs and developing human capacity are essential to adequately use available resources for data use in the wider ecosystem of schools.

In the interviews, brokerage activities such as 'collecting data and building knowledge', 'connecting data supplies to data needs' and 'developing human capacity for data use' were empirically confirmed (Sverrisson, 2001, van Kammen, de Savigny and Sewankambo, 2006). For example, this study showed that collecting data and building knowledge can be undertaken both by internal and external data brokers. However, because a lot of information is made available by external stakeholders, the teachers and principals in our research context do not tend to collect it themselves. As a result, collecting data and building knowledge does not only get stuck in the interpretation phase (Earl and Fullan, 2003), but also in the data collection phase. In most cases, data are made available by data brokers. However, this study confirms that data supplies are seldom connected to data demands (Van Petegem and Vanhoof, 2004; Verhaeghe et al., 2010; Weiss, 2001). In some cases, data are exchanged within the school team, but processes of active knowledge creation are still scarce. Further, the results cautiously indicate that, so far, little is undertaken in schools to develop human capacity for data use. The few examples we found concerned sensitising team members about the use of data, delegating data use responsibilities to team members or helping them to become more professional.

This study shows that, although resources for data use are available in the Flemish ecosystem, these supplies are often not getting aligned to the needs of schools. Possible explanations can be found both in the schools and in the ecosystem itself. A major explanation for the limitations of brokerage activities may lie in the fact that Flemish schools in themselves cannot be considered experienced data users (Verhaeghe et al., 2010; Vanhoof et al., 2014). Particularly not when we compare them to, for example, Dutch schools (Van Gasse, Vanhoof and De Vos, 2014). This lack of experience in Flemish schools implies that the demands in data use activities may not be clear to data users themselves. It is quite likely that the school leaders and teachers interviewed in this study actually do not have a clear vision of where they are heading in terms of data use and what is needed to achieve their data use related goals. Such lack of systematic data use or data use strategies resulted in absence of searching for information, know-how or support in data use. In addition to that, prior research in Flanders has shown that data use is not considered a priority in schools nor a joint responsibility (OECD, 2013; Van Gasse et al., 2017). As such, the absence of strategies and brokerage activities to systematically improve these processes is not surprising. Nevertheless, causes for limited brokerage in Flemish schools can also be partly attributed to the Flemish ecosystem. Compared to, for example, the Netherlands, the Flemish government is less explicit in its expectations towards schools with regard to data use (Van Gasse, Vanhoof and De Vos, 2014). Therefore, clearer expectations may be needed at policy level about how schools should use data to achieve more objective decision making and school improvement.

Next to limited brokerage activities, we found that structural support for data use enhances brokerage within schools. Embedding team work into the daily schedule of teachers creates a stimulating context for brokerage activities and is a way to increase team members' data use and brokerage skills. Embedding time for data use in teachers' daily practice is essential to emphasise the importance of evidence-informed practice and to create a shift in teachers' attitude from the use of data as an additional task to its use in educational improvement.

This study also indicated that a data use-oriented school culture facilitates brokerage. Informal consultation and team members' participation in goal setting are vital to create involvement within the school team, which, in turn stimulates practitioners to take on the role of a broker. However, such a cultural shift is not easy to accomplish. It implies a shift from an individual stance of Flemish teachers towards a culture of mutually shared responsibilities. Therefore, an important facilitator for such a data use-oriented school culture is the formulation of school-wide goals and the formulation of strategies and responsibilities to achieve these goals.

Further, research can improve our understanding of data brokerage in schools. Mixed methods research is advisable; in-depth qualitative data can further delineate and refine the concept and quantitative data can further test these emergent concepts and add breadth. Brokerage is a concept which has been looked at repeatedly from a methodological point of view in social network theory, in which a broker is seen as the connection between several people (Borgatti, Everett and Johnson, 2013). Data use literature would benefit from linking the interpretation of data brokerage as a theoretical concept to brokerage from a methodological point of view.

## Conclusions

This research shows that more structural dispositions will be needed to make data brokerage common sense in schools. As such, schools will become better prepared to define their needs in data use, and to allocate and apply the resources needed to address these within the wider ecosystem. The value of the brokerage concept for schools to cope with their great autonomy implies that incorporating the brokerage idea in future research can be beneficial for further knowledge on how human and social capital in schools can be affected.

## Implications for the research-informed ecosystem

- Data brokers should have job descriptions and working tools.
- Schools should appoint a data broker (or a data coach) to coordinate and support data use activities.
- Data brokers need to engage in professionalising activities.
- Brokerage activities should be integrated into the professional development of future principals and teachers.
- External consultants should be appointed to support and optimise data use activities.

## References

Borgatti, S. P., Everett, M. G. and Johnson, J. C. (2013). *Analyzing Social Networks*. Los Angeles: Sage.

Brown, C., Schildkamp, K. and Hubers, M. D. (2017). Combining the best of two worlds: a conceptual proposal for evidence-informed school improvement. *Educational research*, 59(2), 154–172. DOI: 10.1080/00131881.2017.1304327.

Carlson, D., Borman, G. D. and Robinson, M. (2011). A multistate district-level cluster randomized trial of the impact of data-driven reform on reading and mathematics achievement. *Educational Evaluation and Policy Analysis*, 33(3), 378–398. DOI:10.3102/0162373711412765.

CHSRF. (2003). *The Theory and Practice of Knowledge Brokering in Canada's Health System*. Canadian Health Services Research Foundation, Ottawa.

Datnow, A. and Hubbard, L. (2016). Teacher capacity for and beliefs about data-driven decision making: a literature review of international research. *Journal of Educational Change*, 17(1), 7–28.

Dobbins, M., Robeson, P., Ciliska, D., Hanna, S., Cameron, R., O'Mara, L., DeCorby, K. and Mercer, S. (2009). A description of a knowledge broker role implemented as part of a randomized controlled trial evaluating three knowledge translation strategies. *Implementation Science*, 4(23).

Earl, L. and Fullan, M. (2003). Using data in leadership for learning. *Cambridge Journal of Education*, 33(3), 383–394.

Guest, G., Bunce, A. and Johnson, L. (2006). How many interviews are enough? An experiment with data saturation and variability. *Field Methods*, 18(1), 59–82.

Hoy, W. and Miskel, C. (2001). *Educational Administration: Theory, Research and Practice*. Boston: McGraw-Hill.

Maso, I. and Smaling, A. (1998). *Kwalitatief onderzoek: Praktijk en theorie [Qualitative Research: Practice and Theory]*. Amsterdam: Boom.

Miles, M. and Huberman, M. (1994). *Qualitative Data Analysis*. London: Sage.

Morrow, S. L. (2005). Quality and trustworthiness in qualitative research in counseling psychology. *Journal of Counseling Psychology*, 52(2), 250–260.

Nevo, D. (1995). *School-Based Evaluation: A Dialogue for School Improvement*. Oxford: Pergamon Press.

OECD. (2013). *Synergies for Better Learning. An International Perspective on Evaluation and Assessment*. Paris: OECD Publishing.

Penninckx, M., Vanhoof, J. and Van Petegem, P. (2011). *Evaluatie in het Vlaamse onderwijs. Beleid en praktijk van leerling tot overheid [Evaluation in Flemish education: Policy and Practice from Student to Government]*. Antwerpen-Apeldoorn: Garant.

Schildkamp, K., Poortman, C. L. and Handelzalts, A. (2016). Data teams for school improvement. *School Effectiveness and School Improvement*, 27(2), 228–254. DOI: 10.1080/09243453.2015.1056192.

Schildkamp, K., Rekers-Mombarg, L. T. M. and Harms, T. J. (2012). Student group differences in examination results and utilization for policy and school development. *School Effectiveness and School Improvement*, 23(2), 229–255.

Schildkamp, K. and Teddlie, C. (2008). School performance feedback systems in the USA and in the Netherlands: A comparison. *Educational Research & Evaluation*, 14(3), 255–282.

Sverrisson, A. (2001). Translation networks, knowledge brokers and novelty construction: pragmatic environmentalism in Sweden. *Acta Sociologica*, 44, 313–327.

Vanhoof, J. (2007). *Zelfevaluatie binnenstebuiten. Onderzoek naar zelfevaluatie in scholen [Self-Evaluation Inside-Out. Research on School Self-Evaluation]*. Mechelen: Wolters Plantyn.

Vanhoof, J. and Mahieu, P. (2013). Local knowledge brokerage for data-driven policy and practice in education. *Policy Futures in Education*, 11(2), 185–199.

Vanhoof, J., Vanlommel, K., Thijs, S. and Vanderlocht, H. (2014). Data use by Flemish school principals: impact of attitude, self-efficacy and external expectations. *Educational Studies*, 40(1), 1–15.

Van Gasse, R., Vanhoof, J. and de Vos, W. (2014). Informatiegebruik in verantwoordingsgerichte en schoolontwikkelingsgerichte onderwijssystemen: een Nederlands-Vlaams perspectief [Data use in accountability and school improvement systems: a Dutch-Flemish perspective]. *Pedagogiek*, 34(2), 84–106.

Van Gasse, R., Vanlommel, K., Vanhoof, J. and Van Petegem, P. (2016). Teacher collaboration on the use of pupil learning outcome data: a rich environment for professional learning? *Teaching and Teacher Education*, 60, 387–397.

Van Gasse, R., Vanlommel, K., Vanhoof, J. and Van Petegem, P. (2017). Individual, co-operative and collaborative data use: a conceptual and empirical exploration. *British Educational Research Journal*, 43, 608–626. DOI:10.1002/berj.3277.

van Kammen, J., de Savigny, D. and Sewankambo, N. (2006). Using knowledge brokering to promote evidence-based policy-making: the need for support structures. *Bulletin of the World Health Organization*, 84, 608–612.

Van Petegem, P. and Vanhoof, J. (2004). Feedback over schoolprestatie-indicatoren als strategisch instrument voor schoolontwikkeling [Feedback on achievement indicators as strategic instrument for school improvement]. *Pedagogische Studiën*, 81, 338–353.

Verhaeghe, G., Vanhoof, J., Valcke, M. and Van Petegem, P. (2010). Using school performance feedback: perceptions of primary school principals. *School Effectiveness and School Improvement*, 21(2), 167–188.

Visscher, A. (2002). School performance feedback systems. In A. J. Visscher and R. Coe (Eds.), *School Improvement Through Performance Feedback*. Lisse: Swets & Zeitlinger, pp. 41–71.

Weiss, C. H. (2001). *What Kind of Evidence in Evidence-Based Policy?* Paper presented at the Third International, Inter-Disciplinary Evidence-Based Policies and Indicator Systems Conference, Durham, UK.

# 8

# RESEARCH-INFORMED INITIAL TEACHER EDUCATION

*Tim Cain*

## Aims of the chapter

- To outline the problems that result from student teachers' prior experience of teaching.
- To review some approaches to these problems.
- To consider different conceptions of research-informed ITE.
- To explain the benefits of research-informed reflection.
- To examine some examples of research-informed reflection.

## Introduction: the peculiar problem of Initial Teacher Education

As part of a larger drive to refashion state education as a 'self-improving school system' (Hargreaves, 2010) schools in England are being required to take a leading role in Initial Teacher Education (ITE). This involves ITE being more tightly embedded within the ecosystem of schooling (Godfrey, 2016; Godfrey and Brown, 2018) and the role of universities, which have provided much of the intellectual underpinning for ITE, is consequently reduced. Research-informed ITE has potential to replace this intellectual underpinning but there are at least two competing explanations as to how this might occur. This chapter explores these explanations and uses case study research to argue that one is preferable to the other.

School teaching is an odd profession for the newcomer. Such is the nature of the educational ecosystem that, by the time student teachers start their courses of Initial Teacher Education, they have spent approximately 15,000 hours (Rutter, 1979) in classrooms, experiencing teaching vicariously at close quarters, as students. What is almost unimaginable in other professions – law students with 15,000 hours in courtrooms, say, or dental students with 15,000 hours observing dentistry – is common for student teachers. Furthermore, many student teachers have taught on a casual basis, teaching family members, on work experience, volunteering as youth leaders and so on. So nobody starts a teaching course as a complete beginner; all start with very considerable experience of being taught and many start with some experience of teaching.

The consequences of this 'peculiar problem' are various. One is that some student teachers start their courses already knowing how to teach. In my 25 years involvement with teacher education a small but not insignificant proportion of student teachers (at a guess, 5–10 per cent of any cohort) have made such good use of their personal experiences that they are capable teachers almost from the start of their course. That is, they can convert their subject knowledge into pedagogical content knowledge (Shulman, 1987), they communicate this clearly and at an appropriate level for their pupils, they understand children and form mutually respectful relationships with them, they use questioning and other means to discover what children have, and have not, learned. In some instances they can plan coherent and challenging sequences of lessons. Such students might develop their teaching expertise through informed reflection on practice, but they cannot benefit from being given information about how to teach; they know this already.

At the other extreme there are student teachers who have not learnt how to teach from their personal experience, or perhaps cannot transfer learning from personal experience into new situations. Such students use inappropriate teaching methods, and continue to use them even when they know that they are ineffective. This phenomenon can also be explained with reference to their 15,000 hours of personal experience:

> the role models that novice teachers observed while they were children continue to hold tremendous sway. Often, despite their intentions to do otherwise, new teachers teach as they were taught. The power of their 'apprenticeship of observation,' and of the conventional images of teaching that derive from childhood experiences, makes it very difficult to alter teaching practices and explains in part why teaching has remained so constant over so many decades of reform efforts.
>
> *(Kennedy, 1991, p. 15)*

Whilst some student teachers start their courses already knowing how to teach, and others start resistant to change; the majority are neither wholly competent nor completely resistant, because their 'apprenticeship of observation' has enabled them to be good at some aspects of teaching but not others.

This 'peculiar problem' creates a challenge for Initial Teacher Education (ITE): how can ITE be designed for disparate groups of students, some of whom already possess the essential skills of classroom teaching because they have learned from personal experience, and some of whom are resistant to change for the same reason? The following section considers some of the answers to come out of ITE during the past 100 years or so, in order to provide a background for a discussion of research-informed ITE.

## Some trends in Initial Teacher Education

At the beginning of the 20th century, certainly in the UK, it was common for teachers to learn by observing and assisting a salaried teacher, a practice known as 'Sitting with Nellie' (Zeichner, 1986). Doubtless this worked for some, and we can imagine the occasional students outstripping the teachers they observed. But as society became more sophisticated, work became more demanding, and governments assumed greater responsibility for educating all their population to meet these rising needs, the apprenticeship system was found wanting; presumably it was unable to ensure sufficient teachers with the range of skills and understanding needed to educate all pupils to a sufficiently high standard. So gradually, Higher Education was given a greater role in ITE.

At the beginning, Higher Education Institutions (HEIs) tackled the 'peculiar problem' of ITE by ignoring it; that is, they provided a knowledge base about education which was almost entirely disconnected from the 'practicum'. This knowledge base consisted largely of educational 'theory', drawing on the 'foundation disciplines' of history, philosophy, psychology and sociology (Carr and Kemmis, 1986; Whitty and Furlong, 2017). There was an assumption that, if student teachers could think about the nature and purposes of *education* from a variety of perspectives, their thinking about *classroom teaching* would be more sophisticated and hence, their practice would improve. This approach has been called the 'theory into practice' approach to ITE (Korthagen, Loughran and Russell, 2006). However, whilst it might have produced a more intelligent teaching force (ultimately leading, in many countries, to all teachers having a first degree) the educational theory that was taught was not thought to match the practical demands of teaching. Student teachers and schools complained that the theory seemed useless and irrelevant (Elliott, 1991), partly because, at least in English speaking academic communities if not elsewhere:

> the development of knowledge about education and 'educational phenomena' began to have a dynamism of its own which could sustain momentum almost independently of the development of practice.
>
> *(Carr and Kemmis, 1986, p. 11)*

In the face of mounting criticism, HEIs turned to work around 'the reflective practitioner', often citing Schön's (1983) book of that name. Schön's writing, informed by empirical work, showed that practical learning in various professions occurs through a process of reflecting on experience. At a basic level this might be a matter of trial and error; at a more advanced level it consists of careful thinking about aims and purposes, and the result of practical attempts to achieve these. The 'reflective' approach to ITE did not begin with Schön (1983; 1987); Dewey (1933) had made very similar claims and HEIs were using some versions of the reflective approach before *The Reflective Practitioner* was published. But Schön (1983; 1987) gave teacher educators a useful slogan and some empirical support. It was successful to the point that, in 1991, the Modes of Teacher Education (MOTE) research project found that three-quarters of Teacher Education courses in England were based on the 'reflective practitioner' approach (Miles et al., 1993).

The 'reflective' approach addressed the 'peculiar problem' of ITE by placing practical teaching at its centre. It suggested that all student teachers could improve their practice by thinking deeply about it. However, it was not a single approach: Zeichner and Liston (1996) found five 'traditions' of reflection, each defined by the general orientation of its content. In one tradition, reflection was oriented towards the subject matter being taught, in another, it was about putting educational theory into practice; another tradition emphasised the development of the learners, whilst another focused on issues of social justice and democracy. There was also a 'generic' tradition, which saw reflection as a general good, regardless of its focus.

At about the same time, an Action Research movement took reflection to another level in teacher education, both ITE and in-service education. In the UK this was stimulated by the work including Stenhouse and Rudduck (1985); Elliott (1991); Whitehead and McNiff (2006) and Somekh (2006); there were parallel movements across the English-speaking world. Both Action Research and the 'reflective' approach were conceptualised in terms of recurring cycles of planning, acting, observing and reflecting, but Action Research had a stronger focus on rigour and establishing the trustworthiness (or credibility) of its findings. Action Research was usually seen as including the systematic collection and analysis of data, and the involvement of critical friends or validation groups which serve to establish improvement as a collective, social endeavour, and also guard against idiosyncratic or overly subjective interpretations of data.

## Research-informed practice

The above sketch is extremely incomplete; it ignores major trends in teacher education, including the development of school–university partnerships, the roles of mentors and the role of teacher education in school reform. Nevertheless, it provides a background for understanding research-informed practice in ITE.

On the one hand, research-informed ITE can be conceptualised as a new form of the 'theory into practice' approach. Rather than requiring ITE to teach theory (e.g. about social class, motivation or pragmatism), as occurred previously, research-informed ITE might be expected to teach the findings of empirical studies (chiefly RCTs) of classroom teaching. Student teachers might be taught to access, read and evaluate research findings, and then to act on these findings so that they used only tried-and-tested teaching methods. This appears to be the conceptualisation inherent in some quarters (Godfrey, 2017). For example, the English national annual survey of newly qualified teachers requires these teachers to evaluate how well their ITE has prepared them 'to access educational research . . . to assess the robustness of educational research [and] . . . to understand and apply the findings from educational research' (Gov.uk, 2014). Similarly, the government-sponsored 'Carter Review' of ITE (Carter, 2015) states that new teachers should understand, 'how to access, interpret and use research to inform classroom practice' (p. 8). This conceptualisation sees classroom teaching as a scientific endeavour, rather like medicine (e.g. Hargreaves, 1996; Goldacre, 2013), and ITE as a training in research-endorsed teaching techniques. It is a 'theory into practice' approach, with the difference that the 'soft' educational theory of the previous theory into practice approach is supplanted by 'hard' scientific evidence, and the liberal, person-centred values with which teaching has traditionally been associated with, are replaced by the values of 'what works' (Cain, 2016).

On the other hand, research-informed ITE can be conceptualised as a new approach to reflection, not captured in Zeichner and Liston (1996). In this conceptualisation, student teachers select the research that is most appropriate and useful for their own purposes, and interpret and use this along with their own, situated knowledge (e.g. Hammersley, 2002), guided by the professional values that are acquired through processes of socialisation (e.g. Kelchtermans and Ballet, 2002). Such a conceptualisation sees research as influencing teachers' thinking and thus influencing practice indirectly, rather than the direct influence implied by the research–into–practice approach, described above.

Whilst there might be a place in ITE for the theory into practice version, the 'research informs reflection' approach is, I believe, more congruent with the nature of teaching and ITE, including its 'peculiar problem'. Recent empirical studies have shown that experienced and capable teachers, including middle managers, can learn about teaching through reading and discussing research, and by reviewing their own practice in the light of the research. Specifically, the research texts give teachers material to think about including focuses for enquiring into their own practice, and challenges to their thinking and practice. Research publications can provide teachers with new educational concepts, and can help them to develop their existing concepts. Research texts can also suggest ideas for action. Importantly, published research can influence how teachers think: it can encourage them to be more willing to experiment, more critical; it can develop their understanding of evidence and also their ethical awareness. In short, engagement with research can encourage teachers to think like researchers (Cain, 2015a). Such influence comes not only from research findings but also the whole papers, including literature reviews and discussions of findings (Cain, 2015b). These studies provide good evidence that it is possible for experienced and capable teachers to improve their teaching through reading and discussing research, and relating their own practice to this research in individual and social reflections. This suggests that student teachers who have acquired the basic skills of classroom teaching before they start the course, can nevertheless benefit from a 'research informs reflection' approach to ITE.

## Some cases of research-informed ITE

The following section describes two cases of student teachers learning through a 'research informs reflection' approach to ITE. They were included within an article that was originally published in 2007, entitled, 'Literature-informed, one-turn action research' (Cain et al., 2007). They are cases of Master's level Action Research assignments by music school teachers on a one-year, postgraduate ITE course in secondary school education.

During their first school placement (35 days, before Christmas) the student teachers were required to collect data, in the form of audio or video recordings, from a minimum of three lessons that they taught, obtaining the necessary permissions for so doing. They were advised also to collect other forms of data including lesson evaluations, written reports from mentors and pupils' work. Over the Christmas break they studied the data and came to a general idea as to a pedagogical focus they wished to improve.

They investigated the literature around their chosen focus and, using this literature, developed an action plan for improving their practice in relation to this. Before starting their second school placement (80 days, either side of Easter) they submitted the first part of their report, including a review of the relevant literature, an analysis of data arising from their first placement and an action plan. This was marked and returned to them, noting any aspects that needed strengthening. During their second placement they investigated ways in which their practice in this area developed, again drawing on an analysis of their data, and submitted a final report at the end of their course.

This was only one of the means for developing and assessing reflective teaching on the course; others included lesson evaluations, weekly target-setting, tutorials and weekly meetings with mentors; but because the reports were of 6,000 words, it was the most substantial. The following summaries were chosen because they are good assignments (graded 'A' or 'B') and, since both trainees came to the course directly from a first degree, neither had extraordinary prior experience, such as a Master's degree, which might have made the achievement of high grades more likely.

### Case 1: 'Behaviour management in the classroom' by Joanna Mattock

Mattock's assignment dealt with behaviour management, an area that many trainees find difficult. Her literature review explored the work of Fontana (1985, 1995), Rogers (1998), Cowley (2003) and Jacques and Ellis (2002). She found a great deal of practical advice which was firmly supported with theoretical underpinnings, often from psychology. From Rogers (1998) she understood the functions of behaviour management in terms of socialising individuals, providing for their moral development, their personal maturation and in providing emotional security. From Cowley (2003) she learned the importance of setting clear expectations, appearing authoritative, applying sanctions in a fair and graduated way, of reacting from the head rather than becoming emotionally involved and avoiding confrontation.

Occasionally, she met advice which appeared conflicting. She quoted Philpott (2001):

> Many of the causes of misbehaviour can be pre-empted if the music lesson is well planned, well prepared with, for example, stimulating resources, inter-esting, suitably differentiated [and] musical.
>
> *(p. 70)*

But stated that, whilst she found this 'a very common opinion' it was, 'not one I was entirely convinced about'. She preferred Blum's (1998) approach:

> [Disregard] the current 'inspector speak' which says that pupils behave badly when the quality of teaching is insufficiently stimulating. They often behave badly when lessons are brilliantly planned because they stop the teacher from starting properly.
>
> *(p. 2)*

She video recorded herself teaching and used the recordings to analyse three of the lessons on her first placement. The use of video allowed her to observe herself closely:

> There are moments when I am hunched over, sometimes with my arms folded, which creates a very negative, insecure impression . . . there are occa-sions when I fidget and fiddle for example with a pen lid . . . I think I speak loudly and animatedly which excites the class . . . when issuing instructions I come across as very weak, asking them to do something, rather than telling them in a polite, assertive manner.

Looking at the lessons as a whole, she found:

> The first few minutes were always the worst; uncontrolled and chaotic. However, for the majority of my lessons, once the register had been taken and I actually started to teach, the class settled down, listened and worked well . . . I therefore had to look at the beginnings of my lessons and decide where the problems lay.

At the beginning of her lessons she sometimes felt that she was inconsistent, responding to some pupils' poor behaviour by admonishing them verbally and to similar behaviour in other pupils by sending them out of the room. She found that she became emotionally involved in situations, sometimes becoming defensive and occasionally confrontational:

> Throughout the Y8 lesson I was confrontational; sometimes rude . . . I almost had a full-blown fight with 'Jack' . . . the aggressive manner in which I dealt with the situation led to 'Simon' getting wound up . . . My frustration was demonstrated when I shouted, ordering them to 'shut up'. This is not only rude but exacerbates the situation.

Through applying her reading of the literature to her interpretation of classroom events she began to understand the need some pupils have for attention and said, 'It was important for me to make sure that I did not reinforce negative behaviour through giving students attention when they misbehave'. At the same time, she recognised a need to help the students to develop positive self-images.

Her action plan addressed these problems and included the following points:

- Decide on personal expectations for a class
- Develop a personal plan for responding to misbehaviour
- Stay calm, positive, polite and non-confrontational
- Use non-verbal signals (body language, facial expressions), wait for silence.

As her second placement began she was concerned to discover as much as possible about her students by reading their profiles and talking to their teachers. Her greater knowledge of the students helped both with individuals and with the whole class. She discovered, for instance, that a particular pupil was liable to lose his temper if provoked. When he misbehaved she ignored him but later, when the class was busy working, she spoke to him on his own, and was able to discuss his behaviour without attracting an audience. Her knowledge of individual pupils also enabled her to change the way in which they were grouped, specifically to separate the most difficult students. She says, 'This did not solve all the problems but it made them easier to handle'.

Because most of the poor behaviour happened at the start of her lessons she developed starter activities to focus the class. These were not always whole-class activities. For instance, because a particular class arrived from PE lessons, in twos and threes, she wrote down a simple activity on the board that they could do at their own pace, and was better able to engage students individually.

Through studying her transcriptions of lessons before and after the plan, Mattock analysed her improvements. These were partly a matter of making expectations clear:

> By getting the class to practice, I lay down the rules in a fun and interesting way. By encouraging them to do it better, they felt enthused and wanted to do the best they could . . . by telling them that they were the best class I had heard yet, they felt encouraged.

It was partly to do with self-presentation:

My general body language had improved considerably. I stood up straight, with my arms by my side, keeping my body relaxed and open. I moved freely around the classroom when explaining a point instead of standing behind the desk.

And partly to do with language. In an early lesson she was assertive but confrontational, saying, 'Right, you know the rules. Register in silence or you're in at break'. Later, she was able to give the same instruction in a more positive way saying, 'OK . . . let's see if you can do this. Register in silence. I know you can do it'. She reported that her voice had also changed:

> I found it useful to drop the level of my voice when a class was being particularly noisy, rather than shouting over them . . . I also developed several phrases to use when I wanted their attention, such as, 'OK, headphones off, keyboards off' or 'Everyone turn and face me please'.

In conclusion, Mattock wrote:

> This assignment has allowed me to address the issues that gave me the greatest concern and demonstrate how I have systematically improved in these areas. Developing a discipline plan increased my confidence in dealing with incidents of poor behaviour and implementing my action plan in the classroom meant I had a much better control of the classroom situation. Of course, the work I have done over the past few months does not mean that my abilities in this area are infallible, but it has given me a good foundation to build upon in the future.

### Case 2: 'Freedom to learn' by Alison Larrett

Larrett's work centred around the pupil-focused theories of Carl Rogers (for example, Rogers and Freiberg, 1994). Rogers was a psychologist who developed a humanistic theory of education, drawing partly on his study of child development. Rogers and Freiberg (1994) contrasts traditional methods of teaching, which were characterised in terms of teachers imparting knowledge and information, with child-centred approaches in which the needs of the pupil are paramount. Larrett found that her own approach to teaching had been influenced by traditional assumptions; she was didactic and teacher-centred, lecturing and demonstrating and not expecting input from pupils. Her analysis of her teaching during the first placement revealed three ways in which she fell short of Rogers' ideals. First, she imparted information, rather than encouraging learning by discovery. She wrote:

> On consideration I believe [I am] sending a signal to pupils that I do not expect them to think for themselves; merely that I expect them to listen and recall [this] factual knowledge.

Second, she used questioning more to enact her role as a teacher than to encourage reflection. Her questions to pupils were closed:

> The use of questioning techniques was very narrow and used to check factual knowledge rather than encourage independent thinking . . . although the use of closed questioning is a useful tool for the traditional teacher to check how much knowledge a class has absorbed, I believe I should begin to consider whether these closed questions would motivate a class to respond or discourage them due to a fear of failure.

Finally, her approach to poor behaviour was dominated by 'threats, verbal warnings and enforcing tighter discipline'. She described this as 'largely undemocratic'. In contrast, she wanted to be as Rogers describes:

> A person who is perceived as an authority figure in the situation is sufficiently secure within herself and in relationships with others to experience an essential trust in the capacity of others to think for themselves, to learn for themselves. She regards human beings as trustworthy organisms.
>
> *(Rogers and Freiberg, 1994, p. 212)*

Her reading of Vygotsky helped her to articulate her understanding that learning is essentially social in nature and that pupils' talk assists their learning. She drew on the child-centred literature (e.g. Entwistle, 1970, Aspy and Roebuck, 1977, Darling, 1994) to imagine ways in which she might promote a more person-centred education. She drew up an action plan in which she aimed to become more pupil-centred in her pedagogy and aimed, 'to develop a semi-facilitative role . . . in which students feel valued'.

Larrett transcribed each of her video-recorded lessons and coded the transcriptions according to the activities that took place. She identified the following categories and calculated the time spent on each:

- Lecturing
- Closed questioning
- Questioning encouraging independent thinking and guided discovery
- Musical modelling
- Teacher demonstration
- Pupil demonstration
- Self-evaluation
- Pupil discussion.

Use of these categories enabled her to examine the lessons she had recorded and she found evidence that she had improved in all three aspects she had identified. Her approach became less dogmatic; for instance, in her final recorded lesson she led a rhythmic exercise and, once it had been mastered, asked pupils to come to the front of the class and lead similar exercises while she herself sat with the pupils. Her questioning became more open, asking questions such as, 'What do you think you could have improved?', 'Can you think of any other musical devices that you might use?' and 'Anything else?' She also found evidence of a more facilitative approach to class management than previously. For example:

> When students were asked to sit in a circle it became clear that the circle was not round and some students were left outside . . . I said to the pupils, 'Okay guys, look, at the circle. What needs to happen?' In this way, pupils are encouraged to think for themselves . . . it also eliminates the potential hostility that could be caused through using teacher dictatorship to instruct students.

Although she found such evidence, Larrett was not convinced that her teaching had become pupil-centred:

> Upon reflection, I felt that this research was not sufficient to show whether or not I had met the aims of my action plan. The implementation of more child-centred learning into the classroom is a gradual process which demonstrates a change in the atmosphere of the learning environment which is a joint venture between teacher and pupil. I did not feel that recordings and lesson plans could capture truly how pupils felt about this process.

She therefore administered a brief questionnaire survey of pupils' opinions and, from this, learned that most of her pupils enjoyed, 'having an element of choice in the work', 'taking on responsibilities in the classroom' and agreed with the statement that they 'find it easier to be creative when working with others'. This confirmed that the moves she was making made the pupils feel better about their work. Nearly all of her respondents agreed with the statement 'I understand how to behave in music lessons', which showed that her move towards greater freedom did not produce confusion as to acceptable behaviour although only around 50 per cent agreed that they enjoyed, 'evaluating my own work'.

Larrett did not intend her lessons to be as child-centred as Rogers advocated; what she sought and, to a large extent, found, was a balance in which, 'pupils benefit from an increased amount of freedom and choice in their learning without losing the structure and security of the more traditional practice to which they may have been accustomed'. Through analysis of her lessons against her coding categories, she also found that she had learned to use a much wider range of teaching strategies, including guided discovery, role play, enquiry and self-assessment. She felt that her teaching had improved and concluded that:

> As a direct result of giving pupils 'freedom to learn'. . . teachers [too] can benefit from freedom to experience increased trust . . . teaching and learning become a shared experience rather than a teacher dominated affair.

## Commentary

These cases demonstrate some of the potential for research to inform reflection in ITE, particularly with able students (both achieved the highest possible grade for their practical teaching). In each case, the students chose an aspect of their practice that they wanted to improve; they read and summarised a literature about this aspect; they planned improvements to their practice in the light of these literatures; and they implemented and evaluated their improvements, collecting and analysing data to inform their evaluations. In so doing, they engaged with published research, in order to help them to engage in their own practical research. The literature they used was explicitly grounded in research, although mostly presented for a practitioner readership, and they used it conceptually rather than instrumentally (Cain, 2015b) to guide their own practice and their reflections on their practice. This use of research to guide reflection led to credible improvements in their practice of teaching – improvements which were wholly under the control of the student teachers, throughout the projects. Although they are small scale studies, they demonstrate that student teachers can improve through engagement with a research literature, and they provide some evidence that research-informed reflection can enable even able students to improve their practice.

Nevertheless, my experience of working with these and other students has shown me some of the barriers to be overcome, if research-informed reflection is to be introduced at every level of the ITE ecosystem. First, the reflective process is not necessarily understood by all student teachers, many of whom require some support to select an appropriate focus and to maintain this focus. Many student teachers have multiple problems in their classroom teaching and these shift even within a single day; maintaining a steady focus is not always easy. Second, it is not always easy for student teachers to plan the types of improvement that might be recognised in data. Many started their work with a very general view of what they wanted to achieve, such as to plan more interesting lessons. In some instances, student teachers made several attempts before settling on an action plan that was neither too narrow (e.g. to give fewer punishments) nor too broad (e.g. to improve relationships with pupils). Third, it is very easy for student teachers to collect more data than are manageable. For example, some students made audio recordings of every lesson they taught; others collected examples of work from every pupil. A sensible sampling strategy is essential if the data are to be analysed, not merely collected. Finally, it is not easy for student teachers to set aside overly subjective and emotional approaches to their research. On the one hand, they are understandably keen to demonstrate that their teaching has improved; on the other hand, they are keen to show that they are sufficiently self-critical. These twin pressures can both militate against an approach that involves other people – other student teachers, teachers and pupils – to reach a considered, balanced evaluation.

In most cases, student teachers need support to achieve the level of research-informed reflection, exemplified above. At present this is most likely to come from university staff who also have a responsibility to undertake research. In England,

ITE provision is becoming increasingly school-led and the role of universities more peripheral; this makes support from universities less likely. Nevertheless, even here, as more teachers achieve higher degrees, it is likely that these teachers with experience of research, will be able to support student teachers in becoming research-informed. Such support, and the thinking that will accompany this support, might help to develop the ecosystem of research-engaged schooling more generally, as policy intends (Godfrey, 2017). Because engagement with research enables both established teachers and ITE students to review both what they think about and how they think, over time we might expect research-informed thinking to become embedded within the mindsets of teachers and indeed, the activities of schools.

## Conclusions

There are at least two possible conceptualisations of research-informed ITE. The first sees research-informed ITE as a new version of theory into practice. In this conceptualisation, student teachers are expected to learn about research findings and then to put these into practice in their own classrooms. The second sees research informing their reflection. This conceptualisation is congruent with the nature of teaching and ITE, including its 'peculiar problem': that, because of their prior experience, some student teachers already know how to teach when they start their training, and others are resistant to training. This chapter has presented cases of student teachers whose engagement with and in research has informed their reflection in this way. They provide evidence that, with appropriate support, this is both possible and desirable.

## Implications for the research-informed ecosystem

- At the microsystemic level, student teachers should be encouraged to investigate their own teaching, to identify areas where they might improve. They should be encouraged to read research about these areas, and to use their reading to plan, implement and evaluate, improvements to their practice.
- At the mesosystemic level, experienced teachers should be encouraged to engage with and engage in research, both for the professional development that this can bring, and to enable them to support ITE.
- At the level of the exosystem, government policies should encourage the development of school–university partnerships so that universities' research expertise continues to be available to schools.

## References

Aspy, D. N. and Roebuck, F. N. (1977). *Kids Don't Learn From People They Don't Like.* Amherst, MA: Human Resource Development Press.
Blum, P. (1998) *Surviving and Succeeding in Difficult Classrooms.* London: Routledge.

Cain, T. (2015a). Teachers' engagement with published research: addressing the knowledge problem. *Curriculum Journal*, 26(3), 488–509.

Cain, T. (2015b). Teachers' engagement with research texts: beyond instrumental, conceptual or strategic use. *Journal of Education for Teaching*, 41(5), 1–15.

Cain, T. (2016). Research utilisation and the struggle for the teacher's soul: a narrative review. *European Journal of Teacher Education*, 39(5), 616–629.

Cain, T., Holmes, M., Larrett, A. and Mattock, J. (2007). Literature-informed, one-turn action research: three cases and a commentary. *British Educational Research Journal*, 33(1), 91–106.

Carr, W. and Kemmis, S. (1986). *Becoming Critical: Knowing Through Action Research.* Geelong, Australia: Deakin University.

Carter, A. (2015). *Carter Review of Initial Teacher Training (ITT).* Retrieved 6 January 2019 from: www.gov.uk/government/publications/carter-review-of-initial-teacher-training.

Cowley, S. (2003). *Getting the Buggers to Behave.* London: Continuum.

Darling, J. (1994). *Child-Centred Education and its Critics.* London: Paul Chapman.

Elliott, J. (1991). *Action Research for Educational Change.* Milton Keynes: Open University Press.

Dewey, J. (1933). *How We Think: A Restatement of the Relation of Reflective Thinking to the Educational Process.* Lexington, MA: Heath and Co.

Elliot, J. (1991). *Action Research for Educational Change.* Milton Keynes: Open University Press.

Entwistle, H. (1970). *Child-Centred Education.* London: Methuen.

Fontana, D. (1985). *Classroom Control.* St Andrews: British Psychological Society.

Fontana, D. (1995). *Psychology for Teachers.* London: British Psychological Society.

Godfrey, D. (2016). Leadership of schools as research-led organisations in the English educational environment: cultivating a research-engaged school culture. *Educational Management Administration & Leadership*, 44(2), 301–321.

Godfrey, D. (2017). What is the proposed role of research evidence in England's 'self-improving' school system? *Oxford Review of Education*, 43(4), 433–446.

Godfrey, D. and Brown, C. (2018). How effective is the research and development ecosystem for England's schools? *London Review of Education*, 16(1), 136–151.

Goldacre, B. (2013). *Building Evidence into Education.* Retrieved 3 January 2019 from: http://media.education.gov.uk/assets/files/pdf/b/ben%20goldacre%20paper.pdf.

Gov.uk. (2014). *Newly Qualified Teachers: Annual Survey.* Retrieved 3 January 2019 from: www.gov.uk/government/collections/newly-qualified-teachers-annual-survey.

Hammersley, M. (2002). *Educational Research, Policymaking and Practice.* London: Paul Chapman.

Hargreaves, D. (1996). *Teaching as a Research-based Profession: Possibilities and Prospects.* Teacher Training Agency Annual Lecture. London: Teacher Training Agency.

Hargreaves, D. H. (2010). *Creating a Self-Improving School System.* Nottingham: National College for Leadership of Schools and Children's Services.

Jacques, K. and Ellis, V. (2002). Managing challenging behaviour. In V. Ellis (Ed.), *Learning and Teaching in Secondary Schools.* Exeter: Learning Matters.

Kelchtermans, G. and Ballet, K. (2002). The micropolitics of teacher induction. a narrative-biographical study on teacher socialisation. *Teaching and Teacher Education*, 18(1), 105–120.

Kennedy, M. M. (1991). Some surprising findings on how teachers learn to teach. *Educational Leadership*, 49(3), 14–17.

Korthagen, F., Loughran, J. and Russell, T. (2006). Developing fundamental principles for teacher education programs and practices. *Teaching and Teacher Education*, 22(8), 1020–1041.

Miles, S., Barrett, E., Barton, L., Furlong, J., Galvin, C. and Whitty, G. (1993). Initial teacher education in England and Wales a topography. *Research Papers in Education*, 8(3), 275–304.

Philpott, C. (2001). The management and organisation of music lessons. In C. Philpott (Ed.), *Learning to Teach Music in the Secondary School*. London: RoutledgeFalmer.

Rogers, B. (1998). *You Know the Fair Rule*. London: Financial Times/Prentice Hall.

Rogers, C. and Freiberg, J. (1994). *Freedom to Learn*. Upper Saddle River, NJ: Merrill.

Rutter, M. (1979). *Fifteen Thousand Hours: Secondary Schools and Their Effects on Children*. Boston, MA: Harvard University Press.

Schön, D. A. (1983). *The Reflective Practitioner: How Professionals Think in Action*. New York: Basic Books.

Schön, D. A. (1987). *Educating the Reflective Practitioner: Toward a New Design for Teaching and Learning in the Professions*. San Francisco, CA: Jossey-Bass.

Shulman, L. (1987). Knowledge and teaching: foundations of the new reform. *Harvard Educational Review*, 57(1), 1–23.

Somekh, B. (2006). *Action Research: A Methodology for Change and Development*. Maidenhead: Open University Press.

Stenhouse, L. and Rudduck, J. (1985). *Research as a Basis for Teaching: Readings From the Work of Lawrence Stenhouse*. London: Heinemann.

Whitehead, J. and McNiff, J. (2006). *Action Research: Living Theory*. London: Sage.

Whitty, G. and Furlong, J. (Eds.). (2017). *Knowledge and the Study of Education: An International Exploration*. Oxford: Symposium Books.

Zeichner, K. (1986). The practicum as an occasion for learning to teach. *South Pacific Journal of Teacher Education*, 14(2), 11–27.

Zeichner, K. M. and Liston, D. P. (1996). *Reflective Teaching: An Introduction*. Mahwah, NJ: Lawrence Erlbaum Associates.

# 9

# PROFESSIONAL LEARNING AND RESEARCH

*Graham Handscomb*

## Aims of the chapter

- To outline the ecosystem connectivity between the school as a learning community, professional development and research engagement.
- To explore the relationship between enquiry and professional learning.
- To consider the benefits, status and credibility of practitioner research.
- To examine the power of the insider's knowledge.

## Introduction

Schools are complex, multifaceted sites of learning. This lies at the heart of any understanding of the school as an ecosystem. Clearly the school's core purpose is focused on the learning and achievement of its pupils, but much of the *professional learning community* literature has emphasised that this core purpose is best achieved when learning is seen as the *raison d'être* of the whole school (Stoll et al., 2006; Hord, 2009; Stoll, 2012; Harris and Jones, 2012a). In such learning communities a premium is placed on the importance of the learning and development of adults as well as on that of the children. Teachers, and indeed other staff, become more accomplished professionals through continuing to develop, and to reflect upon and hone their practice.

In turn, enquiry makes an important contribution to this process of continuing professional development. The integral relationship between learning and enquiry is something that is implicitly understood within children's learning but we have been relatively slow to recognise its potency for teacher development. Enquiry and research have now come to be seen as one of nine key contributing factors to effective professional development (Stoll, Harris and Handscomb, 2012). In making this claim, drawing on a review of the literature on effective professional learning, interrelated connections are made between research evidence, improving practice and pupil outcomes, and collaboration between practitioners (Box 9.1).

---

**Box 9.1 Extract from *Great Professional Development that Leads to Great Pedagogy: Nine Strong Claims from Research***

**Claim 6: Effective professional development uses action research and enquiry as key tools**

Commitment to research engagement is an important feature of professional learning because it fosters a proper regard for evidence which can be used to change practice and improve pupil outcomes. It also establishes research communities within and beyond the school that sustain professional learning over time (Stoll, Harris and Handscomb, 2012, p. 6).

---

Identifying these interrelationships is significant. It signals that through its contribution to the professional learning of staff, research engagement also connects with and contributes to a range of features that make up the school ecosystem. Indeed this was precisely at the heart of the thinking that initially pioneered the concept of the *research engaged school* (Handscomb and MacBeath, 2003).

This chapter then will explore the dynamic relationships at play between professional learning and research engagement, and indeed between the related multifarious ingredients of the school ecosystem – including the school as a learning community, the importance of generating school-based knowledge; and the contribution to wider school improvement.

## Research or enquiry – what's in a name?

When exploring the connection between professional development and research engagement it helps to be clear about the nature of each and how this reveals significant implications for how they are intimately bound together. In recent decades there has been a marked shift in the understanding of what is entailed in effective professional development. Long gone is the view that embarking on courses outside the school with limited impact either on the recipient or colleagues is sufficient. Instead there has been a growing and overwhelming consensus that professional learning has most potency when it is school-led, school-owned, focused on teaching and learning and on improving classroom practice (Pollard, 2014). It is within this context that research engagement is seen as making its powerful contribution: 'A pivotal role . . . is that of leading collaborative professional learning and enquiry in order to extend, expand and create new professional knowledge' (Harris and Jones, 2012b, p. 4). So there is a growing compelling view that research use in itself can help to enrich professional development.

However, this poses a range of questions and issues. What is meant by enquiry in this school-embedded professional development context and how does this relate to the concept of research and broader research engagement? How is teacher enquiry different to what a good teacher does in her classroom from day to day? Teachers have long been involved in examining their practice in order to make further improvements, but when may such activity be described as 'research'? What is the relationship between large-scale research, conducted for instance by a university department, and a piece of evidence-informed practice carried out by a teacher within her classroom? And how is such evidence-informed practice different from what good teachers do anyway in refining and honing their craft in day-to-day lesson preparation and evaluation?

One view is that evidence-informed practice typically involves the individual teacher reflecting on her own classroom practice, and sharing this with colleagues in a climate which promotes challenging discourse – in contrast 'research' tends to be seen as involving larger scale, more systematic enquiry. Another view is that these two characterisations are not different in kind but rather two ends of a continuum of practice in which 'evidenced-informed practice' merges into 'research' (Handscomb, 2013).

This is perhaps a rather sterile and unproductive debate, with too sharp a distinction between teacher enquiry/reflection and research. Accepting Stenhouse's (1981) definition of research as 'systematic enquiry, made public' allows us to encompass both the individual teacher focusing on one feature of her craft, as well as large-scale projects involving many schools. The important common element to both is an investigative process undertaken with rigor, concern for evidence and communicated to others. The Stenhouse definition also signals the importance of seeing the contribution of school-based enquiry – through its systematic, collaborative approach – to wider dimensions of the school ecosystem.

So, just as teachers encourage their pupils to engage in enquiry, systematically and with a developing understanding of what constitutes 'evidence', so teachers observe the same principles. It is about turning intuitive and spontaneous judgements into more systematic investigations, and it starts with the everyday questions that teachers ask themselves.

## The relationship between enquiry and professional learning

There are a number of ways in which we can envisage the relationship between enquiry and professional development. Perhaps the most obvious is that of using research and evidence as a pedagogical tool to enrich professional learning and inform practice. However, enquiry can also be seen as the means by which professional learning is undertaken – in other words as the mode or vehicle for how professional development is conducted. This typically involves school practitioners themselves carrying out research investigations. In an early report considering research engagement Dyson (2001) identified three key dimensions:

- Teachers doing research – practitioner researchers
- Teachers using research – drawing on current thinking and learning from the external research community
- Teachers being part of research – being the site of research and part of the investigations of others.

The last point relates to schools being sufficiently engaged and strategic in its research engagement to make informed prioritised decisions as to which research organisations it opens its doors to.

All three dimensions can feature within the professional development process and have implications for what Godfrey (2016) identifies as the *mesosystem* – relating to the professional learning and organisational culture of the school; and the *microsystem* – the immediate environment within the school involving the actions of school leaders, teachers and other members of the school community.

This resonates very much with recent investigations into research-informed teaching practice (RITP) which particularly focuses on the dividends of practitioners' use and application of research. RITP is characterised as a collaborative process in which teachers and school leaders work together to access, evaluate and apply the findings of academic research in order to improve teaching and learning in their schools (Walker, 2017). Brown et al. (2018, p. 39) draw on evidence (e.g. Mincu, 2014) which indicates that 'where research is used as part of high quality initial teacher education and ongoing professional development, it is associated with higher teacher, school and system performance', and they set out a comprehensive range of ways teachers benefit from engaging with research.

## The benefits of practitioner research

What case can be made for teachers investing time and energy in conducting enquiries themselves? Why should teachers – and indeed other staff – engage in practitioner research activity? With all the pressures and demands on teachers, is such involvement an indulgence they can ill afford? Laudable though reflection, enquiry and research are, is there not a danger that teachers will take their eye off the ball of improving teaching and learning and raising standards? (Handscomb and MacBeath, 2008). Despite the growing evidence over a number of decades about the merits of a 'knowledge creating school' (Hargreaves, 1996) and the benefits of this for teachers' development of pedagogy (Baumfield and McGrane, 2001) practitioner enquiry still tends to be perceived as a luxury – desirable but not essential (Handscomb, 2002; 2015).

Well, there is an increasing body of literature and school practice which indicates quite the contrary. Rather than being an effete activity which diverts energies from the school's core business, school-based enquiry and research are now being seen to make an important contribution to self-evaluation, improvement and the professional learning of staff (MacBeath and Mortimore, 2001). Engagement in and with research encourages practitioners to question, explore and develop their practice, making a significant contribution to improved teaching and learning. In fostering a school culture where teachers examine and critique their own practice, research activity can be an important and integral element of professional learning.

Far from being a distraction then, practitioner research can be seen as critical to a school's success. Seeking answers to basic practitioner questions that bubble up in the classroom has always concerned teachers, but never before has it become so critical to a school's survival, growth and success. The third millennium school is required to be self-evaluating, open to scrutiny, evidenced-based, data rich. But, as many commentators have suggested, schools are at the same time often 'information poor' (MacBeath and Mortimore, 2001; Wilkins, 2013). This is, in part, because teachers can feel little ownership of data they are expected to use, questioning both its value and validity. Classroom practitioners can feel 'done to', disempowered, and mere ciphers in an accountability laden culture which tabulates and compares their performance, rather than encouraging self-critique and self-evaluation. Indeed, this issue about lack of ownership of data relating to both our personal and professional lives was at the eye of the storm that raged in the Spring of 2018 about the sharing of Facebook information. This brought into sharp relief fundamental issues about what information is held on people and control rights of individuals over their own data.

Nonetheless, in schools data tends to be a high stakes business, requiring 'delivery' rather than creation, 'implementation' rather than enquiry. Being kept busy undermines teachers' confidence to convert what they know or believe into a form that provides robust counter-evidence. It weakens their ability to speak with conviction that is grounded in their own professional context and experience. The value of CPD which fosters research engagement is that it contains the potential for an 'enquiry' outlook which empowers and re-professionalises teachers: 'Research leads teachers back to the things that lie at the heart of their professionalism: pupils, teaching and learning' (Ruddock, 2001, p. 1). Indeed some see this as the hallmark of the move towards teaching becoming a mature profession – when enquiry as a fundamental form of learning and development is 'integrated into the normal practice for all practitioners' (Wilkins, 2015, p. 25).

## The credibility and status of practitioner research

However positive practitioner research as a core feature of professional development is judged to be, there continues to be heated argument within the wider research community about its importance and status.

In their best evidence synthesis of professional learning and development Timperley and colleagues are coruscating in their stark judgement of the impact of teachers' research engagement and the calibre of any contribution to the research knowledge base:

> With rare exceptions . . . such knowledge has been transitory, likely to be named as the work of researchers rather than teachers, inaccessible to

other teachers, siloed in academic sub-disciplines, and lost amid a plethora of fads or low priority within academic hierarchies of knowledge and reward systems.

*(Timperley and Alton-Lee, 2008, p. 329)*

McLaughlin (2004, p. 1) reflected: 'There has been much debate about the quality, status and type of engagement of practitioners' and goes on to identify a long tradition of tension between two contrasting aspirations for practitioner research and enquiry – its role, nature and purposes. One is that teachers should investigate their own practice to improve it. The other is for practitioner research to contribute to public knowledge about teaching and learning. Fierce conjecture raged when the Centre for Action Research (CARN) advocated strongly that the evidence of teacher enquirers from their own classrooms was more important than that of other external researchers, whilst in contrast researchers like Foster and Gorard 'contested the validity of all teacher research in informing the practice of others' (cited in Bell et al., 2010, p. 27).

At the heart of this often vitriolic debate about the value of practitioner research, and by implication its contribution to wider improvement dynamics within the ecosystem, is the issue of the criteria by which it should be evaluated and whether this should be the same as that by which academic research is judged. McIntyre (2004) provides a helpful reflection by suggesting that we view educational research as a continuum of possibilities. He argues that there are three general criteria for judging educational research: its usefulness, its contribution to knowledge and its methodological rigour; and the application of these criteria would be different depending on the type of research being undertaken (cited in McLaughlin, 2004). So different demands would be made of, for example, reflective teaching, action research and researching teaching and learning. For some this will not be sufficient and will in their eyes leave practitioner research wanting; others, however, will be happy to go with McIntyre's compelling argument that practitioner research be counted as significant within *its fit for purpose* school context:

> There is a term known as 'good enough research' which means generating research designs that are valid and reliable to their purpose and their context, rather than to the purity of knowledge or its generalisability. School-based enquiry is often 'good enough research'.
>
> *(McIntyre, 2004, p. 33)*

Nevertheless, there is a sense that 'the jury is still out' regarding the status of practitioner research, with continuing debate more recently fuelled by Goldacre's 'bad science' challenge and advocacy of randomised control trials (Goldacre, 2013).

## The power of the insider's knowledge

The value of incorporating research engagement – in all its forms – into professional learning has much to do with the way in which it has the potential to empower staff and give them a voice. This is evident, for instance, within initiatives like *Research Learning Communities* (see Chapter 6 for more detailed description). The RLC model is particularly interesting in the way it is founded upon approach where participants are asked to combine school-based knowledge from practitioner enquiry, on topics like growth mindsets or effective grouping, with the insights of investigations from the wider external research community (Brown, 2017). In this way research engagement in schools does not get caught up with the credibility issues aired earlier. What is evident from such initiatives is the way in which research engagement helps to instil in participants a greater sense of efficacy and agency (Durrant, 2014). Much of this is derived from the value of local knowledge, the potency of teachers who are closest to their classroom setting being the ones who conduct investigations into practice. What emerges as powerful is when such local knowledge is harnessed and utilised to problem solve specific improvement issues, facilitated through enquiry communities like RLCs, and connected to wider research knowledge and social developments. So such 'local knowledge is understood to be a process of building, interrogating, elaborating, and critiquing conceptual frameworks that link action and problem posing to the immediate context as well as to larger social, cultural, and political issues' (Cochran-Smith and Lytle, 1999).

This recognition of the potency of local knowledge is longstanding and spans the ages. In the 18th century Giambattista Vico (1725) captured its significance in the following description:

> This is a sort of knowing which participants in an activity claim . . . the knowledge of the actors as against the audience, the 'inside story' as opposed to the 'outside' vantage point; knowledge by 'direct acquaintance' . . . or by sympathetic insight into those of others.
>
> *(cited in Berlin, 1978 and Lieberman, 1992)*

It also features centrally in contemporary thinking and practice. Powerful examples are the work of Bryk, Gomez and Grunow (2011) exploring practitioner engagement in local problem solving through Networked Improvement Communities, and the proposals around design-based research partnerships which take a solutions approach and focus on long-term, in-depth work within a local district (Coburn, Penuel and Geil, 2013).

In all of this, recognition of the importance of the insider's knowledge, coupled with and empowered by an enquiry state of mind, is about acknowledging a different outlook and the improvement leverage that such knowledge can bring:

> Inquiry as stance is neither a top-down nor a bottom-up theory of action, but an organic and democratic one that positions practitioners' knowledge, practitioners, and their interactions with students and other stakeholders at the center of educational transformation.
>
> *(Cochran-Smith and Lytle, 2009, p. 123–124)*

## Case study examples

The following case studies provide examples of how schools have successfully harnessed the benefits of enquiry as an integral feature of professional learning. The first case study (Box 9.2) shows how a group of primary schools collaborated to establish a consortium-wide approach. The second example (Box 9.3) is of a special school which has embedded enquiry at the heart of its approach to staff development linked to school improvement outcomes. The final example (Box 9.4) outlines how a secondary school made school-based enquiry the foundation of its learning community and improvement in student learning. All reflect the dynamic between research engagement, professional learning and school improvement which is at the heart of this chapter. Above all, they demonstrate that 'it is teachers who in the end will change the world of the school by understanding it' (Stenhouse, 1981, p. 104).

---

### Box 9.2 Case Study 1: Collaborative professional learning and research engagement – rural Primary Schools' Consortium

Four small rural schools within a Primary Schools' Consortium in Essex worked in partnership with the University of Cambridge Department for Education on a school improvement research initiative. The group of schools had established themselves into a consortium for some time. The success of the consortium was reflected in the investment each school made in terms of:

- Consortium management – regular management meetings attended by all headteachers; robust consortium management procedures
- Development planning – all schools committed to specific actions to implement in the consortium development plan
- Finance – each school investing £1 per pupil into the consortium finances
- Professional development – common non-pupil days and common weekly staff meetings agreed across the consortium to enable joint professional development linked to the consortium development plan.

This research project arose out of several years' experience of working together for professional development purposes, including work with Cambridge University. At consortium management meetings the schools' headteachers consider the individual needs of schools and identify areas for shared INSET provision and school improvement projects.

The project focused on school-based enquiry. It was decided that three non-pupil days involving all (40) teaching staff at the above schools would

*(continued)*

---

*(continued)*

be devoted to this project and two twilight sessions per term for staff. An accreditation outcome was the award of the Cambridge Certificate of Further Professional Study. Teachers would pursue some school-based enquiry using research methods to study aspects of teaching and learning linked to monitoring and evaluation. Two non-pupil training days were allocated to develop the skills teachers needed to carry out this school-based enquiry.

Following practice in research techniques – carrying out interviews, questionnaires, observations – each school chose to focus on enquiries which were relevant to their own school development. These were:

- How effective is the ICT suite in supporting children's learning?
- Improving writing. Linking writing to motor skills at KS1 and strategies to improve spelling at KS2
- Investigating ways to improve children's ability to read and write for information
- Investigating the development of listening skills
- Developing thinking skills.

Whilst each school pursued its own lines of enquiry it used schools in the consortium to help with planning and to test out ideas and development. Assistance from the university staff with theory and research methodology enabled some rigour to the investigations.

The project involved staff from all schools engaging in research based improvement. Originally, a select range of staff from each school participated. However, as the popularity of the project grew many more took part and in some schools all the staff, including support staff, conducted a research project. This meant that there was a critical mass of research development in each school.

'Both children and staff in each school have benefited from the research and progress has been made in the development of our schools as learning communities' (participating teacher). 'It is hoped that further developments will occur between schools so that this professional learning through enquiry is extended within the consortium' (participating headteacher). The Local Authority has worked actively with the consortium to facilitate opportunities to disseminate outcomes within the authority and through national conferences and networks.

*(Adapted from Handscomb and MacBeath, 2008)*

---

**Box 9.3 Case Study 2: Research engagement embedded into whole approach to professional learning and school improvement: north-east special school**

A special school in the north-east of England developed a clear and in-depth vision for research and the powerful contribution it makes to young people's achievement and well-being, and all aspects of school life. This vision is set through the inspirational leadership of the headteacher, and is shared and renewed by staff, pupils and governors. Research priorities are built into the School Improvement Plan and there are clear timescales, deadlines and review checks specified against research programmes and activity. Research is woven into the whole ethos and nature of the school and involves everyone from headteacher to staff and pupils. The school's enquiry culture fosters a climate in which topics for enquiry are encouraged within a context of school improvement requirement generated by the senior leadership team. There is extensive evidence of engagement with research ideas, publications and approaches. Research engagement is regarded so highly because of the strategic and personal commitment of senior leadership and the way it provides extensive coaching, mentoring and support in terms of time and resources. There is a designated post which has specific responsibility for research and this person plays a crucial role in coordinating the range of activity taking place across the school. School staff – including teaching assistants – lead groups and convene meetings, with SLT being supportive, facilitating members of the group.

The school has developed itself as a community of enquiry which embraces a wide range of participants within and beyond the school. The school used the national Teaching Learning Academy programme to ensure that all staff carry out their own enquiries leading to a TLA award. This generated a momentum of enquiry across the whole school community. There are clear plans to influence the wider engagement of research throughout the Teaching School Alliance and Trust Partnership of which the school is a part.

The school's whole approach to professional learning is founded on research and enquiry which is a key feature of extended practice. Almost all members of staff (teaching and non-teaching) are currently studying for some form of professional accreditation that requires research as a component of their programme. The governors and school, support and pay for staff undertaking Master research. There is a breadth of staff participating in

*(continued)*

*(continued)*

both individual and joint research activity as part of their professional practice. Professional development is seen in terms of ways in which classroom practice is understood and improved, and research is seen as an integral part of this approach. It is built into the School Improvement Plan and in turn informs the school's staff development planning. Staff research activity is tracked and evaluated through the performance management process. Professional development research activity in the school draws on knowledge, research and frameworks from a range of external sources and literature; there is impressive evidence of staff reading extensively to inform their enquiries. Governors have a deep and coherent grasp of how research underpins professional learning and there is potential for proving opportunities for governors to participate more fully in enquiry as part of their development.

A particular and characteristic strength of the school's research engagement is that it clearly has an impact on teaching and learning. Research is used specifically to drive improvements in teaching and learning. Meeting the needs of pupils and improving their learning and well-being are at the heart of the school's whole approach to research and there is a range of evidence that pupils directly benefit from research activity. The school has invested in sustaining research engagement over time and has established a pattern of focusing on major year-long research projects, alongside a wide range of individual and collaborative enquiries. The school's approach to research reflects that of the Enquiring Schools programme, with any individual asking a 'question' and demonstrating how to bring about change within their own practice through looking at existing research and drawing on their own enquiry and experiences.

One of the most powerful features of the school is the quality and depth of its reflection and self-critique. The school takes considerable pains to keep research activity, and the contribution it makes, under review in order to improve this even further. This is exemplified, for instance, in one staff member's approach to using enquiry to try out innovative approaches within his classroom around the open-ended theme of 'shelter', taking care not to proscribe the outcomes, and then reflecting carefully on what he observed in order to change further teaching. The school's investigation into Brain Gym was an example of the school 'letting the data speak' and taking on board negative outcomes. The school invests in knowing itself and this is demonstrated in the considered reflection of everyone ranging from the head and her staff to the governors and students.

(Adapted from Handscomb and Hankin, 2014)

**Box 9.4 Case Study 3: Research engaged professional learning geared to improving student learning and support: Secondary school in the Home Counties**

This secondary school demonstrated a deep and lasting commitment to research-informed professional practice, and to developing a robust and sustainable learning community. The school has a considerable history of encouraging staff to engage in and with research, with the result that it now has a compelling and well-articulated vision for ensuring that research is both a core value and a visible characteristic of the professional practice of teaching; there is a strong collective commitment to nurturing a sustainable learning community involving staff and students across the whole school. There is abundant evidence of a culture where research is valued and perceived to be 'part of what good teachers do'.

The school's rationale for engaging in research is to address more thoroughly and expertly the learning needs of the students. Significant time and resources have been allocated to establishing two cross-departmental teams, the Quality of Learning (QoL) and Quality of Student Support (QoSS) teams, whose work is research-led, supports professional learning and growth, and informs the school's strategic pedagogical and pastoral development. Membership of these teams is, and is seen as, a significant career and professional development stage for staff. Over four years, a number of action research projects that had their origins in QoL or QoSS projects have become embedded into the school's systems, processes and practice. The mutuality and interaction of teams' work – alongside the better use of performance data and the critical use of relevant external research – is a key feature of the school's commitment to a self-evaluative stance.

The leadership for research at senior level is highly effective. Explicit support for school-wide and partnership research activity is provided by the headteacher. Two assistant headteacher posts on the senior management team include roles and responsibilities for research strategy, and both post-holders are energetic leaders of data interpretation and use on the one hand, and research-engagement for professional learning and school improvement on the other.

Teachers are expected to be continually questioning and reflecting on their practice. The different possible starting points for research investigations are recognised and valued, from individual teachers' long-standing interests or intuitive hunches to 'commissioned' evaluations of pedagogic interventions; systematic planning and scheduling are then built into the way the research is conducted.

*(continued)*

*(continued)*

There is a commitment to disseminating and sharing the outcomes of action research through a variety of means, including:

- during INSET days;
- through the Cloud-based virtual learning environment;
- in detailed written report;
- in formal presentations to colleagues on progress as well as outcomes;
- in professional learning / performance management dialogues and
- through informal conversations.

Some staff are participating actively in the wider research community through, for example, ResearchEd. Since the school became an accredited Teaching School, teachers in training are supported in undertaking well-designed research projects which have a link to the school's ongoing research effort. Student engagement in research is a strong feature of the school and there have been a number of investigations which have recruited students as researchers.

Drawing on the depth, breadth and quality of its own research engagement the school shares its knowledge and expertise with other schools, and is strongly committed to creating partnerships and networks widely. Such partnerships revolve around research-based and evaluated interventions and the school provides research training to other partner schools.

Research engagement is demonstrably being used as a powerful vehicle for professional development which in turn is having direct impact on classroom practice and students' learning. The school's rationale for engaging in research is to address more thoroughly and expertly the learning needs of the students. Commitment to improvement of students' learning experiences and outcomes is shown by its investment in major research projects as well as in smaller-scale investigations into how the needs of specific groups of students can be more effectively met.

(Adapted from Saunders, 2015)

## Conclusion

The Cochran-Smith and Lytle (2009) characterisation of the organic interrelationship between practitioner knowledge, the pedagogical process and educational improvement (mentioned earlier on p. 144, this volume) echoes one of the main themes sounded in this chapter. The chapter began by portraying the school as a learning community, embracing the learning of staff as well as pupils. In this context the importance of continuing professional development was emphasised and engagement in enquiry and research was shown to be a crucial element in this. Indeed, it was argued that through its contribution to professional learning, research engagement also connects with, and feeds into, a range of features that make up the ecosystem of the school. The chapter then clarified the terms 'enquiry' and 'research' and the relationship between enquiry and professional learning. This in turn led to a consideration of the merits, credibility and status of practitioner research. The case study exemplars provided rich pictures of how these concepts and principles have lived in practice. Above all this chapter has extolled the value of incorporating research engagement, in all its forms, within professional learning. This value lies fundamentally in its potential to empower and liberate practitioners and 'give voice' to their unique insider's perspective . . . and all the benefits that can accrue from this for the wider school ecosystem.

## Implications for the research-informed ecosystem

- Through its contribution to the professional learning of staff, research engagement connects with and contributes to a range of features that make up the school ecosystem.
- The range of features within research engagement – including practitioner research; using the research of others; and being part of the research of others – have a particular resonance with the school as an ecosystem.
- School-based enquiry entails a systematic and collaborative approach which has an impact on the school ecosystem.
- Establishing research engagement as a fundamental feature of professional learning helps to empower practitioners and draws upon their insider's perspective which can bring dividends for wider school improvement.

## References

Baumfield, V. M. and McGrane, J. (2001). *Teachers Using Evidence and Engaging in and With Research: One School's Story*. British Education Research Association Conference, Leeds.

Bell, M., Cordingley, P., Isham, C. and Davis, R. (2010). *Report of Professional Practitioner Use of Research Review*. CUREE, GTC, and LSIS.

Berlin, I. (1978). *Against the Current: Essays in the History of Ideas*. New York: Penguin Books.

Bryk, A. B., Gomez, L. M. and Grunow, A (2011). Getting ideas into action: building networked improvement communities. In M. Hallinan (Ed.), *Frontiers in Sociology of Education*. New York: Springer Publishing.

Brown, C., Zhang, D., Xu, N. and Corbett, S. (2018). Exploring the impact of social relationships on teachers' use of research: a regression analysis of 389 teachers in England. *International Journal of Educational Research*, 89, 36–46.

Brown, C. (2017). How to establish Research Learning Communities. *Professional Development Today*, 19(2).

Coburn, C. E., Penuel, W. R. and Geil, K. E. (2013). *Research-Practice Partnerships. A Strategy for Leveraging Research for Educational Improvement in School Districts*. White paper prepared for the William T. Grant Foundation.

Cochran-Smith, M. and Lytle, S. L. (1999). Relationships of knowledge and practice: teacher learning. *Communities Review of Research in Education*, 24, 249–305. American Educational Research Association.

Cochran-Smith, M. and Lytle, S. L. (2009). *Inquiry as Stance: Practitioner Research for the Next Generation*. New York: Teachers College Press.

Durrant, J. (2014). Children see differently from us – a fresh perspective on school improvement. *Professional Development Today*, 16(2).

Dyson, A. (2001). *Building Research Capacity*. Sub-group Report chaired by Alan Dyson. National Education Research Forum.

Godfrey, D. (2016). Leadership of schools as research-led organisations in the English educational environment: cultivating a research-engaged school culture. *Educational Management Administration & Leadership*, 44(2), 301–321.

Goldacre, B. (2013). Building evidence into education. Retrieved 3 January 2019 from: https://www.gov.uk/government/news/building-evidence-into-education.

Handscomb, G. (2002). *Educational Enquiry and Research in Essex*. The Forum for Learning and Research Enquiry (FLARE). Essex County Council.

Handscomb, G. (2013). *Empowering Teachers Through Practitioner Research*. London: The College of Teachers.

Handscomb, G. (2015). Researching and learning collaboratively. *Professional Development Today*, 17(2).

Handscomb, G. and Hankin, L. (2014). *NFER Research Mark Report*. NFER 14 July 2014.

Handscomb, G. and MacBeath, J. (2003). *The Research Engaged School* on behalf of The Forum for Learning and Research Enquiry (FLARE), Essex County Council.

Handscomb, G. and MacBeath, J. (2008). The time has come for school-based research. *Principal Matters: Excellence Through Exchange*, Winter, 2008. Australia.

Hargreaves, D. H. (1996). *Teaching as a Research-based Profession: Possibilities and Prospects*. Teacher Training Agency Annual Lecture. London: TTA.

Hargreaves, D. H. (1998). A new partnership of stakeholders and a national strategy for research induction. In J. Ruddock and D. McIntyre (Eds.), *Challenges for Educational Research*. London: Paul Chapman/Sage.

Harris, A. and Jones, M. (2012a). Connect to learn: learn to connect. *Professional Development Today*, 14(4), 13–19.

Harris, A. and Jones, M. (2012b). *Connecting Professional Learning: Leading Effective Collaborative Enquiry Across Teaching School Alliances*. National College for School Leadership.

Hord, S. M. (2009). Professional Learning Communities: educators work together towards a shared purpose – improved student learning. *Journal of Staff Development*, Winter 2009, 30(1), 40–43.

Lieberman, A. (1992). The meaning of scholarly activity and the building of community. *Educational Researcher*, 21(6) (August–September), 5–12.

MacBeath, J. and Mortimore, P. (Eds.) (2001). *Improving School Effectiveness*. London: Open University Press.

McIntyre, D. (2004). Schools as research institutions. In C. McLaughlin, K. Black-Hawkins and D. McIntyre (Eds.), *Researching Teachers, Researching Schools, Researching Networks: A Review of the Literature*. Cambridge: University of Cambridge.

McLaughlin, C. (2004). Practitioner research and enquiry. In C. McLaughlin, K. Black-Hawkins and D. McIntyre (Eds.), *Researching Teachers, Researching Schools, Researching Networks: A Review of the Literature*. Cambridge: University of Cambridge.

Mincu, M. (2014). Inquiry paper 6: teacher quality and school improvement? What is the role of research? In The British Educational Research Association/The Royal Society for the Encouragement of Arts, Manufactures and Commerce (Ed.), *The Role of Research in Teacher Education: Reviewing the Evidence.* Retrieved from www.bera.ac.uk/wp-con tent/uploads/2014/02/BERA-RSA-Interim-Report.pdf. Accessed 8 November 2017.

Pollard, A. (2014). How to develop reflective, school-led teacher education? *Professional Development Today*, 16(2).

Robinson, C. and Pedder, D. (2018). *Workload challenge research projects: overall summary.* Research report. March 2018. National College for Teaching and School Leadership; Social Science in Government and University of Brighton.

Ruddock, J. (2001). *Teachers as Researchers: The Quiet Revolution.* DfES/TTA Conference. London, 7 March.

Saunders, L. (2015). *NFER Research Mark Report.* NFER, 8 July 2015.

Stenhouse, L. (1981). What counts as research? *British Journal of Educational Studies*, 29(2), 103–114.

Stoll, L. (2012). Stimulating learning conversations. *Professional Development Today*, 14(4), 6–12.

Stoll, L., Bolam, R., McMahon, A., Thomas, S., Wallace, M., Greenwood, A. and Hawkey, K. (2006). *Creating and Sustaining Professional Learning Communities: Professional Learning Communities Source Materials for School Leaders and Other Leaders of Professional Learning, Booklet 2.* DfES 0187-2006 with NCSL and GTC.

Stoll, L., Harris, A. and Handscomb, G. (2012). *Great Professional Development that leads to Great Pedagogy: Nine Strong Claims from Research.* The National College with LCLL, Institute of Education, University of London; NFER; Sheffield Hallam University.

Timperley, H. and Alton-Lee, A. (2008). Reframing teacher professional learning: An alternative policy approach to strengthening valued outcomes for diverse learners. *Review of Research in Education*, 32, 328–369.

Vico, G. (1725). *The New Science.* Internet Archive. https://archive.org/stream/.

Walker, M. (2017). *Insights into the Role of Research and Development in Teaching Schools.* Slough: NfER.

Wilkins, R. (2013). Practitioner research and professional identity. *Professional Development Today*, 15(1/2).

Wilkins, R. (2015). Rethinking professional development and professionalization. *Professional Development Today*, 17(3).

# 10

# PROFESSIONAL ENQUIRY

## An ecological approach to developing teacher agency

*Mark Priestley and Valerie Drew*

## Aims of the chapter

- Identify two linked conceptions of the 'teacher-as-researcher': researcher into one's practice; and a more general conception of the research-engaged teacher.
- Describe an emerging landscape of curriculum policy and practice that requires more active engagement by teachers in curriculum making, than has been the case in recent years.
- Introduce and explain how curriculum making can be undertaken through Critical Collaborative Professional Enquiry (CCPE).
- Employ an ecological conception of teacher agency to analyse how CCPE enhances teachers' ability to engage proactively and constructively with new curriculum policy.

## Introduction

It has become fashionable in recent years, resurrecting the ideas of Lawrence Stenhouse (1988), to discuss teacher (or practitioner) research (or enquiry).[1] The recent BERA-RSA enquiry into the role of research in teacher education (Furlong, 2014) identified two linked dimensions to this notion of, to use Stenhouse's expression, the 'teacher-as-researcher': researcher into one's practice; and a more general conception of the research-engaged teacher – someone who is research-literate, and who actively informs their practice through engaging with research. These discussions have taken on a sharper focus following a wave of curricular reforms, characterised as the 'new curriculum' (Priestley and Biesta, 2013), and evident in many national education systems.[2] Following two decades of centralised direction of the content (and at times the methods) of the curriculum, there has been a shift to curricular models which emphasise local flexibility in curriculum making, positioning teachers as autonomous developers of the curriculum and hence agents of change. Yet, arguably, teachers in many countries do not possess much of the professional knowledge necessary for school-based curriculum development. This is attributable to some extent to the prescriptive teacher proof curricula (Taylor, 2013) of previous policy (input regulation), which has deprofessionalised teachers (Biesta, 2004, 2010) and socialised them as deliverers of policy, and also to the persistence of heavy-duty accountability mechanisms (output regulation) (Kuiper and Berkvens, 2013; Kneyber and Evers, 2015), which continue to run parallel to new more permissive curricula.

This chapter focuses on an initiative in Scotland, which sought to enhance teachers' capacity for curriculum making, utilising the methodology of Critical Collaborative Professional Enquiry (CCPE). Through following a process of CCPE, teachers explicitly engaged with the big ideas (purposes and principles) of the Scottish *Curriculum for Excellence* (CfE), framing subsequent curriculum development in terms of fitness-for-purpose – that is fit-for-purpose knowledge content and fit-for-purpose pedagogies. This process involved both dimensions of 'teacher-as-researcher', as highlighted in the opening paragraph of the chapter; it was informed by participants reading research papers, and undertaking a form of research – termed enquiry – as they engaged in curriculum making in their schools. The teachers were supported by university researchers, acting as critical colleagues and providing access to pertinent cognitive resources, including research articles, as they engaged in challenging conversations about research, theories and practices, developing understanding and skills of enquiry. In this chapter, we illustrate, using an ecological understanding of teacher agency (outlined later in the chapter, in the section titled Teacher agency. Also see: Priestley, Biesta and Robinson, 2015), how teachers' agency in curriculum making increased as their confidence and professional knowledge grew, as they developed supportive and focused professional networks and as their contexts for curriculum development were tailored to explicitly encourage sustainable innovation. The chapter draws upon qualitative data generated from three cohorts of participating teachers, including artefacts from the programme, programme evaluations and one-to-one interviews.

## The changing landscape of the curriculum

The 1990s saw the development of policy framed around the notion of input regulation (Kuiper and Berkvens, 2013), often featuring tightly prescribed content and even prescription of methods for teaching. The imperative behind such policy was a desire to ensure fidelity between policy and practice (Cuban, 1998) – to close a perceived 'implementation gap' (Supovitz and Weinbaum, 2008) – accompanied by a rhetoric of school failure that has served to 'create a sense of unease about teaching and justified subsequent government attempts to reconstruct teachers' work' (Helsby, 1999, p. 24). This fundamentally political drive to centralise policy has been widely viewed as nation states assuming control over education, as one of the few remaining levers of economic and political sovereignty in an increasing globalised world (for example: Green, 1999; Halsey et al., 1997). Scotland's curriculum policy during the 1990s broadly fitted with this general trend. The former 5–14 Curriculum, while less prescriptive than England's seminal 1989 National Curriculum, was framed around content expressed as learning outcomes, and came to be associated with highly structured and prescriptive schemes of work in schools (Priestley, 2013).

The period since the start of the millennium has witnessed a curricular turn in many countries as a 'new curriculum' (Biesta and Priestley, 2013) has emerged, characterised by a number of common trends. These include: a shift from the specification of knowledge content as the basis for curriculum planning towards genericism (Young, 2008); an emphasis on the centrality of the learner, active forms of pedagogy and a view of teachers as facilitators of learning (Sinnema and Aitken, 2013); a notion of education as a product, expressed as modular courses and ladders of qualifications (Young, 2008); an articulation of curriculum as assessable outcomes, accompanied by increasingly pervasive regimes of accountability and cultures of performativity (Young, 2008); and (in apparent contradistinction to the previous point) a [re]construction of teachers as agents of change and professional developers of the curriculum (Priestley, Biesta and Robinson, 2015). This evolution of curriculum policy appears to recognise that there need to be more nuanced ways of framing the role of teachers in curriculum making (although as will be made clear in the coming paragraphs of this chapter, such understandings have not been necessarily accompanied by nuanced understandings of the contextual conditions necessary to foster this process). Scotland's CfE is a good example of the 'new curriculum'. For example, it strongly emphasises the key role of teachers in shaping curricular practices.

This curricular shift is a manifestation of a wider transnational discourse that 'teachers matter' (OECD, 2005), characterised by talk of lifelong professional learning, teaching as a Master's level profession, teacher autonomy and teachers as agents of change. Again, Scotland's broader policy landscape manifests similar trends; the influential report *Teaching Scotland's Future* (*TSF*) (Donaldson, 2010) positions practitioners as 'reflective and enquiring teachers who are engaged in continuous improvement' (p. 15) and 'have the capacity to engage fully with the complexities of education and to be key actors in shaping and leading educational change' (p. 19).

This significant shift away from input regulation and teacher-proof curricula is to be welcomed in our view, as it potentially provides the opportunities for teachers to achieve and exercise agency in their professional lives. Nevertheless, currently such aspirations are not achievable for a number of reasons that continue to erode teacher agency. This has become evident in Scotland in the partial (at best) implementation of CfE, as evidenced by research studies (Priestley and Minty, 2013; Wallace and Priestley, 2017) and the recent OECD review of Scottish education (OECD, 2015). First, the pervasive output regulation of teachers' work (Nieveen and Kuiper, 2012; Kuiper and Berkvens, 2013; Leat, Livingston and Priestley, 2013) or outcomes steering (Biesta, 2004) arguably inhibits teacher agency more effectively than has been the case with input regulation. Accountability, surveillance, performance indicators and target setting, as well as governance by data (including attainment data) have been widely viewed as 'a shift from notions of partnership, collegiality, discretion and trust to increasing levels of managerialism, bureaucracy, standardization, assessment and performance review' (Evetts, 2011, p. 407). These factors clearly run counter to the political rhetoric expressed in policy about autonomy and agency. They have been linked to the development of cultures of performativity in professional settings, leading to diminished professional autonomy and instrumental decision-making (Gleeson and Husbands, 2001; Perryman, 2009; Keddie, Mills and Pendergast, 2011). Thus, curricular policy intentions are undermined and diminished by the effects of other policies and associated practices.

Second, the development of aspirational policy to promote teachers' professional agency has not been accompanied by a cultural/discursive environment that might foster such aspirations (Reeves and Drew, 2012). Part of this lies in the above-mentioned performativity; however, the problem is also situated in professional thinking about education and the professional language used to describe and define educational practice. A recent study on teacher agency (Priestley, Biesta and Robinson, 2015; Biesta, Priestley and Robinson, 2017) suggests that many teachers lack an educational language with which to engage critically with policy, and to develop their practice. The study suggests that, in Scotland at least, many teachers simply use the language of the latest policy. There is evidence, mirroring previous studies by scholars such as Cuban (1998) and Swann and Brown (1997) that curriculum change is often superficial, comprising little more than changing the terminology to relabel existing practices as being constitutive of new policy. Moreover, existing educational discourse remains problematic in its technocratic and often linear nature. We offer here two examples of this. The first is the ubiquitous use of 'uneducational' language to describe educational practices, a phenomenon described by Hood (1995, p. 105) as 'new managerial catchwords', which have become so extensive that they constitute a 'new global vocabulary'. The metaphor of delivery is a notable example. One regularly hears about 'delivery' of content, or worse still, 'delivery' of outcomes, or 'delivery' of literacy. This may seem like a trivial issue but it is in fact significant, in that the language and metaphors we use frame the way we think about and enact practice. The continued conceptualising of education as something to be delivered potentially inhibits the enactment of practices, by framing the development of the curriculum as simply the implementation of the curriculum as a product defined by someone else. This is, of course redolent of the sort of linear thinking that seeks to close implementation gaps and ensure fidelity between policy and practice. A second example lies in how we conceptualise the implementation gap. As illustrated above, this is invariably seen as being a gap between policy and practice. A more fruitful way of seeing this is as a gap between educational purposes/principles/values and educational practices. To take this view potentially changes the problematic of enacting policy; instead of being an implementation issue or, as it so often becomes, an issue framed as changing teachers' practices, it becomes an issue of critical engagement with educational principles (including a critical engagement with policy) and a constructive enactment of practice that is fit-for-purpose.

Such an approach, as we shall illustrate in the remainder of this chapter, seeks to avoid a situation where curriculum development is reduced to a process of ticking off of outcomes and the implementation of techniques, as teachers lose sight of the big ideas of the curriculum (Drew, Priestley and Michael, 2016). In the next section, we describe a project, *School-based Curriculum Development through Critical Collaborative Professional Enquiry*, which sought to break the mould of existing curriculum development practices.

## Critical Collaborative Professional Enquiry

This project ran with yearly cohorts of around 25 teachers between 2012 and 2015, within a single Scottish local authority. Throughout the project, there was a strong focus on ensuring that values and beliefs pertaining to issues of social justice were surfaced, examined and challenged through 'asking critical questions of policies and practices' (General Teaching Council for Scotland, 2012). Each cohort comprised small groups of teachers (typically four to six) from early years, primary and secondary schools in the authority, attending six workshops over the academic year.. From the outset, there was an expectation that each school should send a group of teachers, including at least one member of the senior leadership and management team.

There are many frameworks and/or models for similar methodologies of enquiry or action research (for example see: Coghlan and Brannick, 2014; Koshy, 2010). While authors tend to agree that there is no single or correct way of implementing this methodology, a review of 42 studies of collaborative enquiry by DeLuca et al. (2015) identified three principal interrelated structural elements: dialogic processes; taking action; and engaging in reflection. All three elements are embedded in the CCPE model, which comprises a two stage process:

- Stage 1: a conceptual engagement with the 'big ideas' of the curriculum,[3] considering fitness for purpose and addressing contextual conditions.
- Stage 2: undertaking CCPE

The aim of the first stage was to engage practitioners with the principles and purposes of current curricular policy in Scotland and relevant curriculum theory and processes, addressing the issue, highlighted by research, that many teachers have a poor understanding of these (Priestley and Minty, 2013). The emphasis at this stage is not on change *per se*, but on critical engagement. Underpinning this activity is an assumption that existing practices might be fit-for-purpose, but that participants do not necessarily know whether this is the case, unless they are critically evaluated against the CfE attributes and capabilities as well as broader educational purposes, principles and values. An exploration of the principles and purposes or 'big ideas' of the curriculum is accompanied by consideration of fit-for-purpose knowledge/content (something that has been comparatively neglected in CfE; e.g. see: Priestley and Minty, 2013) and pedagogies. Participants are encouraged to think about barriers to and drivers for their planned innovation, stimulating discussion about how, for example, accountability practices and school systems might impede their plans.

This conceptual stage ensures that professional enquiry is rooted in consideration of educational purposes, principles and values. The CCPE stage involves three processes or phases: focusing, interrupting and sense-making (Drew, Priestley and Michael, 2016). During the first phase, the participants engage in professional dialogue about school-based curriculum development to identify an area of interest or concern in their practice related to pedagogy, content or assessment. Throughout this stage the participants develop the focus of the enquiry through engaging critically with ideas in research and academic readings, as they begin to form the enquiry question that will guide their innovation, and attend to principles of social justice and sustainability of practices, underpinned by their codes of professional ethics. By the end of this phase, the CCPE group generate and agree a broad 'critical' question for their enquiry and devise a collaborative plan for implementing the critical enquiry through interrupting practice. In the second phase of CCPE, groups interrupt existing practices through implementing and trialling new approaches. They continue to critique and refine or modify their conceptual framework during this phase, through ongoing critical engagement with reading and professional dialogue, both within the CCPE group and with other members of the educational community including the university researchers and colleagues. The process of engaging in systematic generation and gathering of empirical data (both process and outcomes) takes place throughout all three stages but is perhaps most prevalent during this stage as the practitioners undertake the interruption in practices, and begin to notice changes in their knowledge, understanding and practices, as well as the impact on their students' learning experiences. In the third phase there is a focus on collaborative sense-making through critical analysis of data and interpretation of evidence, as the CCPE group begin to evaluate the impact of the interruption and draft a 'report' for dissemination to their educational community. However, this sense-making process permeates all three phases, as participants invoke professional judgement to make sense of the data generated throughout the enquiry and use this to evidence their claims and assertions about the contribution of the process to: developing pupils' attributes and capabilities; enhancing their professional learning in relation to development of educational practices; and identifying messages for the wider school community.

## Research design

The research was guided by the following research questions:

1.  How did the project impact on educators' knowledge, understandings and practices in their settings?
2.  In what ways did the project shape the agency achieved by teachers in their professional work?
3.  In what ways did the project facilitate school-based curriculum development and affect practices in the participating schools?

Qualitative data were generated from the project. These included data emerging from activities associated with the project, as well as follow-up research, for example:

- Formal semi-structured telephone interviews with six participants, including school leaders
- Programme evaluation questionnaires
- Field notes from participant observation in project workshops
- Artefacts generated by cohorts through various pedagogical activities
- Mid/end of programme feedback from participants
- Artefacts generated for group presentations.

Drawing in this way from multiple data sources allowed the research team to construct a rich picture of the context being researched. Interview data and other written transcripts (for example field notes) were coded following an interpretivist approach (Corbin and Holt, 2005), which allowed for both a process of open coding of data and the subsequent application of theoretical framings (for example, the ecological approach to teacher agency (Priestley, Biesta and Robinson, 2015).

To protect participants, we have sought to minimise the risk of identification by referring to them by role only (e.g. EYCT = early years classroom teacher, PHT = primary head teacher, SDHT = secondary deputy head teacher, SCT = secondary classroom teacher, etc.). Schools are only identified by sector (primary/secondary). All participants are referred to as female, in order to further minimise risk of identification.

## Teacher agency

The data generated by this project have been analysed using the conceptual framework provided by the ecological approach to understanding teacher agency (Priestley, Biesta and Robinson, 2015). It is important to provide a brief overview of this approach here, as it differs from traditional sociological accounts of agency in significant ways. Foremost amongst these is the notion of agency as an emergent phenomenon, rather than as a variable in social action, as characterised in the long-standing structure/agency debate.

> [T]his concept of agency highlights that actors always act *by means* of their environment rather than simply in their environment [so that] the achievement of agency will always result from the *interplay of individual efforts, available resources and contextual and structural factors as they come together in particular and, in a sense, always unique situations.*
>
> *(Biesta and Tedder, 2007, p. 137; emphasis added)*

Agency, in other words, is not something that people have; it is something that people do or, more precisely, something they achieve (Biesta and Tedder, 2006).

It denotes a 'quality' of the engagement of actors with temporal-relational contexts-for-action, not a quality of the actors themselves.

This ecological understanding of agency draws heavily on the social theory of Emirbayer and Mische (1998), who have developed a theory of agency that encompasses the dynamic interplay between three temporal dimensions – influences from the past, orientations towards the future and engagement with the present – and which takes into consideration 'how this interplay varies within different structural contexts of action' (p. 963). They refer to these three dimensions as the iterational, the projective and the practical-evaluative. All three dimensions play a role in social action, but the degree to which they contribute varies. This is why Emirbayer and Mische (1998) speak of a '*chordal triad*' of agency within which all three dimensions resonate as separate but not always harmonious tones' (p. 972; emphasis in original). Thus, they define agency as:

> the temporally constructed engagement by actors of different structural environments – the temporal-relational contexts of action – which, through the interplay of habit, imagination, and judgement, both reproduces and transforms those structures in interactive response to the problems posed by changing historical situations.
>
> *(Emirbayer and Mische, 1998, p. 970)*

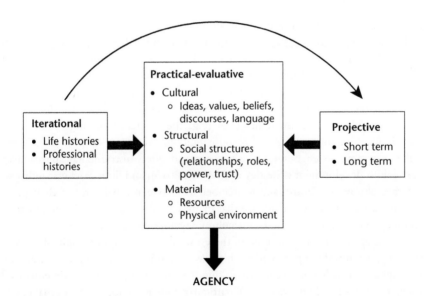

**FIGURE 10.1**   An ecological understanding of teacher agency

*Source:* Priestley, Biesta and Robinson, 2015

Agency thus appears as a

> temporally embedded process of social engagement, informed by the past (in its habitual aspect), oriented toward the future (as a capacity to imagine alternative possibilities) and 'acted out' in the present (as a capacity to contextualize past habits and future projects with the contingencies of the moment).
>
> *(p. 963)*

For a more detailed account of this conceptualisation of teacher agency, readers should refer to Priestley, Biesta and Robinson (2015).

## CCPE and teacher agency

In this final section of the chapter, we examine, through analysis of teachers' voices, the impact that participation in our CCPE project has exerted on teacher agency. We broadly frame this analysis in two areas: 1) the effects of CCPE on teachers' individual capacity to engage with curriculum policy (largely the iterational and projective dimensions, but playing out through teacher's judgements about what is possible in the present contexts of schooling); and 2) the ways in which this project has impacted upon the contexts which shape teachers' responses to curriculum policy (in effect the practical-evaluative dimension).

### *Teacher capacity to engage*

As indicated previously, research (e.g. Priestley and Minty, 2013; Priestley, Biesta and Robinson, 2015) suggests an erosion of Scottish teachers' capacity to develop the curriculum in school. For example, it is evident that many teachers do not possess the professional knowledge required to engage in school-based curriculum development, their practices being limited by strong socialisation associated with previous curriculum policy (e.g. outcomes-based planning with the former 5–14 curriculum), assessment practices (e.g. the influence of subject specifications in examinations syllabi) and accountability practices (e.g. inspections). These influences seem to encourage a risk-averse and often instrumental approach to curriculum development (Priestley and Minty, 2013), and limit teachers' ability to envisage alternative futures and to manoeuvre between repertoires in their practice. In particular, there is evidence that many schools simply recycle old practices and ideas when addressing new curriculum development problematics.

CCPE appears to address some of these issues, by interrupting habitual ways of thinking, by introducing new ideas in a way which is relevant to practice, and by its emphasis on collaborative sense-making. As such, the process clearly enhanced teachers' professional knowledge. Of particular value is the focus on external impetus, through the conversations with university academics and engagement with academic reading. The view of one Secondary Deputy Head illustrates sentiments more widely expressed by participants:

> I led the group; I had a way I wanted to go, a set of rigid ideas of what I considered it to be . . . my vision was narrow; by reading and research and working with Val and Mark, that expanded our thinking . . . Read stuff I had never heard of before . . . it really helped me have a wider perspective – a key driver was research and reading.
>
> *(SDHT1)*

Several teachers spoke about how the project allowed them to develop alternative ways of looking at the process of curriculum development, explaining how this opened up horizons and made new thinking and new practices possible. One Secondary Deputy Head spoke of how the project challenged single-track thinking, which had become deeply embedded in her school:

> Going back to the Four Capacities – refocus, coming back to broader sense of CfE and all the possibilities that are in there – makes you think gosh anything is possible; it opens it up again, you do get very entrenched with what you do on a daily basis.
>
> *(SDHT2)*

Other teachers articulated similar sentiments:

> It has reminded me not to simply accept 'the ways things are' within my classroom and to engage and reflect more critically upon things, which I feel are issues or problems, considering what I can do to improve this by engaging with literature of enquiry within my classroom.
>
> *(PCT8)*

Interestingly, the process seemed to challenge, in some cases at least, the prevailing tradition in Scotland of looking at 'best practice' in other schools, identified within school inspections and often uncritically applied. Instead, the process encouraged a more reflexive approach to developing practice from first principles.

> In terms of matching our interruption . . . to what we were doing, instead of how do we tick all the boxes, based on theory and the connections with critical approaches, rather than going with another school and see what they were doing or applying this because it is the latest initiative.
>
> *(PDHT2)*

For many of these teachers, CCPE represented:

> A change in seeing – it gave them time to see the impact of doing research based enquiry and the impact that professional reading can have directly in your classroom . . . it made them question each other's practice as well.
>
> *(PHT2)*

In turn, this 'allowed practitioners to be creative and innovative, which I believe has given my teachers the ability to do that and not be prescriptive and programmed for them' (PHT2).

In summary, the project appears to have developed teachers' professional knowledge by providing them with alternative ways of curriculum making. In turn, this has opened up new ways of thinking, and afforded opportunities for alternative practices and changes to often axiomatic and routinised ways of teaching. Crucially, it seems to have made participants more critical in their engagement with policy:

> I found that the programme has helped me to be much more analytical about any changes to pedagogy. I think carefully and examine any comments which claim to evidence improvement in a much more detailed way, to ensure that they do provide the evidence which is claimed. In terms of any changes being made in our department, I find myself questioning the rationale more carefully before the process is changed.
>
> *(SCT1)*

In terms of teacher agency, the individual capacity of teachers is clearly important. The project appears to have boosted this, leading to a greater ability in many cases to draw upon a wider repertoire for practice and to envisage alternative futures that had previously been unthinkable. In doing so, these teachers seem to have become less risk averse, more reflexive about their practice and enthused by a new curriculum that had previously often been a source of anxiety. Nevertheless, teacher agency is not just a matter of raising capacity; it is also important to address the structural and cultural constraints and affordances that help shape agency. In the next section of the chapter we examine this issue.

### Contextual issues

The practical-evaluative dimension of agency is largely about two things: the practical constraints and affordances that inhibit agency or conversely make it possible; and the judgements by social actors, such as teachers, that likewise inhibit or afford agency. The achievement of teacher agency, in its orientations to the present, is often about the availability of resources – material, cultural and relational – or the lack thereof, and about judgements of risk made in situ by busy professionals. CCPE, as a structured intervention, subtly altered many of these dynamics, making possible new practices and enhancing teacher agency. The following examples illustrate this change.

First, CCPE seems to encourage the development of more collaborative and collegial cultures in schools. Several teachers spoke about the breakdown of hierarchies and the development of genuinely collegial working, for example:

> It has made me more aware that non-promoted staff are able to bring about a change in the curriculum.
>
> *(PCT6)*

This in turn opened up the availability of what might be called relational resources. There are several dimensions to this, including the development of a supportive and protective environment, where colleagues could experiment and share the risks and benefits of innovation.

> It's a good way to gather a team together, working together, sharing research , sharing your understanding . . . planning changes, how you will look at success and how you will measure it and what changes you are going to make . . . a really good way of working together, working collegiately and joining together. [. . .] we had a shared goal, we had to work, research, evaluate, plan and present together. It was all a team effort; really positive to develop relationships in the staff between HT, DHT, new and existing teachers.
>
> *(PDHT2)*

One effect of this way of working seems to be increased confidence by classroom teachers:

> The process encouraged me to have a more questioning approach to all aspects of my job. This, along with the research approach, has given me a strong wish to ensure that any changes being asked of me are only implemented with carefully thought through reasoning. This has given me confidence to question carefully any claims which are made.
>
> *(SCT1)*

A related effect was a reported increase in teachers' professional engagement in the development of the curriculum:

> It has highlighted that we – as professionals – are able to make a change to our curriculum. It is not always something we are 'made to do' by management.
>
> *(PCT6)*

In Scotland, this has not always been the case. Earlier changes to teachers' working conditions had specified that curriculum development was to be part of a teacher's professional remit, although this has often been slow to develop in a hierarchical system where top-down practices have been widely prevalent.

CCPE appears to be promising in addressing some of the contextual issues. Because the insistence on senior management involvement in the programme, there appears to have been a substantial buy-in from school leaders to the methods and aims of the project, and increased support for resultant practices. This has provided a layer of protective mediation in respect of external demands relating to accountability. It has aided in the development of collaborative professional cultures and school systems, which in combination have enhanced the availability of relational resources in the schools. Moreover, participation in the project has helped to change attitudes and boost staff confidence, meaning that many of the teachers have become likely to engage in different decision-making about curriculum development. This relates to the 'evaluative' aspect.

## Conclusions

Our research on CCPE in one Scottish local authority suggests that it is a powerful mechanism for engaging teachers with curriculum policy and breaking the mould of existing practices. The research suggests that this approach has enjoyed some success in enhancing teacher agency – through augmenting professional knowledge, challenging existing preconceptions and ways of working and through mitigating some of the cultural and structural barriers to curriculum development that currently exist in schools. Moreover, the data suggest (as we have reported elsewhere; see Drew, Priestley and Michael, 2016) that this has led in some cases to sustainable changes to practice in the participating schools.

There are also clear implications in relation to the importance of understanding the ecology within which – and by means of which – the curriculum is made in schools. Governments and other agencies concerned with developing educational policy and practice have tended to overemphasise the importance of teachers as key actors within the system. For instance, the OECD (2005) has claimed that 'teachers matter'. While not denying the importance of good teachers and good teaching, recent research on teacher agency (Priestley, Biesta and Robinson, 2015) has pointed clearly to the vital significance of attending to structural and cultural dimensions of teachers' professional lives, as these can be highly influential shapers of teacher agency.

The CCPE approach is helpful, as it actively addresses these issues. This, and previous research, indicate clearly that the types of structures formed and reproduced in schools are important in shaping what is possible for teachers to do, as they engage with the curriculum (also see: Priestley, Biesta and Robinson, 2015). A key issue lies in the nature of relationships experienced by teachers in their professional contexts, and the relational resources afforded by such structures. CCPE actively addresses this dimension, in particular through facilitating the formation of strong professional ties, with the apparent effect of reducing the effects of hierarchy in schools. CCPE also addresses cultural issues in schools. It promulgates the dissemination of new ideas, through engagement with research and the actions of critical colleagues (in this case, university researchers), both of which can act to interrupt habitual thinking and practices.

This, in turn, points to the crucial role played by school leaders. Early iterations of CCPE were less effective because they did not involve school leaders as active participants in the process. Innovations thus tended to wither on the vine in the absence of senior leadership understanding, enthusiasm and support. In our recent projects, we have insisted on the active engagement of school decision-makers in working groups, and they have tended to become active promoters for the projects in question, playing an important role as advocates for innovation, as protective mediators who shield teachers from external risks (e.g. those associated with accountability mechanisms), and as providers of resources to enable innovations to thrive.

Clearly further experimentation, and more research will be needed to test these claims; however, we would argue on the basis of existing evidence that CCPE is a promising approach with the potential to enhance teacher agency and ultimately to lead to more meaningful curriculum development in schools.

## Implications for the research-informed ecosystem

- Curriculum making is a process that requires the active engagement – and agency – of teachers, as research-engaged and research-literate professionals. Critical Collaborative Professional Enquiry (CCPE) actively fosters these attributes.
- The development of sustainable practices in schools requires an understanding of the ecology of schools: while teachers are important, they can only achieve agency by means of the cultural, structural and material resources available to them. Educational policy and leadership which only focuses on the quality of the teacher, while neglecting the latter dimensions, is less likely to be effective.
- CCPE not only enhances the professional capacity of teachers; it also allows them to identify, navigate and mitigate contextual barriers to their professional engagement, and to actively develop contextual resources, through fostering better understandings of the ecologies of schools and their wider settings.

## Acknowledgements

We wish to acknowledge the enthusiastic participation of around 75 teachers and senior managers over the three years of the project. We also wish to offer our thanks and appreciation to East Lothian Council, particularly Alison Wishart for her support in making this programme happen.

## Notes

1 We use the Scottish spelling 'enquiry' throughout the chapter, in preference to the more commonplace 'inquiry'.
2 First generation new curriculum reforms include the Czech Republic, Scotland and New Zealand. Subsequently, a second wave of countries has moved in similar directions, including the Netherlands, Wales, the Republic of Ireland.
3 In the case of CfE, these are set out in the Four Capacities – the key competencies that form the front-end purposes of the curriculum. They have become a sort of mantra, widely visible as slogans on posters in schools, but often stripped of meaning. In fact, they form a useful starting point for curriculum planning, being broken down into a set of key competences known as attributes and capabilities, which define the skills and knowledge to be acquired by an educated person. See: https://education.gov.scot/scottish-education-system/policy-for-scottish-education/policy-drivers/cfe-(building-from-the-statement-appendix-incl-btc1-5)/What%20is%20Curriculum%20for%20Excellence (accessed 6 January 2019.

## References

Biesta, G. J. J. (2004). Education, accountability and the ethical demand. Can the democratic potential of accountability be regained? *Educational Theory*, 54, 233–250.

Biesta, G. J. J. (2010). *Good Education in an Age of Measurement: Ethics, Politics, Democracy*. Boulder, CO: Paradigm Publishers.

Biesta, G., Priestley, M. and Robinson, S. (2017) Talking about education: the significance of teachers' talk for teacher agency. *Journal of Curriculum Studies*, 49, 38–54.

Biesta, G. J. J. and Tedder, M. (2006). *How is Agency Possible? Towards an Ecological Understanding of Agency-as-Achievement. Working Paper 5*. Exeter: The Learning Lives Project.

Biesta, G. J. J. and Tedder, M. (2007). Agency and learning in the lifecourse: towards an ecological perspective. *Studies in the Education of Adults*, 39, 132–149.

Coghlan, D. and Brannick, T. (2014). *Doing Action Research in Your Own Organisation*, 4th edition. London: Sage.

Corbin, J. and Holt, N. J. (2005). Grounded theory. In B. Somekh and C. Lewin (Eds.), *Research Methods in the Social Sciences*. London: Sage, pp. 113–120.

Cuban, L. (1998). How schools change reforms: redefining reform success and failure. *Teachers College Record*, 99, 453–477.

DeLuca, C., Shulha, J., Luhanga, U., Shulha, L. M., Christou, T. M. and Klinger, D. A. (2015). Collaborative inquiry as a professional learning structure for educators: a scoping review. *Professional Development in Education*, 41, 640–670.

Donaldson, G. (2010). *Teaching Scotland's Future: Report of a Review of Teacher Education in Scotland*. Edinburgh: Scottish Government.

Drew, V., Priestley, M. and Michael, M. (2016). Curriculum development through Critical Collaborative Professional Enquiry. *Journal of Professional Capital and Community*, 1, 1–16.

Eady, S., Drew, V. and Smith, A. (2014). Doing action research in organizations: using communicative spaces to facilitate (transformative) professional learning. *Action Research*, 13, 105–122.

Emirbayer, M. and Mische, A. (1998). What is agency? *The American Journal of Sociology*, 103, 962–1023.

Evetts, J. (2011). A new professionalism? Challenges and opportunities. *Current Sociology*, 59, 406–422.

Furlong, J. (2014). *Research and the Teaching Profession Building the Capacity for a Self-Improving Education System*. Final report of the BERA-RSA inquiry into the role of research in teacher education. London: BERA.

General Teaching Council for Scotland (2012). *The GTCS Professional Standards*. Available: www.gtcs.org.uk/standards/standards.aspx. Accessed 4 September 2015.

Gleeson, D. and Husbands, C. (Eds.) (2001). *The Performing School: Managing, Teaching and Learning in a Performance Culture*. London: RoutledgeFalmer.

Green, A. (1999). Education and globalization in Europe and East Asia: convergent and divergent trends. *Journal of Education Policy*, 14, 55–71.

Halsey, A. H., Lauder, H., Brown, P. and Wells, A. S. (Eds.) (1997). *Education, Culture, Economy and Society*. Oxford: Oxford University Press.

Helsby, G. (1999). *Changing Teachers' Work*. Buckingham: Open University Press.

Hood, C. (1995). Contemporary public management: a new global paradigm? *Public Policy and Administration*, 10, 104–117.

Keddie, A., Mills, M. and Pendergast, D. (2011). Fabricating an identity in neo-liberal times: performing schooling as 'number one'. *Oxford Review of Education*, 37, 75–92.

Kelly, A. V. (2004). *The Curriculum: Theory and Practice*. 5th edition. London: Sage.

Kneyber, R. and Evers, J. (Eds.) (2015), *Flip the System: Changing Education from the Bottom Up*. London: Routledge.

Koshy, V. (2010). *Action Research for Improving Educational Practice: A Step-By-Step Guide*. 2nd edition. London: Sage.

Kuiper, W. and Berkvens, J. (Eds.) (2013). *Balancing Curriculum Regulation and Freedom Across Europe, CIDREE Yearbook 2013*. Enschede, the Netherlands: SLO.

Leat, D., Livingston, K. and Priestley, M. (2013). Curriculum deregulation in England and Scotland: different directions of travel? In W. Kuiper and J. Berkvens (Eds.), *Balancing Curriculum Regulation and Freedom Across Europe, CIDREE Yearbook 2013*. Enschede, the Netherlands: SLO, pp. 229–248.

Nieveen, N. and Kuiper, W. (2012). Balancing curriculum freedom and regulation in the Netherlands. *European Educational Research Journal*, 11, 357–368.

OECD (2005). *Teachers Matter: Attracting, Developing and Retaining Effective Teachers*. Paris: OECD.

OECD (2015). *Improving Schools in Scotland: An OECD Perspective*. Paris: OECD.

Perryman, J. (2009). Inspection and the fabrication of professional and performative processes. *Journal of Education Policy*, 24, 611–631.

Priestley, M. (2013). The 3–18 Curriculum in Scottish education. In T. G. K. Bryce, W. M. Humes, D. Gillies and A. Kennedy (Eds.), *Scottish Education: Referendum*, 4th edition. Edinburgh: Edinburgh University Press, pp. 28–38.

Priestley, M. and Biesta, G. J. J. (Eds.) (2013). *Reinventing the Curriculum: New Trends in Curriculum Policy and Practice*. London: Bloomsbury Academic.

Priestley, M., Biesta, G. J. J. and Robinson, S. (2015). *Teacher Agency: An Ecological Approach*. London: Bloomsbury Academic.

Priestley, M. and Minty, S. (2013). 'Curriculum for Excellence': A brilliant idea, but . . ., *Scottish Educational Review*, 45, 39–52.

Reeves, J. and Drew, V. (2012). Relays and relations: tracking a policy initiative for improving teacher professionalism. *Journal of Education Policy*, 27, 711–730.

Sinnema, C. and Aitken, G. (2013). Trends in international curriculum development. In M. Priestley and G. J. J. Biesta (Eds.), *Reinventing the Curriculum: New Trends in Curriculum Policy and Practice*. London: Bloomsbury, pp. 141–164.

Stenhouse, L. (1988). Artistry and teaching: the teacher as a focus of research and development. *Journal of Curriculum and Supervision*, 4, 43–51.

Supovitz, J. A. and Weinbaum, E. H. (2008). Reform implementation revisited. In J. A. Supovitz and E. H. Weinbaum (Eds.), *The Implementation Gap: Understanding Reform in High Schools*. New York: Teachers College Press.

Swann, J. and Brown, S. (1997). The implementation of a national curriculum and teachers' classroom thinking. *Research Papers in Education: Policy and Practice*, 12, 91–114.

Taylor, M. W. (2013). Replacing the 'teacher-proof' curriculum with the 'curriculum-proof' teacher: toward more effective interactions with mathematics textbooks. *Journal of Curriculum Studies*, 45, 295–321.

Wallace, C. and Priestley, M. (2017). Secondary science teachers as curriculum makers: mapping and designing Scotland's new curriculum for excellence. *Journal of Research in Science Teaching*, 54, 324–349.

Young, M. (2008). From constructivism to realism in the sociology of the curriculum. *Review of Research in Education*, 32, 1–28.

# 11

# RETHINKING RATIONALITY WITHIN AN ECOSYSTEM APPROACH TO FOSTER RESEARCH-INFORMED PRACTICE

*Chris Brown*

## Aims of the chapter

- To suggest that an ecosystem approach provides an opportunity to rethink how we examine why research-informed practice does (or doesn't) occur in schools.
- To introduce the concepts of Optimal Rationality, Optimal Rational Positions and the analytical framework of semiotics into the ecosystem model. To use these to show how teachers interpret and respond to signals such as the current push for research-informed practice.
- To provide an overview of how these concepts were used in relation to one case study of research-informed practice: a federation of three infant schools in Hampshire, England. Furthermore, to examine the clues this case provides for how to make research-informed teaching a reality.

## Introduction

Envisaging teachers' engagement with research evidence via an ecosystem lens provides the opportunity to radically rethink our understanding of research-informed practice. In particular it enables researchers to consider which concepts and analytical approaches might best suit the ecosystem model. Correspondingly, the empirical analysis that is presented in this chapter is framed by two pertinent theoretical and methodological perspectives: 1) the concept of Optimal Rationality, which represents an alternative to Rational Choice Theory and suggests that rational behaviour is related to how individuals interpret particular signals: e.g. actions, requirements, ideas or concepts; and 2) the analytical approach of semiotics, which provides a lens through which we can analyse individuals' myriad interpretations and their responses to signals. Using these two perspectives to examine the case of the Chestnut Learning Federation, I explore what research use means to teachers, why they do or do not seek to use research evidence to improve teaching and how these positions might be shifted in favour of research-informed teaching practice (RITP).

## Optimal Rational Positions

The concept of Optimal Rational Positions (ORPs) represents the idea that there are certain acts, states or situations that society deems beneficial – generally these benefits accrue in terms of the longer term and in relation to the wider population (Brown, 2018). For example, the need to reduce carbon emissions to minimise the impacts of climate change is an ORP, as is the need for us to eat five items of fruit and vegetables a day. Other examples of ORPs include the suggestion that we should limit our alcohol consumption to 14 units per week[1] and that we should exercise for 30 minutes at least three times a week.

In terms of how they might be recognised or defined, *Optimal Rational Positions* typically emerge as a result of four key factors:

1.  a robust and credible evidence base in relation to current or potential new behaviours;
2.  a well-reasoned argument (or theory of change) which provides this evidence with meaning;
3.  a social, moral or value-based imperative setting out the need for change based on this meaning (or conversely, the consequences of not changing);
4.  and buy in to this imperative from a range of credible stakeholders.

These four factors will be illustrated using the example of RITP below.

Underpinning this chapter are two key arguments in relation to ORPs. The first is that, because they comprise a pragmatic 'coming together' of hard facts with a general imperative to improve people's lives, Optimal Rational Positions present us with a substantive requirement to engage in change. Second, we should want to pursue ORPs because they espouse the types of behaviours that will enable us to live healthier, happier or more productive lives; that can improve the lives and outcomes of others; or that can help us ensure social and/or environmental sustainability.

At the same time the concept of Optimal Rational Behaviour – of which ORPs form part – accepts that people may not necessarily pursue ORPs because of the freedom we have to choose what we believe in, how we act and the many goals we may seek to aim for. In other words, the notion of Optimal Rational Behaviour suggests, much in the same way as animals in natural ecosystems respond in relation to specific signs and signals that occur in the environment surrounding them, that people will respond to ORPs depending on how they interpret such positions. Clearly, however, interpretation by humans occurs at a much more cognitively complex level than for other animals. It also occurs in a much more complex environment. For instance, the need to respond to messages suggesting we should gear our diet so that we consume five portions of fruit and/or vegetables whilst also reducing the use of plastics, appears to require more cognitive effort than those suggesting responses such as 'mate', 'hunt', 'survive' etc. At the same time, these two simple ORPs are just the tip of iceberg in terms of the myriad goals and sometimes conflicting demands we face in our information-rich social world. As a result, sometimes individuals will know about ORPs but not engage in actions that cohere with them or they may be rejecters of ORPs.

Correspondingly, this means we can consider people's responses to *Optimal Rational Positions* according to their *attitudes* towards the ORP and their *engagement* with the ORP. In other words whether: 1) individuals believe that the ORP is something that reflects how they and others should be behaving; and 2) whether they are indeed acting in accordance with the ORP. Assuming that both beliefs/attitudes and actions can be assigned to the dichotomous categories of 'yes' or 'no' then this specific division of attitudes and actions can be represented by the 2 x 2 matrix set out in Figure 11.1.

As a result we can begin to consider individuals as belonging to one of four types as relates to any given ORP. Here 'Type 1' individuals are those that believe that the OPR represents the right thing to do and act in accordance with it. In other words, Type 1 individuals are achieving the Optimal Rational situation of maximising welfare (i.e. welfare for the long-term self or long-term universal). 'Type 2' individuals are those who believe that the ORP represent the right thing to do but are yet to act in accordance with it: for instance they may lack required knowledge, skills or resource to fully engage with the ORP. Type 2 individuals may also require a greater incentive to move away towards more preferential activities. 'Type 3' individuals do engage in actions that cohere with the ORP but

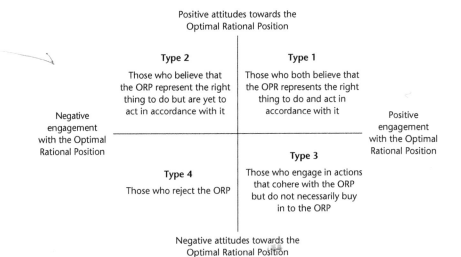

FIGURE 11.1  Rationality types

do not necessarily buy in to the ORP. This may mean, for example, that the fact that their actions cohere with the ORP is simply coincidence or that their actions are driven by other factors (such as budget restraints). As such, it seems likely that without positive buy in to the ORP, the coherence of the actions of 'Type 3' individuals with the ORP is only likely to be temporary. Finally 'Type 4' individuals totally reject the ORP.

As a result of allocating people to the types set out in Figure 11.1 we can determine whether rationality 'gaps' exist: in other words we can ascertain whether outcomes could be more objectively beneficial than they currently are. This is because it is only 'Type 1' individuals who maximise well-being. While Types 2–4 are engaging in rational acts (according to the notion of rationality espoused by ORP: Brown, 2018), this will not be in accordance with what a given ORP suggests is required over the long term. As noted above, people in these situations will instead typically be acting in the interests of the short-term self. Rationality gaps in essence then represent the proportional differences between those people who might be considered 'Type 1' and all others (i.e. those who could potentially be 'Type 1').

Key to filling rationality gaps, meanwhile, is understanding the relationships that exist between people and things, such as objects and ideas. To provide a means to engage in the type of analysis of relationships to fill rationality gaps, I turn to *semiotics; a theory which holds that all phenomenon and things convey meaning to individuals.* As Umberto Eco, observes, semiotics is something that is 'concerned with everything that can be *taken* as a sign. A sign is everything which can be taken as significantly substituting for something else' (Eco, 1979, p. 7). In other words, semiotics is concerned with the interpretations that you, I and others associate with words, images, objects or anything else that can be used to signify [indicate] some meaning or other. Semiotics has a key role to play in relation to ORPs because what is signified to us by particular ideas, objects, people etc. is instrumental to how we make choices.[2] In fact, we may think of signification as affecting decision-making in three ways: 1) what the ORP 'signifies' to individuals, and what individuals believe engaging with an ORP enables them to signify to others; 2) the benefits individuals perceive will result from acting in accordance with an ORP; and 3) cost, and whether individuals can 'afford' to, or will find it difficult to act in ways required by the ORP. I now explore these in more detail.

**Signification:** Part of the reason we may choose to engage with an Optimal Rational Position is that it reflects who we perceive ourselves to be. This reflection may represent our current behaviour or behaviour we aspire to. In both cases, however, what the ORP signifies is seen as desirable – it represents something that we can connect to and that we want to be regarded as being associated with.[3]

**Benefits:** Optimal Rational Positions also need to clearly signify their benefits to enable us to choose between the ORP and other attractive options. The benefits of attending the gym or eating healthily, for example, are generally self-apparent and tangible: doing these things will make us fitter and healthier, they will enable us to live longer and they reduce the risks of us suffering from heart disease and cancer, of developing type 2 diabetes and of becoming obese. The benefits of other types of ORP are perhaps less apparent and so may require us to consider impacts that reside beyond the immediate self and instead serve the good of the long-term collective. This can be hard for people to do and easy for them to ignore.

**Costs:** Finally, ORPs need to signify their costs to ensure individuals understand what is required to engage with them. With some ORPs costs will involve an element of price: we can establish how much a monthly gym membership costs and so ascertain how to incorporate this into our budget. Likewise, it is easy to find out the cost of using public transport compared to cars or the price of purchasing particular types of food. With many ORPs however there are non-financial costs that need to be considered. Such non-financial costs include the time it takes to engage in a particular type of activity. There is also the cost of perceived effort, which affects how hard we think it will be to access particular benefits.

Adding this understanding of benefits, costs and signification to the matrix set out in Figure 11.1 now provides a framework that can be used to develop a more in-depth understanding of why people respond to ORPs in different ways. By exploring what is signified to different people when they consider ORPs we can begin to understand the essential variations in their perceptions of meaning, usefulness and cost: why an ORP is viewed as attractive, useful and easy to attain to one set of individuals and not to another. Furthermore, why individuals may prefer to choose alternatives to the ORP. This is illustrated in Figure 11.2. We can also begin to explore what factors or phenomenon might alter what is signified and, correspondingly, the likelihood that people will engage with the ORP.

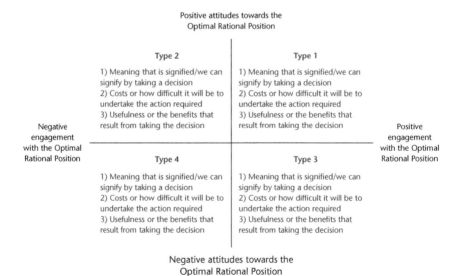

**FIGURE 11.2**  Incorporating semiotic analysis into the Optimal Rational matrix

## Research-informed teaching practice

Research-informed teaching practice (RITP) represents a collaborative process in which teachers and school leaders work together to access, evaluate and apply the findings of academic research in order to improve teaching and learning in their schools (Walker, 2017). There is now a longstanding recognition by both teachers and policy makers that academic educational research can be used to improve practice but only limited evidence on how this might be facilitated at the school level (Graves and Moore, 2017). As a result this leaves only sporadic instances of RITP occurring within and across schools; with other factors such as intuition and experience instead solely driving much of the decision-making undertaken by teachers (Vanlommel et al., 2017). Yet at the same time RITP very much represents an Optimal Rational Position and so should be encouraged and fostered within schools. That RITP is an ORP can be illustrated below using the four factors that comprise ORPs:

## RITP as Optimal Rational Position

Factor 1: Collaborative RITP can have positive benefits for both teachers and students. For example, correlational data reported by Mincu (2014) suggests that where research is used as part of high quality initial teacher education and ongoing professional development, it is associated with higher teacher, school and system performance. More recently Rose et al. (2017), using a randomised control trial across a sample of 119 schools, showed that increased levels of collaborative research use by primary school teachers had a positive impact on primary school student's exam results. CUREE (2010), meanwhile, lists a range of positive teacher outcomes that emerge from collaborative RITP including both improvements in pedagogic knowledge and skills, and greater teacher confidence.

Factor 2: A theory of change for why RITP should improve teaching and student outcomes is set out in Brown et al. (2017). Broadly this argues that there is a multitude of research that currently exists that can help teachers in a number of areas of their work. For example research can be used to: 1) aid teachers in the design of new bespoke strategies for teaching and learning; 2) help teachers expand, clarify and deepen their own concepts, including the concepts they use to understand students, curriculum and teaching practice, or; 3) provide teachers with specific programmes or guidelines, shown by research to be effective. Thus, if teachers are able to engage with this research in a way that enables them to undertake any of 1–3) above, their teaching quality should be improved. Correspondingly, improved teaching quality should then lead to improved student outcomes.

Factor 3: Given that it is possible to use research evidence to improve teaching practices then teachers *should* engage in RITP. This imperative stems from advocates such as Oakley; who argues that evidence-informed approaches ensure that 'those who intervene in other people's lives do so with the utmost benefit and least harm' (2000, p. 3). Oakley thus contends that there exists a moral imperative for practitioners to only make decisions, or to take action, when armed with the best available evidence. In other words that:

> we [all] share an interest in being able to live our lives as well as we can, free from ill-informed intervention and in the best knowledge we can gather of what is likely to make all of us most healthy, most productive, most happy and most able to contribute to the common good.
>
> *(2000, p. 323)*

More recently England's Chartered College of Teaching recently suggested that teachers engagement with research should be viewed as the hall-mark of an effective profession.[4]

Factor 4: It is evident that there now exists a general position in favour of teachers pursing collaborative RITP. For instance, the direction of travel of recent educational policy in England and elsewhere (including for example, Australia, Netherlands, Norway, Ontario, and the USA) focuses strongly on promoting, assisting and requiring teachers to better engage with research. It is also apparent from recent announcements by organisations, such as the Education Endowment Foundation (EEF), who in 2014 launched a £1.4m fund to improve the use of research in schools (EEF, 2014) and in 2016 launched the *Research Schools* initiative.[5] In addition, this position can be associated with the rise of bottom up/teacher led initiatives, such as the emerging network of 'Teachmeets' and 'ResearchED'[6] conferences designed to help teachers connect more effectively with educational research. One recent prominent example of such teacher led initiatives was the 2017 launch of England's Chartered College of Teaching: an organisation led by and for teachers in order to support the use of evidence-informed practice.

### The Chestnut Church of England Learning Federation

The case that forms the focus of the analysis in this chapter is that of the Chestnut Church of England Learning Federation; a family of three small Church Infant Schools based in the Hampshire villages of Rosebush, All Saints and Southampton Common. These three schools all work closely together under the leadership of the Federation principal and governing body and share a vision of ensuring children grow up to lead safe, happy, healthy and successful lives by benefitting from the highest standard of education and the opportunity for each child to attain their own, full potential.

One of the Federation's improvement plan objectives for the academic year 2016/2017 was for it to become an evidence-informed Federation where teachers and schools collaborate to rigorously evaluate the quality of the education they offer, understand what they need to do to improve, to take appropriate evidence-informed action and to evaluate the impact of their actions, enabling them to achieve together. To meet this objective, the Executive Principal proposed a school improvement plan to move school professional development in the Federation away from traditional professional development models and towards one in which all teachers are engaged in evidence-informed enquiry. In particular, the aim of Chestnut Learning Federation's model for evidence-use was to enable teachers to use research-informed enquiry to trial and evaluate the impact of new approaches to teaching and learning. Furthermore, to ensure teachers are facilitated to work collaboratively so that impactful innovations and effective pedagogic practices are modelled and embedded across all three schools.

Correspondingly, this chapter uses combined semiotic/Optimal Rational approach (referred to here as ORS) to explore the context for the roll out of the evidence-informed school improvement model developed by Chestnut Learning Federation, and to show what the ORS approach indicates was needed for the Federation to move towards the Optimal Rational Position of RITP. The research questions addressed by the ORS approach were, in terms of the Chestnut Learning Federation model of evidence-informed improvement:

1.  What are the pre-intervention perceptions of staff in relation to collaborative RITP?
2.  What is the signification initially associated with RITP within the Chestnut Learning Federation?
3.  What might be required to shift the current signification associated with evidence-use within Chestnut Learning Federation towards that of the Optimal Rational Position of RITP?

To address these questions a qualitative methodology was employed. For research question 1) in-depth semi-structured interviews were used to collect pre-intervention data on the attitudes towards and engagement in RITP by Chestnut's staff. Data was collected using qualitative versions of questions employed by Brown and Zhang's 2016 study of research-use; these measures are set out in Table 11.1.

For research questions 2) and 3) questions were developed in relation to the three factors signified to us when we are required to make choices concerning an ORP. These are 1) what the ORP's 'brand' means to us, and what we believe engaging with it enables us to signify to others (sample question: 'When I say research-informed teaching, what image does that convey to you?'); 2) the benefits

**TABLE 11.1** Measures of research use from Brown and Zhang (2016)

1.  Information from research plays an important role in informing my teaching practice
2.  I have found information from research-useful in applying new approaches in the classroom
3.  I do not support implementing a school-wide change without research to support it
4.  I do not support implementing a Federation-wide change without research to support it
5.  In the last year, I have discussed relevant research findings with colleagues in my school
6.  In the last year, I have discussed relevant research findings with colleagues in the Federation

we perceive will result from acting in accordance with an ORP (sample question: 'in terms of ways of improving practice, how effective is using research evidence? Why?'); and 3) cost, and whether we can 'afford' to, or will find it difficult to act in ways required by the ORP (sample question: 'In terms of ways of improving practice, how "costly" is using research evidence? Prompt in terms of time, money, training etc.'). Questions were also asked in relation to the background, values and beliefs of respondents.

A total of 15 teachers were interviewed in September 2016 (representing the whole of the Federation's teaching staff). The characteristics of the respondents are set out in Table 11.2. Interviews were recorded and these recordings transcribed. Data from the recordings were analysed thematically, first to ascertain the Optimal Rational *type* of participants and then to ascertain their perspectives in relation to the three signifying factors above.

Beginning with the analysis of the Optimal Rational *type* of participants, here type was determined by looking at teachers' responses to questions 1 and 4 in Table 11.1. In other words by examining teachers' beliefs as to whether they subscribe to the notion of RITP driving Federation level changes to teaching and learning and whether they themselves engage in RITP to improve teaching and learning. It can be seen in Figure 11.3 that there was a fairly wide distribution of respondents according to whether they believed they used research to improve their practice (or not) – question 1 in Table 11.1 AND/OR whether respondents were in favour of a school or federation level commitment to using research to improve practice (or not) – question 4 in Table 11.1. Overall a third of respondents indicated they believed in and acted in accordance with the ORP (i.e. were 'Type 1'). The remaining two thirds were predominantly Types '2' and '3' although one respondent was an out and out rejecter of the ORP ('Type 4') (in other words there was a rationality gap of 66 per cent).

Following this initial allocation of participants, thematic analysis was subsequently employed to identify all germane perceptions or perspectives from the interview data in terms of the signification (meaning), benefits and costs associated with RITP. Specifically, a hierarchy of thematic codes was developed to explain interview responses, with the development of codes occurring both inductively and deductively (Lincoln and Guba, 1985). The resulting coding tree is set out in Figure 11.4 and the allocation of codes by quadrant is set out in Figure 11.5.

**TABLE 11.2** Characteristics of the interview respondents

| | |
|---|---|
| Gender | 12 Female (92%), 1 Male (8%) |
| Average time in post | 9 years |
| Average age bracket | 46–50 |
| Number with postgraduate qualifications | 5 (38%) |
| Middle or senior leaders | 6 (46%) |

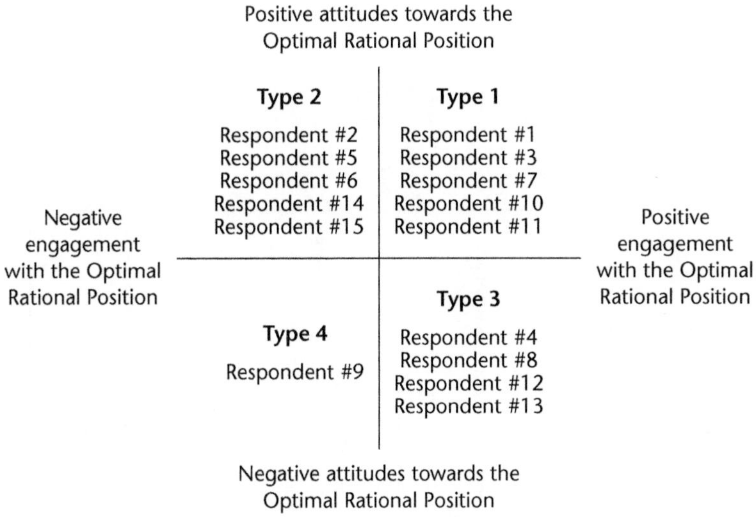

Positive attitudes towards the
Optimal Rational Position

| Type 2 | Type 1 |
|---|---|
| Respondent #2 | Respondent #1 |
| Respondent #5 | Respondent #3 |
| Respondent #6 | Respondent #7 |
| Respondent #14 | Respondent #10 |
| Respondent #15 | Respondent #11 |

Negative
engagement
with the Optimal
Rational Position

Positive
engagement
with the Optimal
Rational Position

| Type 4 | Type 3 |
|---|---|
| Respondent #9 | Respondent #4 |
| | Respondent #8 |
| | Respondent #12 |
| | Respondent #13 |

Negative attitudes towards the
Optimal Rational Position

**FIGURE 11.3**  Allocation of respondents according to Optimal Rational type

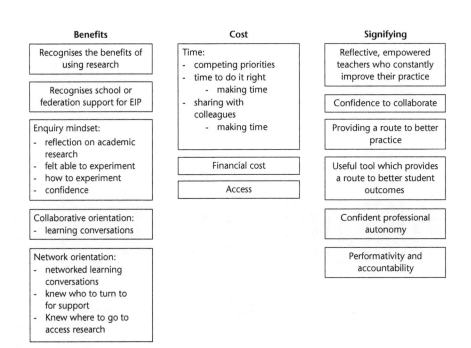

**FIGURE 11.4**  The hierarchy of thematic codes

Positive attitudes towards the Optimal Rational Position

**Negative engagement with the Optimal Rational Position** (left column)

**Benefits**
- Recognises school or federation support for EIP
- (+ve) Enquiry mindset
- (+ve) Collaborative orientation
- (+ve) Network orientation

**Cost**
- Time – 3 sub categories
- Access

**Signifying**
- Providing a route to better practice
- Confidence to collaborate

**Benefits**
- Cynicism
- (?) Valued activity
- (–ve) Enquiry mindset

**Cost**
- Time
- Access

**Signifying**
- Performativity and accountability

**Positive engagement with the Optimal Rational Position** (right column)

**Benefits**
- Recognises the benefits of using research
- Recognises school or federation support for EIP
- (+ve) Enquiry mindset – 3 sub categories
- (+ve) Collaborative orientation
- (+ve) Network orientation – 3 sub categories

**Cost**
- Time – 2 sub categories
- Financial cost

**Signifying**
- Reflective, empowered teachers who constantly improve their practice
- Confidence to collaborate

**Benefits**
- Recognises the benefits of using research
- (–ve) Recognises school or federation support for EIP
- (+ve) Enquiry mindset – 2 sub categories
- (local) Purpose
- (–ve) Network orientation

**Cost**
- Time

**Signifying**
- Useful tool which provides a route to better student outcomes
- Confident professional autonomy

Negative attitudes towards the Optimal Rational Position

**FIGURE 11.5** Allocation of thematic codes according to respondent's ORP type

Following coding, a comparison was then made between the codes sitting under each BCS value domain within in each quadrant. This was done in order to ascertain whether there were any meaningful differences in respondents' semiotic perspectives vis-à-vis their differing ORP *types*. For brevity, in this chapter I have provided a summary of the main findings.

### Type 1 (positive attitudes towards and positive engagement with the ORP)

Beginning with the *benefits* that were signified by RITP, five mid-level and nine initial codes were identified within the Type 1 quadrant. The first of these mid-level codes was *recognises the benefits of using research*, which highlights respondents' beliefs that the regular use of research to inform practice would result in better outcomes for children. Responses within the Type 1 quadrant also highlighted that this group knew how to maximise the *benefits* of RITP. For example they displayed an *enquiry mindset* illustrating they *felt able to experiment* with research and that they knew *how to experiment* with research, thus meaning they were happy to trial new approaches to teaching and learning. Participants engaged in *learning conversations* as a way of assessing whether and how new evidence-informed practices should be adopted. Furthermore, participants also displayed a *network orientation* in that they *knew who to turn to for support*: i.e. that they were able to identify who within the federation might support them with engaging in RITP if required. Also that respondents *knew where to go to access research*; i.e. they could identify who and where they might go to access research.

Moving to the *cost* value, two mid-level codes were identified. The first of these was *time*, which was often regarded as a barrier to achieving even more (with the initial level coding reflecting the need to find *time to do it right*). Included here was the time needed to ensure sufficient good quality research could be drawn on. *Sharing with colleagues* or the brokerage of research or research-informed strategies was also seen as key but time consuming, since it was recognised that sharing is only effective when research is 'effectively translated'. Finally, in terms of the *signifying* values of RITP, respondents suggested that, to them, RITP signalled the presence of *reflective, empowered teachers who constantly improve their practice*. At the same time, findings here also suggest that respondents viewed the use of research as something that would provide the *confidence to collaborate* with others across the federation: the use of research thus seen as providing a firm basis upon which to debate and engage in discussion around effective forms of teaching and learning.

### Type 2 (positive attitudes towards but no engagement with the ORP)

Moving now to the Type 2 quadrant and beginning again with the *benefits*, four mid-level and initial codes were identified. In all cases the benefits related to how RITP could augment existing practices. For example participants already *felt able to experiment*; thus teachers could see how research could strengthen this process. As with the Type 1 quadrant, *learning conversations* (reflecting participants' *collaborative orientation*) were often used and seen as a beneficial way of challenging entrenched practice that might not always be effective: learning conversations were thus seen as something that could be potentially strengthened by research. Respondents in this quadrant also actively connected with colleagues in other schools in order to collaborate and learn from each other through *networked learning conversations* (again reflecting their *network orientation*) and again saw how research could augment such conversations.

Four mid-level codes were identified for *cost*, of these three were related to the time costs associated with engaging in RITP. For this quadrant, such costs were associated with the *time [needed] to do it right*: i.e. engaging with research effectively and meaningfully. What's more, the cost of time also stretched to *sharing with colleagues*: ensuring that colleagues, such as teaching assistants (TA), understood how to use the approach as well. In both cases there was an anxiety about finding this time (*making time*), but it was felt that such issues would be manageable if protected time was allocated. One final cost value code was the cost of *access*. Here some expressed a worry as to whether they might understand formal academic research.

In terms of the *signifying* values, it was clear that respondents in this quadrant associated RITP with the qualities of the *enquiry mindset* expressed by others those already engaged in research-use (i.e. those in quadrants Type 1 and Type 3) with that mindset then *providing a route to better practice*. More specifically, RITP was associated with teachers who reflect using research and develop deeper pedagogic knowledge as a result; who are willing to try new approaches; and who experiment to take risks to improve practice. What's more, research-use was also seen to providing *confidence to collaborate* and a secure basis for evidence-informed teachers to be both collaborative and network orientated.

### Type 3 (positive engagement with the ORP but negative attitudes towards it)

Within the Type 3 quadrant there were five *benefit* codes, one *cost* code and one *signifying* code. In contrast to the first two quadrants, however, two of the *benefit* codes indicated negative perspectives and a further use code represented a localised focus. The first of the positive benefit codes was: *recognises the benefits of using research*. In other words, respondents in this quadrant thought that using research could result in better practice. Others noted that because they had just taught a difficult cohort of children, they had turned to research to provide them with specific pedagogic strategies. It was also apparent that respondents within this quadrant exhibited an *enquiry mindset*. This was indicated first by participants' *reflection on academic research*. Here, as before, this code often applied to the responses of those who had relatively recently completed a degree, or postgraduate qualification.

In terms of the negative codes, it was clear that participants in this quadrant could not point to examples of leadership support directed at encouraging RITP more widely (*recognises school/federation level of support for RITP*). This meant that this group did not tend to experiment and further stressed that the focus of the research-use activity needed a recognisable purpose if they were to buy into it. Sometimes this meant that they felt the locus for RITP should be at the level of the classroom rather than the level of the federation.

What's more, the *network orientation* of participants indicated a lack of depth of engagement with others. While those in the Type 1 and Type 2 quadrants employed *networked learning conversations*, those in this quadrant were more likely to engage in more superficial collaboration with networked peers. For example, the simple sharing (i.e. cost) of resource, rather than deep engagement with peers that centred on how to use the resource effectively. Finally, a key issue for those in this quadrant was the number of *competing priorities* that often seemed to 'get in the way' of research-use (the cost value of *time*). With these factors combined, it is perhaps no surprise that when it came to the *signifying* values associated with research-use, respondents within this quadrant tended to articulate a practical purpose. For instance, evidence use was regarded as a *useful tool* which *provides a route to better student outcomes*. A research-informed teacher meanwhile was seen as having good pedagogic knowledge: research-use thus seen as providing the basis for *confident professional autonomy*. In keeping with the analysis above, the imagery associated with RITP also had a local focus that involved teachers operating in their class-rooms in their own way.

## Type 4 (neither positive attitudes towards or any engagement with the ORP)

Only one respondent provided responses to suggest that they held Type 4 beliefs. Triangulating their responses with the analysis above shows that, in terms of *benefit*, unlike with other quadrants, this participant did not *feel able to experiment* (they thus demonstrated a negative *enquiry mindset*). In terms of *cost* value, this respondent also flagged the issue of *competing priorities*. Finally while respondents located in the other three quadrants universally linked RITP to solving problems, developing an enquiry habit of mind, becoming a reflective practitioner and developing 21st century learners, this respondent linked RITP directly to *performativity and accountability*.

## Conclusion

Moving forward, these findings (derived from the application of Optimal Rationality and semiotic analysis to the study of RITP) provide vital insights if schools and federations such as Chestnut Learning Federation are to become evidence-informed: i.e. are to shift the perspectives of its teachers towards the Type 1 quadrant. In particular, the analysis above suggests a number of perceived *cost* and *benefit* factors were contributing to teachers behaving in less than optimal ways in relation to collaborative RITP. These include: a lack of opportunities to engage with research evidence and so a dearth of experience in terms of the benefits of using research-evidence to improve practice (Type 2 respondents); a lack of access to research (Type 2 and some Type 3 respondents); respondents worrying whether they would be able to understand research evidence (Type 2 respondents); concerns such as having enough time to engage effectively with research evidence, or having time to show others how to engage with evidence-informed interventions (Type 2 and Type 3 respondents); and worries regarding *how* to engage with research evidence and whether they would engage in the 'right' way (Type 2 and Type 4 respondents). Some respondents also viewed RITP as a localised and reactive activity, rather than something that could be used collaboratively and proactively to drive continuous improvement (Type 3 respondents).

In addition, a number of *benefit* and *signifying* related factors also contributed to respondents holding less than optimal beliefs regarding RITP. For instance, there were concerns that not engaging 'properly' with research evidence would have professional consequences; meaning RITP as a concept was rejected because of its perceived relationship to performativity. This position was exemplified by the Type 4 respondent's perception that they were currently 'not allowed' to experiment to improve classroom practice). In some cases, respondents also believed there was little benefit in engaging in wider collaborative endeavours in relation to RITP, or that the competing priorities they faced meant that such collaboration was not possible (Type 3 and Type 4 respondents); also that these kind of collaborative endeavours would not be supported by the Chestnut Learning Federation's school leadership team (Type 3 and Type 4 respondents).

At the same time, looking across the responses of those who did use research in some form or other (i.e. Type 1 and Type 3 respondents), it could be seen that participants' first hand understanding of the benefits of using research was key to driving *actual engagement with research-evidence*. Often these individuals had had recent formal experience of *reflection on academic research*, possibly via postgraduate study. A key driver of respondents' positive attitudes towards RITP meanwhile (irrespective of whether they were Type 1 or 2) was that RITP was seen as representing a community wide endeavour: in this respect RITP was viewed as representing a culture rather than an activity, since it involves schools engaging with research to focus on strategic as well as local priorities. It would seem therefore that a fundamental part of what drives optimal attitudes towards collaborative RITP is the extent to which research use is perceived as being something that should extend beyond the local setting. That is, optimal attitudes towards RITP relate both to respondents' *collaborative* and *networked* orientations (e.g. their use of learning conversations and networked learning conversations) and the extent to which evidence-use signifies not just a tool, but something that leads to 21st century teaching and learning within what the OECD refers to as 'learning organisations' (OECD, 2016). Alongside this is the recognition from teachers that senior leaders within the federation are encouraging of the RITP agenda (*recognises school/ federation level of support for RITP*) and, vitally, that leaders are also engaging in acts (such as timetabling) to enable networked collaboration.

## Implications for the research-informed ecosystem

- The ecosystem approach provides the opportunity to recast and revision how we investigate research-informed teaching practice. While this chapter provides one set of new tools to do so: a combination of semiotics and Optimal Rationality – there are likely to be other exciting analytical approaches that could be profitably explored.
- In practical terms, the analysis above suggests that school and system leaders need to be attuned to how actors within the ecosystem are facilitated to engage with and collaborate in relation to RITP. Efforts here should be directed towards helping teachers fully understand the benefits on offer; also to support teachers in overcoming the costs associated with research-use.
- Vital however is the role of signals and signalling in the ecosystem. Teachers must perceive that collaborative RITP is a priority and is supported by school leaders; they must feel that engaging in it will not be judged in a performative and instrumental way; but perhaps most of all teachers must perceive RITP as now part of what professional teachers and the 21st century teaching workforce can and *should* do.

## Notes

1 See: https://patient.info/health/recommended-safe-limits-of-alcohol (accessed 16 January 2019).
2 Understanding how we make choices is widely regarded as key to understanding how we might enact behavioural change (e.g. see Elster, 2007).
3 Desirability in this sense could also include social duty since it can be attractive for people to know that they are doing 'something good' or 'the right thing to do'.
4 See: https://chartered.college/chartered-teacher-professional-principles (accessed 16 January 2019).
5 See: https://educationendowmentfoundation.org.uk/our-work/research-schools/ (accessed 16 January 2019).
6 See: www.workingoutwhatworks.com (accessed 16 January 2019).

## References

Brown, C. (2018). *How Social Science Can Help us Make Better Choices: Optimal Rationality in Action.* London: Emerald.
Brown, C., Schildkamp, K. and Hubers, M. (2017). Combining the best of two worlds: a conceptual proposal for evidence-informed school improvement. *Educational Research,* 59(2), 154–172.
Brown, C. and Zhang, D. (2016). Is engaging in evidence-informed practice in education rational? Examining the divergence between teachers' attitudes towards evidence use and their actual instances of evidence use in schools. *British Educational Research Journal,* 42(5), 780–801.
Coldwell, M., Greany, T., Higgins, S., Brown, C., Maxwell, B., Stiell, B., Stoll, L., Willis, B. and Burns, H. (2017). *Evidence-Informed Teaching: An Evaluation of Progress in England.* London: Department for Education.

CUREE (2010). *Report of Professional Practitioner Use of Research Review: Practitioner Engagement in and/or with Research.* Coventry: CUREE, GTCE, LSIS and NTRP. Retrieved 24 December 2017 from: www.curee-paccts.com/node/2303.

Eco, U. (1979). *A Theory of Semiotics.* Bloomington, IN: Indiana University Press.

EEF (2014). EEF launches £1.5 million fund to improve use of research in schools. *Retrieved* 16 January 2019 from: https://educationendowmentfoundation.org.uk/news/eef-launches-15-million-fund-to-improve-use-of-research-in-schools/. Accessed 27 September 2015.

Elster, J. (2007). *Explaining Social Behavior: More Nuts and Bolts for the Social Sciences.* Cambridge: Cambridge University Press.

Graves, S. and Moore, A. (2017). How do you know what works, works for you? An investigation into the attitudes of school leaders to using research evidence to inform teaching and learning in schools. *School Leadership & Management,* 38(3), 259–277.

Lincoln, Y. and Guba, E. (1985). *Naturalistic Inquiry.* Newbury Park, CA: Sage Publications.

Mincu, M. (2014). Inquiry paper 6: teacher quality and school improvement – what is the role of research? Retrieved 16 January 2019 from: www.bera.ac.uk/wp-content/uploads/2014/02/BERA-RSA-Interim-Report.pdf. Accessed 8 November 2017.

Oakley, A. (2000). *Experiments in Knowing: Gender and Method in the Social Sciences.* Cambridge: Polity Press.

OECD (2016). *What Makes a School a Learning Organization?* Retrieved 25 January 2016 from: www.oecd.org/education/school/school-learning-organisation.pdf.

Rose, J., Thomas, S., Zhang, L., Edwards, A., Augero, A. and Rooney, P. (2017). *Research Learning Communities: Evaluation Report and Executive Summary,* Retrieved 15 December 2017 from: https://educationendowmentfoundation.org.uk/public/files/Projects/Evaluation_Reports/Research_Learning_Communities.pdf.

Vanlommel, K., Van Gasse, R., Vanhoof, J. and Van Petegem, P. (2017). Teachers' decision-making: data based or intuition driven. *International Journal of Educational Research,* 83, 75–86.

Walker, M. (2017). *Insights into the Role of Research and Development in Teaching Schools.* Slough: NfER.

# 12

# MAINTAINING (ECOSYSTEMS FOR) A BROAD VIEW OF EDUCATIONAL RESEARCH AND ITS RELATIONSHIP TO PRACTICE

*Emma Wisby and Geoff Whitty*

*Geoff and I worked on this chapter over a number of months, and it was finalised in the last few weeks of Geoff's life, in June 2018. It covers a topic that we had written together on extensively – first in 2005 in preparation for his British Educational Research Association (BERA) Presidential Address, but particularly so since 2015 in relation to the book* Research and Policy in Education *(Whitty, 2016). I hope that Geoff would have been pleased with this final iteration of the chapter; I have endeavoured to keep in mind his particular concerns – to maintain a broad church of educational research and to support models of teacher education and teacher professionalism that reach beyond instrumental concerns – but any shortcomings are of course my own.*

## Aims of the chapter

- To show how the relationship between educational research and practice and the ecosystem in which they sit have evolved, particularly in England.
- To highlight the range of different knowledge traditions in the field of educational research and their shared relevance to teacher professionalism.
- To reflect on the phenomenon of 'post-truth' and its implications for how we think about evidence and evidence-informed practice.

## Introduction

One of the criticisms of the school effectiveness movement that was dominant in England and elsewhere during the 1990s was that it tended to view schools out of context. As a result, it greatly exaggerated their capacity for self-improvement as well as their role in broader movements for social justice (Mortimore and Whitty, 1997; Thrupp and Lupton, 2006). This problem has subsequently become exacerbated – now by a fetish among policy makers and some education researchers for what is usually termed evidence-informed policy and practice.[1] This evolved out of the 'what works' movement in the US, itself reflective of a particular medical model of research and intervention.

This trend has not gone unchallenged, as illustrated most recently at the time of writing by a 2018 editorial in the *British Educational Research Journal* (*BERJ*) (Aldridge et al., 2018). In the editorial the authors make an impassioned plea for the nature of educational research to 'remain contested' (p. 1). The authors suggest that, while educational researchers need to engage in public debates, criticism of the idea of establishing an 'educational science' is also legitimate. Indeed, they might have pointed to the limitations of such an approach identified over 40 years ago by the founding president of the British Educational Research Association (BERA), who noted that we had already moved away from 'the naïve idea that problems are solved by educational research' or what he called the 'old educational science idea' (Nisbet, 1974).

The *BERJ* editors' welcome statement of intent nicely complemented the argument we mounted in 2016 in *Research and Policy in Education: Evidence, Ideology and Impact* (Whitty and Wisby, 2016a), where we expressed concern about the implications for education research of an over-concentration on the agendas of 'evidence-informed policy' and 'research impact'. While these agendas have not been exclusive to England, England's tying together of 'what works' with research funding and research assessment under the guise of a drive for 'impactful research' has meant that it has pursued these causes particularly avidly. Our argument in *Research and Policy* was that (1) advocates of these agendas failed to recognise that research evidence is, rightly (certainly in a democracy), only one of a number of influences on policy decisions, and (2) in the process these agendas could skew research commissioning and narrow the field of education research by disproportionately favouring trials and systematic reviews. Not only, we suggested, could this be detrimental to education research, it would also, ultimately, be detrimental to political debate and policy making on education (see also Whitty, 2006; Whitty and Wisby, in press). In this regard, it is vital that education policy making is understood as a part of broader social, economic and political processes – or, in the terminology of the present volume, that it is addressed as part of the 'ecosystem' of which it is inevitably a part.

More recently in England, the advocacy of evidence-informed policy has focused its attentions on a new constituency – that of the professions and the cause of evidence-informed *practice*. We remain concerned that this movement too could become similarly caught up in simplistic ideas about the nature of research and how it can have impact – in this instance, on classroom practice – which in turn could have its own implications for the research base in education. As the present volume makes clear, classroom practice itself cannot be treated as an isolated target for analysis or intervention independently of the ecosystem of the school and community in which it takes place. Even school-based educational research needs to ask and answer questions that go well beyond 'what works' and a range of modes of enquiry therefore needs to be part of the repertoire employed.

In this chapter we rehearse in some detail a critique of recent tendencies in school-based research not with a view to dismissing them out of hand but to point to the importance of their being seen as part of a wider field of research. We also argue that teachers themselves should be properly engaged with a range of approaches to educational enquiry as part of their professional practice. In doing so, we want to recover the memory of other important school-focused traditions of research that have been at least as important in enhancing the quality of education as the current enthusiasm for 'what works', and reflect on the kind of ecosystem that can support that diversity. To set the scene, before exploring a case study of recent developments in England, we identify something of the richness of educational research around the world.

## Traditions in the study of education

It is the case that in virtually every country today there is a growing emphasis on what we termed in Whitty and Furlong (2017) the 'New Science of Education', and this is partly driven by the influence of OECD PISA tests on national policies. However, there is also a much broader tradition of educational research, much of which is also relevant to understanding the ecosystem of education itself. Our analysis suggests that there are three main traditions in the study of education. Firstly, there are academic knowledge traditions. Following the work of Bernstein, these include both 'singulars' (the disciplines of education such as the psychology of education or the history of education) and 'regions' (multidisciplinary traditions such as comparative and international education or management education). Secondly, there are practical knowledge traditions such as the competency movement or what we call 'Networked Professional Knowledge Production'. Finally, there are integrated knowledge traditions that attempt to combine both academic and practical knowledge. These include established approaches such as action research and newer models like 'Education Sciences', which is based on engineering principles. Rather than being a single discipline, let alone a single approach, the study of education is, then, made up of a range of different intellectual traditions, each with its own distinctive epistemological assumptions and each with its own distinctive relationship to the world of practice (see also Furlong, 2019).

## The evolution of policy on evidence-informed practice in England

Within the English schools system school-based and teacher research has a longer history than the advocacy noted above, although the current extent of its visibility as a mainstream concern for school leaders and teachers is relatively new. The roots of a much richer vein of teacher engagement with and in research can be traced back to the work of Stenhouse in the 1960s and 1970s (e.g. Stenhouse, 1975). His model of curriculum as enquiry was a critique of the rational-linear model of curriculum development beginning to be advocated by some governments at the time. More recently, and more in tune with the current rational-linear model, the ideas of David Hargreaves in the 1990s (e.g. Hargreaves, 1996), influenced by his understanding of medical education, has informed the development of research-rich models of professional and school development, especially in the autonomous schools in which he has worked (Hargreaves, 2006).

Taking an ecosystems approach, Godfrey (2014) relates these different conceptualisations of evidence-informed practice to the wider policy frameworks in place at the time, as seen across the Anglophone world – from the relative permissiveness of the 1960s to the 'devolution and choice' and 'third way' agendas of the 1990s (see also Whitty, Power and Halpin, 1997; Whitty and Wisby, 2016b). England has since pursued a distinctive path internationally, forging ahead with a relatively extreme model of school autonomy and accountability. This has, in turn, generated a relatively extreme version of the rational-linear model of evidence-informed practice (with actual and potential implications for research commissioning). In the face of ostensibly greater school autonomy, schools need to be equipped to make the most effective decisions in relation to the indicators against which their performance is measured, with more autonomous and more accountable schools enjoined to seek out evidence of what works and to base their practice on that evidence. Presented in less political terms, this shift is at the very least driven by a concern to direct scarce funds in the most cost effective way (as defined by government).

The step change in these respects came in 2011 with the government's establishment of the Education Endowment Foundation (EEF), a 'What Works Centre' for education. This move was reinforced by a 2013 report for the government by the popular science writer and campaigner Ben Goldacre, *Building Evidence into Education* (Goldacre, 2013). The report argued that schools should be helping to build 'the' evidence-base for education – a systematic, external research base, rooted in RCTs and systematic reviews, which would in turn directly inform their practice. The introduction of the EEF saw a significant tranche of government spend on research transfer to the EEF and its favoured methodologies of RCTs. Its key resource is the 'Teaching and Learning Toolkit', which, by 2018, summarised educational research on 34 topics, showing what different interventions can achieve in terms of learning gain and their relative resource-intensiveness. Versions of the toolkit are being launched around the world. There are loose similarities with John Hattie's influential work on 'Visible Learning' (Hattie, 2012).

In 2017 these developments were coupled with the government's introduction of a network of 'research schools', tasked with working directly with local schools to 'build their capacity to use evidence in their decision-making'. The EEF plans to spread what is learnt from the research schools across the country, thereby encouraging the development of the emergent knowledge tradition we have termed 'Networked Professional Knowledge Production' (Whitty and Furlong, 2017). More generally, schools are encouraged to evaluate their spending (for example, the additional funding they receive to support pupils from disadvantaged backgrounds) against the EEF Toolkit, whilst RCT evidence of an intervention's effectiveness has become a criterion for accessing some other strands of government funding.

Developments in other quarters have aligned themselves to a greater or lesser extent with the broad framework provided by Goldacre and the EEF. A prominent example, and a 'ground-up' example, is ResearchEd, which aims to improve teachers' research literacy and research use, seeking to 'dismantle myths in education, and get the best research where it is needed most'. ResearchEd originated in England in 2013 but is now operating conferences around the world. As one point of comparison, 2017 saw the launch of the independent Chartered College of Teaching, an organisation led by and for teachers 'to support evidence-informed practice' – though its website refers to 'promoting the learning, improvement and recognition of the *art, science and practice* of teaching for the public benefit' (Esner, 2017 [emphasis added).

In this sense, there is not a universally shared definition of what is being aimed for when it comes to supporting and realising 'evidence-informed practice'. The government's rational-linear agenda is relatively clear, but others seem to be working on the basis of a broader definition – or at least hedging their bets to a greater extent. Is education an art and/or a science? Does the evidence necessarily need to be an RCT? Should we start from research evidence, or practitioners' own experience? What would the accepted indicators of success be – teacher engagement, changes in practice, and/or improved pupil outcomes? From the kinds of developments outlined above we could infer that all of these options stand.

## Evidence-informed practice in practice

What the rational-linear model most demands is evidence of its impact on pupil outcomes. As yet, that evidence is scant. The EEF is itself aware of the issues around knowledge mobilisation and evidencing its impact in this regard (Turner, 2015; Collins, 2016). In 2014 it invested £1.5 million in five projects to explore the impact of research use in schools in terms of the impact on pupils' attainment. Early reporting has highlighted the challenges in demonstrating a causal link between evidence use and improved outcomes (Speight et al., 2016). A possible exception in the evidence base is Rose et al.'s (2017) evaluation of the EEF-funded 'research learning communities' programme. This did suggest a small possible link between the collaborative use of research by teachers and positive outcomes for pupil attainment. The 'intervention' or model of research use in question is not, however, on a strict reading of the rational-linear model, of that mould. And this reflects how the rational-linear model may already be evolving, or mutating, in practice, into something less prescriptive.

A commonly used typology of research use comprises three categories: instrumental, conceptual, symbolic (see Godfrey, 2017). Instrumental use relates to the rational-linear model and the use of research to replicate interventions shown through (RCT) research to be effective. Symbolic use is merely recourse to the research evidence (ideally RCT evidence in the English context) to justify existing practice. One reading of the conceptual use of research is not so far from the instrumental model: the concern is still with the replication of evidenced interventions with a focus on improving pupil outcomes, but here replication involves adaption of the intervention as opposed to its replication or adoption. By implication, the gold standard of evidence remains external research and, in particular, the RCT. The argument is not that *equivalent* replication should no longer be pursued but to add more nuance into what it means to scale up a research-informed approach (Brown and Flood, 2018: 153. See also Brown and Zhang, 2016). One might also go as far as to say there is an underlying assumption that, even if more modest ambitions in this respect may have to be accepted for now, the rational-linear model will 'come of age'. For the time being at least, though, this model affords more agency to the teacher in engaging with external research. It also highlights the potential in weaving together different knowledges, something that we return to later on.

Another possible reading of the conceptual model is much more nebulous and diffuse – using research more loosely to, for example, make phenomena more visible, challenge one's thinking, or as a prompt for thought and action (see Godfrey, 2017). This reading would seem inherently more accepting of a broader range of research evidence, right through, potentially, to more theoretical work. It also suggests that Nisbet's (1974) insistence that the relationship between research and policy is often an 'indirect' and 'sensitizing' process may apply to the relationship between research and practice as well. It would certainly appear to offer a better fit with evidence-informed practice as it is playing out in England's schools, at least to date.

The wider evidence from England is that teachers are much more focused on local action research than RCT data. Furthermore, often the supposed 'action research' reported in studies taken as evidence of the benefits of evidence-informed practice is not really research in the conventional sense – it is engagement with school data, through to curriculum development projects, or ad hoc lesson observation, learning walks/school visits and conference attendance. It might even include simply reading a magazine article about teaching (e.g. Sebba et al., 2012; Downing et al., 2004; Furlong and Salisbury, 2005. See also Bell et al., 2010; BERA-RSA, 2014; and, on England, Coldwell et al., 2017). More 'advanced' or sophisticated engagement with research might include reading groups/journal clubs, or undertaking research as part of accredited professional studies (see, for example, Saunders, 2007), though this activity could sit at very different ends of the spectrum of the conceptual use of research as set out above. Some would prefer to call it research-informed professional development.

Many have called for a greater recognition and acceptance of this broader view of research use, emphasising that the findings from local, small scale action research are closer to teachers' experience and more engaging and useful to them. The 2014 BERA-RSA report, for example, focuses more on teacher-led enquiry than teachers working with evidence created by others. Several of the contributing research papers refer to practice from elsewhere, such as Japan's lesson study approach. Saunders (2017) cites the value of teacher engagement in/with research as making the implicit explicit such that teachers can articulate the precise reasons – ethical, emotional, intellectual – for the decisions they have made during any given lesson. Whatever the methodology, this requires teachers to relate actively to the research in question. Nutley, Jung and Walter (2008) suggest that simply engaging in a research project, not just as a research subject but as an investigator, can lead to change in ways of thinking and behaving.

Some prominent education researchers have highlighted what they regard as the poor quality of and lack of robustness in much practitioner and school-based research (see, for example, Furlong and Oancea, 2006, 2008 – cited in Godfrey, 2014). In their review of the 2000–2003 government-funded Best Practice Research Scholarship programme, which was a form of officially funded 'action research', Furlong and Salisbury (2005) are clear on the limitations of such practice in terms of identifying 'what works', on the grounds of the relatively poor quality of the activity in research terms, and, thereby, the limits to useful dissemination. As they note, with one or two exceptions, many of the case studies reported 'what can only be described as "soft", more impressionistic, evidence' (p. 66); much of the 'knowledge' that is produced is not only context specific but also 'located in the individuals themselves and their practices [such that] it is often hard for individuals to articulate or even to recognise' (p. 69). Nevertheless, that does not lead Furlong and Salisbury to dismiss the value of such activity. As they continue: 'What the [programme] gave teachers access to (albeit in different degrees) was the "discourse" of research – reading and research-based procedures' (p. 57). This is about engagement with or in research as, first and foremost, a development activity and a more systematic approach to reflecting on practice.

As with Coldwell et al. (2017), Furlong and Salisbury (2005) do though call for clearer definition/delineation as to what counts as research worthy of wider dissemination. Different approaches to research use need not be mutually exclusive, but we do need to be clear on what each approach can and cannot offer. As one important development in this regard, BERA is currently seeking to build a shared understanding of what constitutes quality in what it terms 'close-to-practice educational research' (BERA, 2018).

Some of course would respond that teachers' preference for local action research simply reflects teachers' failure to understand the potential power of engaging in or with 'robust' research, or their lack of skills and confidence to do so. But this debate is not just about methodological concerns; it is also about the implications of different models of research use for understandings of the nature of teacher professionalism.

## Research use and teacher professionalism

While action research – and even conceptual use of research that is more towards the instrumental end of the spectrum – offer teachers more than the technician status of merely implementing approaches used elsewhere (see Brown and Flood, 2018), we might want to see a fuller definition still of teacher professionalism. But what kinds of research 'evidence' would a richer conception of teacher professionalism need?

Even on the broader definitions of evidence-informed practice outlined above, teacher engagement in or with research is all contained within a school effectiveness perspective. It is purely concerned with school improvement in terms of raising pupil attainment. In this sense, even action research can also become an (albeit distant) off-shoot of the rational-linear, instrumental model. But, as Leat, Lofthouse and Reid (2013) set out, there are other potential motivations for teachers to engage in research, including personal and political motivations. This requires us to distinguish between research as a body of knowledge, research as a professional learning process, and research as a social practice. The latter stance is one in which teachers may begin to think differently and may adopt an altogether more critical position. It may have repercussions for their identity and result in them experiencing some difficulty in working within the parameters of their school or the underpinning assumptions of national policy within which those schools operate. Leat et al. spell out the risks of evidence-informed practice in this sense: 'One of the potential consequences of research which provokes contradictions and causes dissatisfaction is that teachers may choose to leave the classroom as they find it increasingly difficult to live with those contradictions' (p. 6).

Evidence-informed practice as currently conceived by policy in England puts such risks to one side; engagement in or with research that asks more challenging questions, such as 'what is the curriculum for?' and 'what represents socially just schooling?' is generally not on the agenda.

As we argued in the 2005 BERA presidential address (Whitty, 2006), the professional literacy of teachers surely involves more than purely instrumental knowledge. Accordingly, it is appropriate that a research-based profession should be informed by research that questions prevailing assumptions, and considers such questions as to whether an activity is a worthwhile endeavour in the first place. Others have pointed to the dangers of eschewing the moral purpose of education (e.g. Biesta, 2006; Hammersley, 2005), while Atkinson (2000) has considered the role that educational theories or philosophies can play for practitioners. Chiming with this perspective, Winch, Oancea and Orchard (2013) emphasise three interconnected and complementary prongs to a richer notion of teacher professionalism: practical wisdom, technical knowledge *and critical reflection*.

At present, however, within the current ecosystem, it is clear that many teachers in England feel something of a disconnect with the more theoretical end of research. Where they engage with external research, these teachers usually value research that matches their professional experience and can be translated into tangible and practical outcomes in terms of classroom practice. They want research that is readily accessible and applicable, that makes limited demands on time, and does not require special knowledge or research skills. As Cordingley points out:

> Concepts like criticality which make an important contribution to the development of [understanding of the underpinning rationale for different approaches or practical theory] may seem like self-justifying virtues

to researchers but their purpose is less apparent to teachers who may instead be alarmed by what appears to be unnecessary and possibly even dysfunctional negativism.

As she continues:

> There is work to do in developing a shared language for and about [professional development] that includes a role for theory and criticality.
>
> *(Cordingley, 2013, p. 249)*

It seems that educational researchers themselves will need to make the argument for maintaining a broad church of education research in this regard – and make greater effort to show external audiences, not least education practitioners, how their professionalism can grow by engaging with a breadth of material. Just as some are keen for teachers to be better able to engage with and judge the findings of quantitative research, so there remains a place for critical studies within their reading. This need not be to the exclusion of engagement with RCT evidence and attempts to adapt – even adopt – interventions from elsewhere. The two need not be seen as mutually exclusive. But it is this criticality that arguably takes the teacher from being a technician to one degree or another, to being a professional who is able to engage with debates about underpinning values as well as the nuts and bolts of practice – as well as one who is able to understand the ecosystem within which s/he is practicing and perhaps even act to change it. That would seem to us to be an important marker of a contemporary professional, whether of the 'managerial', 'collaborative' or 'democratic' variety (Whitty, 2008).

## Squaring the circle – the challenge of combining different knowledges

There are different views as to where the English system (and other systems) goes from here. It may be that we accept a pluralistic approach, recognising that it is unlikely that all traditions of evidence-informed practice can be reconciled either epistemologically or practically – even if they were realisable on their own terms in practice. Equally, few would take the view that any one of the existing approaches is sufficient on its own. So it would seem that the most fruitful path would be to focus on the weaving together of different knowledges – that of practical experience, action research and external evidence, as well as of different kinds of external evidence, broadly conceived. For some questions, specific academic and practical forms of enquiry are appropriate, while others will demand the development of new and complicated integrated knowledge forms.

A major current debate centres on what counts as '*powerful*' knowledge in professional contexts, an issue recently brought to life in discussions of Michael

Young's work with Joe Muller (Guile et al., 2017). In their view, the 'problem' for the field of education research is that the closer to the world of practice one moves, the less 'rigorous' and less cumulative become the forms of knowledge that are developed – as the aforementioned 2005 Furlong and Salisbury study of teacher research scholarships illustrated. While Young and his colleagues reassert the role of formal academic knowledge in the development of education both as a discipline *and* as a field of practice, others see practical and integrated knowledge traditions, as advocated in the work of Schön (1983) and his followers, as the way forward in professional education. Crucially, and perhaps most plausibly, Maton (2014) argues that powerful professional knowledge entails mastery of *how different knowledges are brought together and changed*.

## Conclusions

In this chapter we have drawn out the different dimensions of the debate on what we have referred to as 'evidence-informed practice' – the question of whether that evidence should ideally be external to the teacher, and preferably in the form of a trial; whether there is any place for small-scale, teacher-led research; whether teacher professionalism requires or benefits from engagement with critical or theoretical work under the banner of research use. In the process we have shown the slippage between different definitions of research use in practice. From there we have made the case for an inclusive and pragmatic model of evidence-informed practice.

We would argue that such a model need not be seen in deficit terms when contrasted with idealised models, typically taken from the medical field. This pluralism and the debate it has prompted in relation to 'powerful knowledge' can be seen as a strength in and of itself. Equally, it arguably represents a more realistic model in practice – something that is in fact borne out in studies of evidence-informed practice in medicine as it is enacted on the ground (e.g. Bell et al., 2010).

But adding another dimension to the debate, we write this at a time when certainly the 'gold standard' of the rational-linear, instrumental model, if not the 'less exacting' alternatives, faces new challenges of its own, with the political context, at least in the UK and the US, having grown seemingly less hospitable. And this challenge to taken for granted assumptions about the status of academic research and evidence and what they represent prompts us to look again at our conclusions.

In *The Death of Expertise: The Campaign Against Established Knowledge and Why it Matters*, Tom Nichols expresses the concern that 'the average American' is not simply 'uninformed' but moving towards being 'aggressively wrong'. As well as showing ignorance, Nichols asserts, American citizens are actively resisting new information that might threaten their beliefs. He talks about the conflation of information, knowledge and experience, and how this has been reinforced by the ubiquity of Google. He also talks about the triumph of emotion over expertise (Nichols, 2017).

Here in the UK, particularly following the EU referendum and vote for Brexit (and the election of Donald Trump in the US), there has been a spate of publications reflecting on what has become known as 'post-truth' (e.g. D'Ancona, 2017). This literature picks out similar trends, contrasting veracity vs impact; facts vs story/connecting with people emotionally; the honestly complex vs the deceptively simple; the rational vs the visceral; veracity vs solidarity/identity. Perception is all and the battle becomes one of defining reality. This is accompanied by the discrediting of traditional sources of authoritative knowledge, be that the mainstream media or academia, the so called 'experts'.

Once again, the impact of the internet, but particularly social media, is implicated – for exacerbating people's tendency to retreat to echo chambers and filter bubbles, now compounded by algorithms. Also implicated are Freud and the paradigm of therapy; behavioural economics and the emphasis on psychological impulses in decision-making (something that Brown and Zhang, 2016, have discussed in relation to research use); and the emphasis on emotional intelligence and the role played by emotional competencies in social relations. Postmodernism and social constructionism, leading to cynicism, relativism, hyperreality, are said to have had their own corrosive effect in terms of 'putting the ideologically driven layman at the advantage of the scholar' (see also Calcutt, 2016).

Nichols, D'Ancona and others arguably put too positive a gloss on science and academia, ignoring academia's own tendency towards echo chambers and filter bubbles, as well as the limitations of (even positivistic) research itself – its fallibility, its temporal nature, its being open to different interpretations. Equally, in laying blame at the door of postmodernist perspectives, they arguably discount too easily the possibility of accommodating a range of epistemological positions. Nevertheless, the trends they describe would seem to have a bearing on debates about the role and status of research and evidence in relation to classroom practice and the nature of teacher professionalism.

This latest development does not change our overriding support for seeking to maintain a broad church of educational research and, linked to that, a wide remit for research use in schools. What it highlights are the issues for education as a field of research and a field of practice in weaving together different types of knowledge and accommodating different epistemological traditions, and the need for clear quality criteria across those traditions. As for practitioners, what it would seem useful to pursue in response is a renewed commitment to *systematic reflection*, whatever form the research and research use sitting behind it takes. This requires (after Stenhouse, 1981) that the process of enquiry is conscious, that it addresses clear questions, has a sense of purpose and timescale, that records are maintained, that there is engagement with the wider literature, and that attention is paid to authenticity. Such a model will also require an ecosystem in which policy rhetoric, research funding and commissioning, school accountability, and models of teacher professionalism (among system and school leaders and teachers alike) each sees value across the spectrum of research methodologies and purposes of research engagement. In the case of England, that will require adjustments on all sides.

## Implications for the research-informed ecosystem

- A need to challenge ecosystems that threaten the maintenance of a broad church of educational research and a broad definition of what counts as research among teachers and in schools.
- The need to explore the scope for bringing together aspects of different knowledge traditions to develop more powerful professional knowledge in schools.
- The need for researchers and research commissioners to maintain humility about their role within the schools ecosystem.

## Note

1 While we are aware of the significance (and slipperiness) of language in these debates – with commentators often contrasting 'evidence/research-*based*' and 'evidence/research-*informed*', among others – throughout this chapter we stick with the term 'evidence-informed practice' for the sake of simplicity.

## References

Aldridge, D., Biesta, G., Filippakou, O. and Wainwright, E. (2018). Why the nature of educational research should remain contested. *British Educational Research Journal*, 44(1), 1–3.

Atkinson, E. (2000). In defence of ideas, or why 'what works' is not enough. *British Journal of Sociology of Education*, 21(3), 317–330.

Bell, M. et al. (2010). *Report of Professional Practitioner Use of Research Review: Practitioner Engagement in and/or with Research*. Retrieved 3 January 2019 from: www.curee.co.uk/files/publication/1297423037/Practitioner%20Use%20of%20Research%20Review.pdf.

Biesta, G. (2006). *Beyond Learning: Democratic Education for a Human Future*. Boulder, CO: Paradigm Publishers.

BERA (2018). Close-to-practice research project. Retrieved 3 January 2019 from: www.bera.ac.uk/project/close-to-practice-research-project.

BERA-RSA [British Educational Research Association and Royal Society for the Arts] (2014). *Research and the Teaching Profession: Building the Capacity for a Self-Improving Education System*. Retrieved 3 January 2019 from: www.bera.ac.uk/project/research-and-teacher-education.

Brown, C. and Flood, J. (2018). Lost in translation? Can the use of theories of action be effective in helping teachers develop and scale up research-informed practice?, *Teaching and Teacher Education*, 72, pp. 144–154.

Brown, C. and Zhang, D. (2016). Is engaging in evidence-informed practice in education rational? What accounts for discrepancies in teachers' attitudes towards evidence use and actual instances of evidence use in schools? *British Educational Research Journal*, 42(5), 780–801.

Calcutt, A. (2016). The surprising origins of 'post-truth' – and how it was spawned by the liberal left. *The Conversation*, 18 November. Retrieved 3 January 2019 from: https://theconversation.com/the-surprising-origins-of-post-truth-and-how-it-was-spawned-by-the-liberal-left-68929.

Coldwell, M., Greany, T., Higgins, S., Brown, C., Maxwell, B., Stiell, B., Stoll, L., Willis, B. and Burns, H. (2017). *Evidence-Informed Teaching: An Evaluation of Progress in England. Research Report July 2017 (DFE-RR696).* Department for Education. Retrieved 3 January 2019 from: www.gov.uk/government/uploads/system/uploads/attachment_data/file/625007/Evidence-informed_teaching_-_an_evaluation_of_progress_in_England.pdf. Appendices: www.gov.uk/government/uploads/system/uploads/attachment_data/file/625477/Evidence-informed_teaching_-_an_evaluation_of_progress_in_England_Appendices.pdf.

Collins, K. (2016). Disciplined innovation: harnessing evidence to support and inform improved pupil outcomes. Lecture at the What Works Global Summit, London, 27 September.

Cordingley, P. (2013). The contribution of research to teachers' professional learning and development. Report for the Research and Teacher Education: The BERA-RSA Inquiry. Retrieved 3 January, 2019 from: www.bera.ac.uk/wp-content/uploads/2013/12/BERA-Paper-5-Continuing-professional-development-and-learning.pdf.

D'Ancona, M. (2017). *Post-Truth: The New War on Truth and How to Fight Back.* London: Ebury Press.

Downing, D. et al. (2004). *Sabbaticals for Teachers: An Evaluation of a Scheme Offering Sabbaticals for Experienced Teachers Working in Challenging Schools.* London: DfES.

Esner, M (2017). Why we need the chartered college of teaching. Retrieved 3 January 2019 from: https://chartered.college/why-we-need-the-chartered-college.

Furlong, J. (2019). Quality, impact and knowledge traditions in the study of education. In A. Brown and E. Wisby (Eds.), *Knowledge, Policy and Practice: The Struggle for Social Justice in Education – Essays in Honour of Geoff Whitty.* London: UCL IOE Press.

Furlong, J. and Salisbury, J. (2005). Best practice research scholarship: an evaluation. *Research Papers in Education,* 20(1), 45–83.

Godfrey, D. (2014). Leadership of schools as research-led organisations in the English educational environment: cultivating a research-engaged school culture. *Educational Management Administration & Leadership,* 44(2), 301–321.

Godfrey, D. (2017). What is the proposed role of research evidence in England's self-improving' school system? *Oxford Review of Education,* 43(4), 433–446.

Goldacre, B. (2013). *Building Evidence into Education.* London: DfE. Retrieved 3 January 2019 from: www.gov.uk/government/news/building-evidence-into-education.

Guile, D., Lambert, D. and Reiss, M. J. (Eds.) (2017). *Sociology, Curriculum Studies and Professional Knowledge: New Perspectives on the Work of Michael Young.* London: Routledge.

Hammersley, M. (2005). The myth of research-based practice: the critical case of educational inquiry. *International Journal of Social Research Methodology,* 8(4), 317–330.

Hargreaves, D. (1996). Teaching as an evidence-based profession: possibilities and prospects. Teacher Training Agency Annual Lecture. Retrieved 3 January 2019 from: https://eppi.ioe.ac.uk/cms/Portals/0/PDF%20reviews%20and%20summaries/TTA%20Hargreaves%20lecture.pdf.

Hargreaves, D. (2006). *Education Epidemic: Transforming Secondary Schools Through Innovation Networks.* London: Demos.

Hattie, J. (2012). *Visible Learning.* Abingdon: Routledge.

Leat, D., Lofthouse, R. and Reid, A. (2013). Teachers' views: perspectives on research engage-ment. Report for the Research and Teacher Education: The BERA-RSA Inquiry. Retrieved 3 January 2019 from: www.bera.ac.uk/wp-content/uploads/2013/12/BERA-Paper-7-Teachers-Views-Perspectives-on-research-engagement.pdf?noredirect=1.

Maton, K. (2014). Building powerful knowledge: the significance of semantic waves. In B. Barrett and E. Rata (Eds.), *Knowledge and the Future of the Curriculum*, London: Palgrave Macmillan, pp. 181–197.

Mortimore, P. and Whitty, G. (1997). *Can School Improvement Overcome the Effects of Disadvantage?* London: Institute of Education.

Nichols, T. (2017). *The Death of Expertise: The Campaign Against Established Knowledge and Why it Matters.* NY: Oxford University Press.

Nisbet, J. (1974). Educational research: the state of the art. Address to the Inaugural Meeting of the British Educational Research Association, Birmingham, April.

Nutley, S., Jung, T. and Walter, I. (2008). The many forms of research-informed practice: a framework for mapping diversity. *Cambridge Journal of Education*, 38(1), 53–71.

Rose, J. et al. (2017). Research learning communities: evaluation report and executive summary. London: EEF. Retrieved 3 January 2019 from: https://educationendowmentfoundation. org.uk/public/files/Projects/Evaluation_Reports/Research_Learning_Communities.pdf.

Saunders, L. (2007). *Supporting Teachers' Engagement in and with Research*. London: TLRP.

Saunders, L. (2017). Just what is 'evidence-based' teaching? Or 'research-informed' teaching? Or 'inquiry-led' teaching? IOE London blog. Retrieved 3 January 2019 from: https:// ioelondonblog.wordpress.com/2017/03/23/just-what-is-evidence-based-teaching-or-research-informed-teaching-or-inquiry-led-teaching/

Schön, D. (1983). *The Reflective Practitioner: How Professionals Think in Action.* New York: Basic Books.

Sebba, J., Tregenza, J. and Kent, P. (2012). Powerful professional learning: a school leader's guide to joint practice development. Nottingham, National College for School Leadership. Retrieved 3 January 2019 from: www.gov.uk/government/uploads/system/uploads/attachment_data/file/329717/powerful-professional-learning-a-school-leaders-guide-to-joint-practice-development.pdf.

Speight, S., Callanan, M., Griggs, J. and Farias, J. (2016). *Rochdale Research into Practice: Evaluation Report and Executive Summary.* London: EEF. Retrieved 3 January 2019 from: https://educationendowmentfoundation.org.uk/public/files/Projects/Evaluation_Reports/EEF_Project_Report_ResearchintoPractice.

Stenhouse, L. (1975). *An Introduction to Curriculum Research and Development.* London: Heinemann.

Stenhouse, L. (1981) What counts as research? *British Journal of Educational Studies*, 29(2), 103–114.

Thrupp, M. and Lupton, R. (2006). Taking school contexts more seriously: the social justice challenge. *British Journal of Educational Studies*, 54(3), 308–328.

Turner, J. (2015). Weighing up the evidence. Retrieved 3 January 2019 from: www.sutton trust.com/newsarchive/weighing-up-the-evidence/.

Whitty, G. (2006). Education(al) research and education policy making: is conflict inevita-ble? *British Educational Research Journal*, 32(2), 159–176.

Whitty, G. (2008). Changing modes of teacher professionalism: traditional, managerial, collaborative and democratic. In B. Cunningham (Ed.), *Exploring Professionalism*. London: IOE Press.

Whitty, G. and Furlong, J. (Eds.) (2017). *Knowledge and the Study of Education: An International Exploration.* Oxford: Symposium Books.

Whitty, G. and Wisby, E. (2016a). Education(al) research and education policy in an imperfect world. In G. Whitty et al. (Eds.), *Research and Policy in Education: Evidence, Ideology and Impact.* London: UCL IOE Press.

Whitty, G. and Wisby, E. (2016b). Education in England – a testbed for network governance? *Oxford Review of Education,* 42(3), 316–329.

Whitty, G. and Wisby, E. (in press). Evidence-informed policy and practice in a 'post-truth' society. *Handbook of Education Policy.*

Whitty, G., Power, S. and Halpin, D. (1997). *Devolution and Choice in Education.* London: Open University Press.

Winch, C., Oancea, A. and Orchard, J. (2013). The contribution of educational research to teachers' professional learning – philosophical understandings. Report for the Research and Teacher Education: The BERA-RSA Inquiry. Retrieved 3 January 2019 from: www.bera.ac.uk/wp-content/uploads/2014/02/BERA-Paper-3-Philosophical-reflections.pdf?noredirect=1.

# 13

## MOVING FORWARD – HOW TO CREATE AND SUSTAIN AN EVIDENCE-INFORMED SCHOOL ECOSYSTEM

*David Godfrey*

### Aims of the chapter

- To synthesise the arguments and research evidence from the chapters in this book in terms of the ecosystem levels.
- To bring out further implications of ecosystems thinking as applied to the research-engaged schools.
- To present a revised ecosystems conceptualisation of the research-engaged school.
- To suggest the role for policy makers, researchers and leadership of a research-engaged school ecosystem.

### Introduction

In this chapter I restate our ecosystem framing and build a richer picture of what a highly research-informed ecosystem of schools could look like, synthesising the learning from the preceding chapters. The chapter also builds on this from an ecosystems perspective, suggesting some theoretical and methodological ways forward; these include suggestions for study of the ecosystem and elements within the system. Finally, this chapter proposes some recommendations for policy makers about how to support a richly research-engaged ecosystem and for the role of leadership within this system. The aim throughout is to stimulate further thinking rather than have the last word, in particular the roles of various stakeholders, institutions, types of research and the role of government in the ecosystems theoretical framework.

It is worth clarifying what we have meant in this book when referring to the 'ecosystem'. We see this term increasingly used by companies like Apple and

Google to show the inter-connectivity of programmes, data storage and hardware – to explain how each part of this system needs to be 'surrounded' with supporting procedures, protocols and structures. In education, some have suggested the need for an 'architecture' of evidence-based practice for teachers (Goldacre, 2013). However, Goldacre's suggestions rather limit the nature of the research-engagement ecosystem, focusing almost entirely on the construction of knowledge that has its foundation built from randomised controlled trials of teaching strategies. He proposed that this foundation should support a layer of diffusion via teacher journal clubs, taking inspiration from the way some medical practitioners discuss research knowledge. In this book we have aimed for a more ambitious model of the ecosystem and a more inclusive notion of research-informed practice. The ecosystem involves an interplay between people, knowledge and 'things' i.e. physical resources, structures, processes and also cultures (including meanings, language and values). An 'effective' ecosystem would be adaptable, dynamic, resilient and sustainable.

We have looked at the ecosystem in two related ways:

1. The notion of an ecosystem as a supportive, nourishing environment in which research-engagement can flourish (and lead to learning and improvement).
2. School education as an ecosystem with multiple levels.

The first approach relies on an assumption, held by both of us, that research-engagement – i.e. doing and 'using' research is inherently of importance and adds great value to the school education system, both to practice and in policy making. Research-engagement in schools is the focal system with 'soft boundaries' (McGinnis and Ostrom, 2014) and is a subsystem of the wider educational ecosystem. There are clearly a near infinite number of other potential foci in the wider education system, such as teacher recruitment, maintaining school buildings, the incorporation of information technology and so on. The educational ecosystem also interacts with other ecosystems, for instance social care, health, transport, employment and the business world. We have looked at multiple levels of this focal ecosystem (macro, chrono, exo, meso and micro), pivotal being the concept of research-engaged schools (see Chapter 1). The book has included many, but by no means all, elements in the ecosystem that have a direct effect on research-engagement in school education. For instance, there has been no direct analysis of the role of government in this system. This chapter turns to the latter in the concluding section.

By picking out some of the key findings from the chapters above, Table 13.1 summarises some of the elements we can expect to see in a school system that is highly research-engaged. Alongside each level there is a list of ecological conditions that support this ecosystem. Following the table summary, I extend the analysis of these levels, incorporating a range of approaches from the ecosystem literature.

**TABLE 13.1** Elements of a highly research-engaged school ecosystem

| Level | Indicators of high research-engagement | Ecological conditions |
|---|---|---|
| Macrosystem | – Schools are institutions that successfully promote high-level societal aims such as equality, diversity and social justice as well as excellence in learning and achieving qualifications and skills<br>– Research-engagement helps to achieve these aims | – High levels of trust and stakeholder involvement<br>– Belief in key role for professional practitioners and academics<br>– Clear and inclusive narrative about research-informed practice to encourage optimal rational choices<br>– Consensus about the aims of education and thus how research can help achieve those aims |
| Chronosystem | – Changes to policy making and practice are incremental, coherent and informed by research-engagement | – Strong professional bodies/political systems to act as buffer against short-termist policy or practitioner fads<br>– Research–practice models that take the learning from research through to implementation |
| Exosystem | – School collaborations, networks and partnerships enable research knowledge to be effectively mobilised and combined with other professional knowledge<br>– Practitioners, schools and networks actively engage in research and enquiry as well as 'using' research | – Long-term resourcing of knowledge mobilisation networks, including online resources and social networks, plus quality assured, effective distribution and translation of research for professionals<br>– An accountability system and middle tier that supports collaboration and promotes trust<br>– Changes to funding and structure of work for some practitioners and academics in order to traverse communities of practice<br>– Universities and other research organisations support schools, providing high quality professional learning, expertise, support and critical friendship |

| | |
|---|---|
| Mesosystem | – Schools operate with learning and enquiry at their heart for adults as well as their young learners<br>– Research-practice projects are integrated into the developmental cycle of schools<br>– School staff use data effectively to inform school improvement | – Leaders with skills to promote research-engagement within and across schools<br>– Teachers with time to engage in and with research and enquiry in order to develop practice<br>– Universities and other research staff afforded time and career incentives to engage in research-practice collaborations<br>– Support from data-brokers from within and outside schools to help practitioners take effective evidence-informed action |
| Microsystem | – Teachers and other professionals have skills and knowledge to implement societal aims for education system<br>– Mutual trust high between school staff, parents and students due to increased (research-informed) professionalism | – Initial education and professional learning of teachers and school leaders gives research-engagement a clear priority<br>– Coherent system of teacher professional bodies that set the goals, criteria and standards for research and research-informed practice<br>– Responsibility to engage in and with research backed with entitlement to appropriate training, support and funding |

## The macrosystem

While it has not been the focus of this book to comment in depth about the purposes and goals of the education system, rather to focus on the first proposition above, the two intentions go very much hand-in-hand. The values held in the macro-level permeate down to policy enactment, to institutional and organisation arrangements and ultimately to the micro-level. If we add that management of ecosystems requires regular monitoring and evaluating of actions, then there is a synergy between 1 and 2 above, in that research enables us to achieve the end of an 'effective' ecosystem (values, purposes).

In Chapter 1 we outlined the need to think of the school as an institution as well as an individual organisation. This way we reaffirm the values behind education and the purposes for and in society of the school system. In a research-engaged school system, research would be clearly directed towards helping achieve such aims. In order to do so, there will be a need for some consensus about where this system should be heading and why. In order for there to be sufficient uptake or demand for research-informed practice, the narratives that emerge from government, the research community, schools, universities and other institutions need to be clear about its value. In this way, teachers and other practitioners are more likely to make the kind of optimal rational choices that Brown analyses in Chapter 11. Professional bodies (and even quasi-independent political processes which have at their core a commitment to establishing long lasting educational values) have a clear role in taking the lead in this respect and can offer a buffer to the turbulence caused as new governments come in and propose their own new sets of requirements and fads (see Chapter 5). They can do so by outlining a clear professional ethic and promoting wider educational values of equality, diversity and social justice, for instance. A clearer balance between the aims of building 'qualities' in young people, such as resilience (character), and to finding ones place in democratic society are also possibilities around which, we would contend, there would be widespread agreement. Given the current, and dominant view worldwide, fuelled by national and international league tables of schools and education systems that education is primarily about achieving qualifications, sometimes to the detriment of children's (and teachers) well-being, this would provide welcome balance.

Research not only helps educators to achieve wider educational ends and means, but they can also inform the debate. For instance, in England we have seen the research community make a robust challenge to the idea of increasing the number of schools that select by academic performance in tests at age 11, this is despite the covert ways that schools and government have sought to increase the capacity of existing schools and thereby increase the number of places available.[1] Arguments about the social inequity caused by school academic selection, have provided powerful counterarguments to further expansion of 'grammar schools' nevertheless (e.g. Burgess et al., 2017).

We have seen also, that building trust plays a vital role when promoting learning from school research-engagement (see Chapter 6 and exosystem below).

Therefore, the accountability system (including the media) needs to balance the need to punish underperformance with a developmental and co-constructive approach that supports learning and growth. It also makes less sense to blame others, if we accept our own responsibility in the same ecosystem. Therefore public condemnation of 'failing schools',[2] often fuelled by inspection reports, are counterproductive to the aim to promote high trust and encourage innovation through research and development.

In Chapter 12, Wisby and Whitty pointed out that our ecosystem for research-engaged schools should be empowering, inclusive and adoptive of a broad church of research practice. If, as has been argued, the push is for narrow ideas of technical-rationalism in teaching and educational leadership, expressed through dominance of a 'what works' agenda in research-engagement (Godfrey, 2017c) then we are in danger of falsely applying certainty to a complex system. In doing so, rather than producing teachers who are empowered to use their professional judgement to meet these complexities, teaching may instead be reduced to a mechanical process of implementation of 'evidence-based' strategies.

## The chronosystem

In Chapter 1, I gave one example of the analysis of the development of schools as research-engaged organisations. There, I drew upon research of eight secondary schools in England on different trajectories (Godfrey, 2017a). The development of these school organisations was determined by entrenched and ongoing contradictions in the object of their activities. For instance, the learning derived from PLC activity was sometimes in contrast to the performative aims of the school leadership, driven particularly by the external inspection system. These contradictions had to be negotiated over time, leading to a new 'object' of their activities, often leading to an expanded idea of what it meant to be a professional (to include research-engagement), to an expansion of the community of practice (to include research organisations or advice). Mediating this 'expansive learning' (Engeström, 2001), a new language derived from the world of research acted as a tool to leverage change, enabling teachers to achieve the kind of ecological agency described in Chapter 10. The contradictions found in the developmental cycle of change described in my case studies above, are also found in discussions of transformational change and leadership described in the ecosystems literature (e.g. Westley et al., 2013).

Contradictions or tensions in ecosystems are sometimes described in terms of a search for *dynamic equilibrium*, i.e. where the forces in the ecosystem are sustainable but not entirely static or without elements of refinement, expansion or even destruction. If an ecosystem is 'static' it fails to accommodate new innovations or trends in society, while one in constant flux does not create the conditions to institutionalise policies and practices. Social ecological systems (SESs) have been described as 'self-organising', and involving:

the interaction of cultural, political, social, economic, technological and other elements, [wherein] parts of an SES respond to changes in other components, sometimes triggering feedbacks that can amplify change in the whole system or can have a stabilizing effect. Through these interactions, SESs can self-organize (i.e., adjust themselves through interactions among their components), novel configurations can emerge, and adaptation is made possible.

*(Resilience Alliance, 2010)*

This 'diagnosis' of ecosystems has warranted the development of a framework to extract various elements in detail (McGinnis and Ostrom, 2014). Within this analysis of the resilience of ecosystems, the nature of institutional development has been an interesting source of study and to which I turn below.

It has been proposed that SESs go through four phases of adaptation, powered by the degree to which capital is stored or released and the degree to which the system is either homogenous or heterogeneous in certain features. These four phases of the adaptive cycle: exploitation, conservation, release and reorganisation describe a double repeating loop, where the front loop is characterised by institutionalisation and the back loop is the destructive, change part of the loop where innovation occurs (Westley et al., 2013). Where there is a multiplicity of organisational forms, this can lead to more connections and overlap that can help to mobilise action and resources for innovation. However, too much multiplicity leads to fragmentation and therefore makes it hard to release resources in large quantities.

Institutional entrepreneurship looks at the opportunity contexts that the adaptive cycle presents. Using Westley et al.'s model, a number of education systems could be said to have gone recently through a phase of 'creative destruction' in which there has been fertile ground for innovation and much entrepreneurial 'land grab' as new opportunities for the release of resources and capital have emerged. This would be my characterisation of the landscape in England, for example, that has gone through a period of structural changes to school institutions and the way they work in networks (Godfrey, 2017b). This has been accompanied by many opportunities for researchers to look into these changes and the effects they are having on educational outcomes. Assuming England is now moving towards a more stable phase in which there is a great deal of heterogeneity of structures and institutions, then this calls for research that helps identify which practices, policies and institutional arrangements should be connected together, consolidated and reinforced or indeed, cut.

Research and development also plays an essential role in this system to encourage innovations to be trialled, evaluated, refined and spread more widely across the system. An understanding of the scalings in the ecosystem is important, however it is also necessary to appreciate the drivers of change at each level and the varying rates of implementation, embedding and institutionalisation of innovations. The leadership challenges in diffusing innovations in research-engaged schools across the ecosystem is discussed later in this chapter.

## The exosystem

One of the major shifts in ecological systems theories is from the idea of the organisation as a discrete 'sealed' unit to one that has 'semi-permeable boundaries' (Godfrey, 2016b, p. 23). This is important in Pollock et al.'s discussion of the 'middle-tier', specifically of the KNAER network in Chapter 2. They explain that to promote research-engaged schools in a healthy educational ecosystem, it is necessary to actively mobilise multiple forms of evidence through multiple processes of communication, collaboration and interaction. These networks are more than the sum of their parts, as they cannot work independently to the same extent, benefiting from sharing resources and harnessing collective knowledge. In a symbiosis, the individual school organisations can benefit the network and the network also is of value to practitioners operating on a daily basis in the 'core business' of the school. The knowledge created within the network can come from individuals, departments, whole schools or within cross-school partnership levels. Some of these may also involve multidisciplinary projects with outside organisations, such as universities, the KM network allowing there to be gains from working at scale and allowing greater diffusion of innovations emerging through research-engagement. Furthermore, through the kinds of thematic networks and communities of practice, illustrated in the Ontario KM case, these can engage resources from the government level and also to achieve aims collectively in a way that individual schools would be unable to do on their own.

For these kinds of KM networks are to come about and to lead to positive changes that permeate down to the microsystem, new ways of working will need to be embedded across the ecosystem. As Pollock et al. point out:

> there has been a shift from the traditional relationship models toward new models that are more interactive and value partnerships and networks has developed. Although this is a positive move, it is becoming increasingly recognized that there needs also to be attention to the wider ecosystem in which research and evidence are part of a culture and infrastructure of co-development, critical inquiry, genuine collaboration and attending to existing structural challenges in accessing, adapting and applying research in and for education.
>
> (Chapter 2, p. 28)

However, for these KM networks to promote learning, improvement, resilience and adaptability through research, the regulatory and accountability mechanisms need to work in a way that does not lead to too much standardisation and control. In Chapter 3, Ehren outlines the many ways in which schools change their understanding of educational quality in high stakes accountability regimes by adopting the external inspection framework for their own school evaluation, in lesson observations and by becoming overly preoccupied with being 'inspection ready'. Schools concerned with being judged on an individual basis will not work effectively in networks, and the value of such networks can be wrongly assessed by the accountability system in terms of the aggregate of the quality of individual schools, rather than network level outcomes (Ehren and Godfrey, 2017). Ehren explains how the external accountability environment can lead to *coercive isomorphism*:

> Schools are part of an exosystem in which they interact with other schools, local community organisations, parents, and suppliers of services and resources (e.g. suppliers of textbooks). These organisations and stakeholders exert pressure on schools (both formal and informally), particularly when schools are dependent on these organisations.
>
> *(Chapter 3, p. 44)*

She goes on to suggest that, 'Inspections play an important role in creating such coercive pressures and in defining how schools are expected to be structured and formed' (p. 3). In order to build the high levels of trust needed to encourage research-engagement, the co-construction of the goals of the network level accountability are a crucial area of alignment in the exosystem.

## The mesosystem

An implication of the semi-permeable organisation boundaries in the exosystem is for a new kind of ecological understanding of the mesosystem too. This will need to be multifaceted and enable numerous connections to occur at the network level, with outward-looking organisational foci being essential in the formation and sustainability of strategic alliances. In successful ecosystems, organisations gain nourishment from these connections as well as feeding into the success of the ecosystem of which they form a part.

I propose furthermore, that an extension of our notion of the research-engaged school is the aim of being an *adaptive organisation* (e.g. Fulmer, 2000); i.e. one that matches its capacity to meet the demands of the external environment. Referring to Stelzner's (2005) work in the ecological leadership literature, several challenges emerge for leaders of adaptive, research-engaged schools:

1. The need to balance the swift decision-making possible in traditional, hierarchical models of leadership with the more open ended participatory leadership that allows for greater flow of feedback and information.
2. The need to devote time to thoroughly understand the context for taking decisions.
3. In order to build organisational adaptability, rich 'feedback loops' are needed to understand practices, policies and procedures from the evaluations of learners, employers, governors and parents, triangulated with the analysis of peer reviews, inspection visits or other enquiries by staff.
4. Adaptable organisations should scan the horizon by taking into account the views of people from a variety of cultural backgrounds. However, this drive for diversity and inclusion can conflict with the need to make single-minded decisions.

5. School leaders need to exercise courage in their own vision to pursue a course of excellence, rather than relying purely on external, accountability driven measures.

The above challenges require a shift in thinking from mechanistic, industrial ideas of bureaucratic organisation towards more organic, ecological, systems thinking and managing a series of 'tensions'. There should be less emphasis on singular, positional leaders to direct activities and more on seeing leadership of organisations as emerging in a number of ways and afforded in particular circumstances and contexts. This ecological leadership is discussed further on in this chapter.

## The microsystem

The aim in our microsystem is to have research-informed professionalism where practitioners (especially teachers) are empowered to take decisions, exercise good and wise judgement and expertly execute the kind of approaches that enable students to fulfil their potential. The link to the macrosystem is essential; the values that society, government, parents, business leaders and so on want from schools are largely in the hands of the professionals that work in them. Therefore the research-engaged school ecosystem needs to empower such practice, be inclusive, set standards for this work and shape the agenda.

Staff in research-engaged schools will be motivated and supported in their engagement through a number of levels and dimensions in the ecosystem. In Chapter 10, Priestley and Drew draw attention to the 'ecological conditions' necessary for the achievement of agency and that can be promoted through enquiry approaches to teacher learning and thus enabling teacher leadership of school improvement. Such enquiry approaches can be nourished and sustained through a variety of means, many originating outside the school and passing through the semi-permeable boundaries of the organisation. The practices that occur will then be reconfigured, influenced by the context, the leadership and many cultural influences of the individual school. We have seen earlier in this book how teacher research-engagement can be directly supported during initial teacher training (Chapter 8), through the encouragement and support of professional bodies (Chapter 5) and also by virtue of the school's membership to a knowledge mobilisation network or a research-practice project with a university (Chapter 2).

## An ecosystem of research-engaged schools

Figure 13.1 proposes an ecosystems conceptualisation of research-engaged schools, building on the arguments and research discussed in this book (summarised above), an article I published previously about leadership of research-led schools (Godfrey, 2016b) and another paper that I co-wrote on the research and development ecosystem in the English school system (Godfrey and Brown, 2018). The elements of the model comprise the macrosystem values level that underpin the ecosystem. These values foreground the policy enactment, institutional configurations and surrounding mechanisms in the exosystem that provide support, nourishment or alignment for research-engagement to thrive. In the case of KM networks and schools the arrow is bi-directional in flow, recognising the mutual benefits for both the schools and the network as a whole of the alliance. In Chapter 4, Dimmock described the importance of leadership in promoting the kind of effective PLCs that are essential to research-engaged schools. But the notion of the school as a learning organisation is not limited to how it creates opportunities for its members to take part in and learn from research but also to how the school learns from their partnerships and links with other institutions. These semi-permeable boundaries of the mesosystem as mentioned above are represented by the dotted lines in Figure 13.1.

The microsystem practices by individuals (professionals) emerge within the research-engaged school mesosystem as described in Chapter 1 of this book: i.e. a school that promotes engagement in and with research, is connected to the wider educational system and makes decisions and adopts practices, based on its members' research-engagement. The chronosystem element reflects the cyclical renewal of the elements in the system: the adaptive institutional cycle and the need for ecological leadership to cohere and align the various forms of capital and emergent resources needed to keep the ecosystem in dynamic equilibrium.

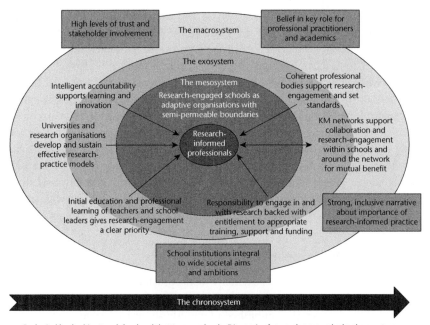

Ecological leadership at each level and that traverses levels. Diagnosis of research-engaged school ecosystem according to the adaptive cycle in order to maintain a resilient ecosystem in dynamic equilibrium

**FIGURE 13.1** An ecosystems conceptualisation of the research-engaged school

The conceptualisation in Figure 13.1 suggested as a starting point, inviting further thought about additional or missing concepts and elements or refinements. It also serves to stimulate thought about the precise nature of the relationship between elements and how such an ecosystem model for research-engagement could be used to think about systemic reform of schools.

## Leadership of the research-engaged school ecosystem

In this section I elaborate the leadership aspects of the above conceptualisation of the research-engaged school ecosystem that have as yet been underdeveloped in this model. In particular, the discussion of: 1) leadership of adaptive organisations (adaptive management) and 2) of an ecological model of system leadership. For the former, I will refer partly to a review I wrote for the Further Education Sector in the UK (Godfrey, 2016a). For the latter, I will rely heavily on the work of Toh et al. (2014) who describe features of 'ecological leadership'.

## Adaptive management

Research in adaptive management has defined ecosystems as, 'complex adaptive systems that require flexible governance with the ability to respond to environmental feedback' (Olsson et al., 2004, p. 75). Part of the leadership challenge of adaptive systems lies in the recognition of the complexity and uncertainty faced in the environment. Such issues have been defined as 'wicked problems' (Rittel and Webber, 1974). Wicked problems are difficult to define; have no correct solution, they are inextricably linked to the context, there may be no obvious cause and effect and they are likely to be the cause of much debate, disagreement and conflict. Many of the concerns facing the schools sector are wicked problems, for instance, the knotty question of how schools can help reduce inequalities of outcome, the role of technology, the best pedagogical strategies to use in various subjects or how to best organise the curriculum. There are often no agreed solutions to these issues, neither is there an agreed series of 'steps' that need to be taken to go from A to B (whatever B is). No one person or organisation can know everything that is necessary to meet this challenge. In addition, given the interplay of factors such as changes in funding, policy decisions and local contexts, the path from cause to effect is less than clear.

In short, the major issues facing the sector are complex – and need to be acknowledged as such. Heifetz (1994) goes further in calibrating problems in terms of their wickedness thus:

- Type I (tame) problems. These are technical in nature and have clearly defined questions and mechanical, straightforward solutions.
- Type II problems that are clearly definable but have no clear-cut solution.
- Type III problems that have neither clear-cut definitions nor technical solutions.

Meeting these problems requires commitment to the kind of inclusive ecosystem of research-engagement advocated in this book with different kinds of research and evidence informing different levels of problems. In relation to the above, solutions to type II problems are only proposals that must be tested and refined on the basis of outcomes. While type III problems are the most wicked and require continual learning to formulate the problem and adaptively work toward solutions (DeFries and Nagenda, 2017, p. 266). The same authors warn against falsely assuming tame solutions to wicked problems and also inertia caused by overwhelming complexity.

The above challenges require new forms of leadership that bring people together to co-construct the future and to face up to these problems. However, as leaders may not like to admit that they do not have all the answers, or are unwilling to communicate uncertainty, there can also be a strong pull towards adopting a more managerial approach. While 'management' issues call for rational, procedural and calculative responses, leadership approaches that tackle wicked problems require the 'soft skills' of managing relationships and emotions.

Adaptive and resourceful leadership approaches require leaders to: monitor external changes; identify relevant strategies; articulate an appealing vision; identify reasons for resistance to change and seek to convert opponents; build realistic optimism; keep people informed of progress and evaluate the outcomes of strategic decisions in order to refine mental models (Yukl and Mahsud, 2010, p. 98). In other words, leaders need to articulate theories of action for their proposed changes and to monitor the implementation of these agreed alternatives course of action (see Chapter 5 and Robinson, 2017). This cycle of organisational learning then is integral to leaders and leadership within and beyond institutional boundaries. The next issue is how to spread this learning and enable improvements throughout the ecosystem, to which the section on ecological leadership below addresses.

## Ecological leadership

Through case studies of two exemplar schools in Singapore that have been successful in spreading curriculum innovations across networks of schools, Toh and colleagues (2014) looked at the kind of ecological leadership required to do so. Also referring to Bronfenbrenner's ecosystem levels, they describe five thrusts of the diffusion process, summarised with the acronym SCALE:

(i) Systems thinking to benefit more schools so as to bring forth collaboration and imbue communitarian perspective in the system.

(ii) Converge vision and contextualize innovations in relation to overarching mandates.

(iii) Align efforts by mitigating tensions and paradoxes within and across the subsystems in the ecology.

(iv) Leverage collective wisdom and resources emanating from any level of subsystem to diffuse innovations.

(v) Emergence of new adaptive capacities for sustainability.

*(Toh et al., 2014, p. 843)*

Toh and colleagues describe this ecological leadership as more encompassing than traditional descriptions of system leadership. They describe the latter as, 'still predominantly centred on nurturing positional leaders, especially head teachers with macro views of benefitting the school system' (Toh et al., 2014, p. 845). Rather, and drawing on research by Wielkiewicz and Stelzner (2005), ecological leadership capitalises on collective voices emanating from the ecology; staff at various levels of formal and informal leadership and layers of the ecosystem contribute to the scaling up of innovations. Ecological leaders in the exemplar schools looked at by Toh and colleagues, acted as:

> a mediating layer to broker the interpretation of macro policies, benchmark them against the multifarious affordances of the school, make careful selection of innovations that they want to develop, translate them into micro implementation, consolidate the insights that arose from the processes and re-strategize for innovation diffusion to other schools.
>
> *(p. 844)*

Scaling up innovations involves the communication and translation of a clear narrative that aligns and converges the institutional processes and aims with those of the exosystem. This alignment of approach to implementation also has to recognise the autonomy of each institution while:

> common cultural artefacts of learning and teaching such as the pedagogical approach of inquiry-based learning and the co-designed lesson plans [will] act as unifying boundaries for the community
>
> *(p. 841)*

Thus a common language and set of principles are adopted but adapted to context in each school, creating both alignment and convergence. As part of the exosystem, Toh and colleagues also document the important long-term role played by partnerships with university researchers in conducting evaluations of impact and feeding back on the process of implementation (p. 841).

Leaders in this ecosystem required the sort of social skills described above in relation to adaptive leaders. This social capital of key leaders enabled resources in the ecosystem to be harnessed that would otherwise have been difficult to obtain directly from the Ministry of Education. Throughout this process, leaders took opportunities to seed conditions for 'social memory' (captured sense-making experiences of actors) to become 'ecological memory' (Olsson et al., 2004, in (Toh et al., 2014, p. 842). The coherence emerging from this approach created, 'virtuous cycles of collaborative capital that can be harnessed by others' (Toh et al., 2014, p. 847). This 'emergence', i.e. the tendency for agents in a social system to interact synergistically to produce new capacities and novel order, is different from the individual local actions that engendered them (Toh et al., p. 841).

The beauty of the ecological leadership approach, when applied to the ecosystem concept of the research-engaged school, is that we can avoid the tendency to get into the polarised debate about whether centralised top-down approaches are superior to local, bottom-up ones. Rather we look for synergy and emergence that can be viewed as an interconnected system. This leads us to the role of government and policy.

## Conclusions

### Implications for policy and research of the ecosystem

The political dimension has been under-explored so far in this book and it is beyond the scope of this chapter to do so in detail here. However, there is clearly an important role for government at all levels in the ecosystem. Above, Toh and colleagues (2014) argue that systems leadership needs to be expanded to a more holistic ecological leadership that builds alignment and convergence throughout the levels of the ecosystem. However, as they themselves suggest, the political context in the Singapore system is characterised by collectivism, which does not apply universally, such as in 'Anglo-Saxon' contexts. They do not mention, but it is also the case, that there is also great consensus about the role and aims of the school system in society. In such a context, the alignment between the macrosystem and other levels may be much easier to sustain. If the aims for the education system as a common good are not stated clearly enough or broadly shared, there is a danger of giving in to a market narrative that hijacks the language of ecosystems. We have seen how these market and hierarchical forces still pervade in the English school system, despite much talk of the vital role of networks and collaboration in the so-called 'self-improving system' (see Greany and Higham, 2018).

An ecosystem is by its nature complex and this presents challenges for its analysis. Traditional science has tended to favour unidirectional, linear and parsimonious explanations of cause and effect. However, in complex social ecosystems the variables are often more dynamic and the outcomes of research may be less certain. However, as has been shown throughout this book, the need for research to test, diagnose, propose solutions and redefine problems is ever present. Research and development therefore needs to take place both of the system and in the system. External accountability structures can play a key role in taking the 'temperature' of the ecosystem, identifying weaknesses and areas for further support as well as emergences from the ecosystem to be further developed.

More work that explores the research-engaged school ecosystem is warranted too, for instance, using the social-ecological framework to diagnose ecosystem resilience (McGinnis and Ostrom, 2014) or to examine longitudinal changes (the chronosystem) in school networks (e.g. Ehren and Godfrey, 2017). Research that looks at ecological and adaptive leadership in the school sector will help understand the kinds of collaborative and social capital that add convergence, alignment and the emergence of new resources in the ecosystem.

## *Implications for government policy level and decision-making*

So many of the problems facing the education system cross professional, geographical, disciplinary and governmental boundaries. The need to broker multi-agency cooperation has been explained in many of the examples in this book. Government has a key role in this. We can look outside of the education sector to find inspiration for how to encourage an ecosystem towards dynamic equilibrium. Finegold (1999) researched the growth and success of Silicon Valley, in particular the way that this area attracted and developed a highly skilled workforce. Finegold suggested four forces in high skills ecosystems: a catalyst, fuel or nourishment, a supportive host environment and a high degree of interdependence. Applying this to a research-engaged school system, we could identify a government role to act as a *catalyst* to marshal sources of funding for research and KM networks, to *nourish* the development of capacities for leadership in the research-engaged school system, in schools, KM networks and universities. A *supportive environment* could include access to specialist advice, local arrangements to support peer review and other research-practice collaborations, and extensive virtual learning environments to store and share resources developed from research and development activity. In terms of *interdependence*, support for a professional identity that looks beyond allegiances to single organisations could be reinforced by government as well as formed by the kind of strong and coherent professional bodies that have been discussed elsewhere in this book.

In our macrosystem there needs to be further consideration of the future relationship between the school ecosystem and related ecosystems such as the economy and the state. For instance, some authors have recognised the importance of schools in developing the so-called 'knowledge-economy' and have speculated on how this would need to lead to radical changes to the nature of schools and the curriculum (MacDonald, 2005). With some economists suggesting the need for a more active and entrepreneurial role for the state in generating and commercialising innovation (e.g. Mazzucato, 2015), then schools could play a key role in the future economic ecosystem. Finally, if we broaden out to 'humans-in-nature' – the logical end-expression of ecosystems thinking – we would also want to ask about how school education feeds into the sustainability of the planet's resources. It is hard to see how we can achieve such ambitious aims for our school ecosystem, without the existence of flourishing research-engaged institutions that promote enquiry and the synthesis of knowledge, autonomy in decision-making, and a high level of collaborative learning among the professionals that work in them.

## Implications for the research-informed ecosystem

- The characteristics of a research-engaged school ecosystem have been set out in terms of the macro, chrono, exo, meso and microsystems.
- The research-engaged school is more likely to succeed under particular ecological conditions at each level of the ecosystem.

- An ecosystem of research-engaged schools requires ecological leadership in order to develop adaptive organisations and to spread learning and innovation across the system.
- While this book has provided a good starting point for thinking about notions of ecosystems and research use, there are still many empirical and conceptual gaps to be filled.

## Notes

1 www.bbc.co.uk/news/education-44727857 (accessed 6 January 2019).
2 e.g. www.itv.com/news/2017-12-13/ofsted-annual-schools-report/ (accessed 6 January 2019).

## References

Burgess, S., Crawford, C. and Macmillan, L. (2017). Assessing the role of grammar schools in promoting social mobility (No. 17-09). Department of Quantitative Social Science-UCL Institute of Education, University College London.

DeFries, R. and Nagendra, H. (2017). Ecosystem management as a wicked problem. *Science*, 356(6335), 265–270.

Ehren, M. C. and Godfrey, D. (2017). External accountability of collaborative arrangements; a case study of a Multi Academy Trust in England. *Educational Assessment, Evaluation and Accountability*, 29(4), 339–362.

Engeström, Y. (2001). Expansive learning at work: toward an activity theoretical reconceptualization. *Journal of Education and Work*, 14(1), 133–156.

Finegold, D. (1999). Creating self-sustaining, high-skill ecosystems. *Oxford Review of Economic Policy*, 15(1), 60–81.

Fulmer, W. E. (2000). *Shaping the Adaptive Organization: Landscapes, Learning, and Leadership in Volatile Times*. Nashville, TN: Amacom.

Godfrey, D (2016a). A review of the leadership of thinking in Further Education. A review for the Further Education Trust for Leadership (FETL). Retrieved 28 August 2018 from: http://fetl.org.uk/wp-content/uploads/2016/09/Lit-review-LR.pdf.

Godfrey, D. (2016b). Leadership of schools as research-led organisations in the English educational environment: cultivating a research-engaged school culture. *Educational Management Administration & Leadership*, 44(2), 301–321.

Godfrey, D. (2017a). *Exploring Cultures of Research Engagement at Eight English Secondary Schools*. Doctoral dissertation, University College London.

Godfrey, D. (2017b). Global perspectives of educational leadership: the English context. Symposium presentation for International Congress for School Effectiveness and Improvement, Ottawa.

Godfrey, D. (2017c). What is the proposed role of research evidence in England's 'self-improving' school system? *Oxford Review of Education*, 43(4), 433–446.

Godfrey, D. and Brown, C. (2018). How effective is the research and development ecosystem for England's schools? *London Review of Education*, 16(1), 136–151.

Goldacre, B. (2013). Building evidence into education. Retrieved 13 September 2018 from: www.gov.uk/government/news/building-evidence-into-education.

Greany, T. and Higham, R. (2018). Hierarchy, markets and networks: analysing the 'self-improving' school-led system agenda in England and the implications for schools. Retrieved 6 January 2019 from: www.ucl-ioe-press.com/ioe-content/uploads/2018/08/Hierarchy-Markets-and-Networks.pdf.

Head, B. W. (2008). Wicked problems in public policy. *Public Policy*, 3(2), 101–118.

Heifetz, R. A. (1994). *Leadership Without Easy Answers* (Vol. 465). Cambridge, MA: Harvard University Press.

MacDonald, G. (2005). Schools for a knowledge economy. *Policy Futures in Education*, 3(1), 38–49.

Mazzucato, M. (2015). *The Entrepreneurial State: Debunking Public vs. Private Sector Myths* (Vol. 1). London: Anthem Press.

McGinnis, M. D. and Ostrom, E. (2014). Social-ecological system framework: initial changes and continuing challenges. *Ecology and Society*, 19(2), 30–41.

Olsson, P., Folke, C. and Berkes, F. (2004). Adaptive comanagement for building resilience in social–ecological systems. *Environmental Management*, 34(1), 75–90.

Resilience Alliance. (2010). Assessing resilience in social-ecological systems: Workbook for practitioners. Version 2.0. Retrieved 6 January 2019 from: www.resalliance.org/files/ResilienceAssessmentV2_2.pdf.

Rittel, H. W. and Webber, M. M. (1974). Wicked problems. *Man-made Futures*, 26(1), 272–280.

Robinson, V. (2017). *Reduce Change to Increase Improvement*. Thousand Oaks, CA: Corwin Press.

Toh, Y., Jamaludin, A., Hung, W. L. D. and Chua, P. M. H. (2014). Ecological leadership: going beyond system leadership for diffusing school-based innovations in the crucible of change for 21st century learning. *The Asia-Pacific Education Researcher*, 23(4), 835–850.

Westley, F. R., Tjornbo, O., Schultz, L., Olsson, P., Folke, C., Crona, B. and Bodin, Ö. (2013). A theory of transformative agency in linked social-ecological systems. *Ecology and Society*, 18(3), 27.

Wielkiewicz, R. M. and Stelzner, S. P. (2005). An ecological perspective on leadership theory, research, and practice. *Review of General Psychology*, 9(4), 326–341.

Yukl, G. and Mahsud, R. (2010). Why flexible and adaptive leadership is essential. *Consulting Psychology Journal: Practice and Research*, 62(2), 81.

# INDEX